ArtScroll Series®

Rabbi Nosson Scherman / Rabbi Meir Zlotowitz

General Editors

by
Yair Weinstock

translated by
Libby Lazewnik

Published by
Mesorah Publications, ltd

for the SOUL 5

A famous novelist retells classic stories with passion and spirit

FIRST EDITION
First Impression … November 2004
Second Impression … July 2005

Published and Distributed by
MESORAH PUBLICATIONS, LTD.
4401 Second Avenue / Brooklyn, N.Y 11232

Distributed in Europe by
LEHMANNS
Unit E, Viking Business Park
Rolling Mill Road
Jarow, Tyne & Wear, NE32 3DP
England

Distributed in Australia and New Zealand by
GOLDS WORLDS OF JUDAICA
3-13 William Street
Balaclava, Melbourne 3183
Victoria, Australia

Distributed in Israel by
SIFRIATI / A. GITLER — BOOKS
6 Hayarkon Street
Bnei Brak 51127

Distributed in South Africa by
KOLLEL BOOKSHOP
Shop 8A Norwood Hypermarket
Norwood 2196, Johannesburg, South Africa

ARTSCROLL SERIES®
TALES FOR THE SOUL 5
© *Copyright 2004, by* MESORAH PUBLICATIONS, Ltd.
4401 Second Avenue / Brooklyn, N.Y. 11232 / (718) 921-9000 / www.artscroll.com

ISBN:
1-57819-439-3 (hard cover)
1-57819-440-7 (paperback)

Typography by CompuScribe at ArtScroll Studios, Ltd.

Printed in the United States of America by Noble Book Press Corp.
Bound by Sefercraft, Quality Bookbinders, Ltd., Brooklyn N.Y. 11232

Table of Contents

Tales for the Soul 5

En Route to the Chupah

THE MEMBERS OF THE HOLY BA'AL SHEM TOV'S ENTOURAGE were a merry group. Together with their rebbe, they were on their way to attend the wedding of his eldest grandson, R' Moshe Chaim Efraim, known as the "Degel" because of his *sefer, Degel Machaneh Efraim*. R' Moshe Chaim Efraim lived in the city of Sadlikov. The Ba'al Shem Tov greatly respected the young man, who was the son of his righteous daughter, Udele. In a letter to his brother-in-law, R' Gershon, he had referred to his grandson with the words, "And my grandson, the outstanding *chasan*, R' Moshe Chaim Efraim, is also a great *ilui* in learning."

The Ba'al Shem Tov had honored his holy and brilliant student, R' Yaakov Yosef of Polonya, author of the *Toldos Yaakov Yosef*, with the role of *mesader kiddushin*, and R' Yaakov Yosef had accepted the honor.

In due course, they entered the town where the "Degel's" wedding was to take place. Descending from the carriages, the disciples flanked their rebbe in rows as they proceeded toward the *chupah*. Happiness infused their every step. The students' eyes were riveted on their rebbe on this joyous occasion in his life. The Ba'al Shem Tov's face shone as though lit by torches from within.

As they walked through the city streets, they saw a simple Jew walking toward them. The atmosphere of joy seemed not to touch him at all. To the students' astonishment, the Ba'al Shem Tov left his place, went over to the man, he whispered something in the man's ear and then, without waiting for an answer, returned to his place in line.

The incident surprised the Ba'al Shem Tov's disciples, and piqued their curiosity. Apparently, they surmised, that Jew must be one of the secret individuals with whom their rebbe maintained discreet contact. What could the Ba'al Shem Tov have whispered in the other fellow's ear, if not one of the secrets upon which the world hangs?

They were anxious to unravel the mystery, and to learn the identity of the hidden *tzaddik* whom the Ba'al Shem Tov had stepped out of line to greet on the way to his grandson's *chupah*. Most of all, they wanted to know the secret their rebbe had whispered in the man's ear.

The older disciples felt that it would be unseemly for them to leave the entourage. Instead, they signaled to some of the younger men to follow the stranger and see what they could find out.

Silently, the disciples trailed after the man until he entered the courtyard of a modest inn. In one hand he carried a small bundle, tied with cord. Just as the man was about to enter the inn, the students stopped him with hands outstretched in greeting. "*Shalom aleichem*, Rebbe!"

Startled, the man stared at them the way a frightened chicken might gape at a human being.

"You've got the wrong address. I'm no rebbe, nor the son of a rebbe!"

"We know that Your Honor is an important man," the disciples persisted. "It's useless to try and hide it."

"But I'm not a rebbe!"

"Your Honor, we wish you would confess to us," the disciples pressed, assuming that the man was not only a hidden *tzaddik,* but also extremely modest.

"I don't understand why you're starting up with me!" the man exclaimed. "Not only am I not a *tzaddik* or a rebbe, but the opposite: I am a sinner! A sinner who deserves to have scorn heaped on his head!"

Momentarily at a loss, the students soon rallied. Stubbornly, they said, "With our own eyes, we saw the way our rebbe, the Ba'al Shem Tov, came over to Your Honor on this, his big day, on the way to his grandson's wedding, and whispered something in Your Honor's ear. It's useless to deny it: Your Honor is no ordinary person."

The man saw that he would not easily be rid of his interrogators. He thought a while, and then spoke.

"I see that you are all curious and won't leave me alone. I'll tell you the secret that your rebbe whispered in my ear, and that will reveal something of his enormous power. But, to do that, I must roll the scroll back a bit, and return to an earlier time ..."

My name is Dov Ber, but everyone calls me Berel. I live in a city not far from here, where my little house sits right next door to the home of my dear friend, Menachem Dovid.

Menachem Dovid has been my best friend since childhood. We are the closest and most devoted of friends — even closer than brothers,. I think the correct expression is, "One soul in two bodies."

Menachem Dovid earns his living as a peddler. From time to time, he borrows money from rich people and takes the money with him on his travels to various towns and villages, buying cheap goods such as bundles of flax, wax tablets, and pots of honey, which he then goes on to sell in the big cities. The money he earns in this way is used to repay the loans and cover his expenses, with a bit left over for his family's support. He is not often at home, for when he returns from his travels he must set out again almost at once if he doesn't want his family to starve.

One day, Menachem Dovid returned from the big city. As always, friends and acquaintances dropped in to say hello. I, naturally, was one of them. A group of us sat in his home, chatting amicably, as Menachem Dovid told us of his experiences on his latest trip.

I suddenly felt an overwhelming urge to smoke. Being perfectly at home in my friend's house, I went into the inner room and opened the cupboard where he keeps his bags of tobacco. I wanted to take some to fill my pipe. Don't be surprised at my behavior — going over to someone else's cupboard as if I owned it. This was the great thing about our friendship; we were no strangers to one another. Menachem Dovid did the same thing in my home. That was the kind of friendship we had.

I opened the cupboard door, and what did I see? The purse of money that Menachem Dovid had just brought back, the profits from his peddling in the big city. It was lying there carelessly, exposed to all eyes.

I was angry at my friend. Was this any way to take care of money? It was Menachem Dovid's good luck that I was the one who had opened the cupboard this time. What if it had been someone else? Another person would certainly have been tempted to take the money!

I decided to teach my friend a lesson he would have never forget. I would hide the purse for a while, and return it only after he would searched frantically and learned the hard way that you have to guard your profits. It never occurred to me that I was performing the transgression of *lo signov* (thou shalt not steal), for our Sages have determined that taking for the purpose of causing distress is also considered stealing. I simply thought that, as he searched for the purse, I would remove it from my pocket as proof of his negligence. I would tell him exactly where and in what condition I had found his money.

I went into action. I took the money and went home.

Of course, I never intended to do him any harm. As I said, I intended to return the money as soon as he had discovered it was missing ... But things did not turn out the way I had envisioned them. To put it bluntly, the situation quickly became so complicated that it spiraled out of control.

My friend went over to the cupboard a few minutes later and discovered that the money was gone. He burst into heart-rending cries and began racing around the house like a madman. He searched for the money on every shelf, in every cupboard, even under the beds, between the chairs, and behind the door. The purse was gone. All along, it was in my pocket. I sat at home, heard the outcry, and smiled with pleasure. I knew that I was the one who had caused all the commotion. After a few minutes, I decided that the "lesson" was over. Enough. I prepared to leave my house in order to return what Menachem Dovid had lost, and to treat him to a well-deserved lecture.

But things were happening too quickly. Shaken to the core, Menachem Dovid fainted. His wife, seeing him collapse, fainted as well. Their small children stood by, wailing in fear and bewilderment. The entire household was in an uproar. I realized that this was no time to return the money, in front of all the neighbors who had congregated there in an effort to rouse the unconscious couple. I waited for the crowd to disperse — but just the opposite occurred. The more time passed, the larger the crowd grew and the greater the commotion became.

At long last, they managed to awaken Menachem Dovid. He opened his eyes and remembered what had happened. Leaning his head against the wall, he groaned, "The money. *Oy*, the money," and fainted again.

I saw the gravity of the situation. If I took out the purse now, I would be stoned by the neighbors. I'd get scolded to within an inch of my life for the "smart" trick I had played, taking my friend's money and causing him to keel over. I decided to wait for evening and return the money when there were no witnesses present, so that no one would know it had been my doing. I had already forgotten the notion of teaching my friend a lesson. My heart was filled with remorse over what I had done.

But, from that moment on, Menachem Dovid's house was never empty. Neighbors lingered there, to watch over the situation. My friend mourned endlessly, and everyone who heard him felt compelled to offer some comfort. He lay in bed, half-dead, surrounded by people giving him advice. Perhaps he had left the money in this place; perhaps in that one. I, too, sat at his bedside to console him in his time of difficulty. To tell the truth, I didn't find the proper words, for I knew the bitter truth, but the din was so loud and continuous that no one paid attention to what I did or didn't say. I wandered through the house, waiting for the right moment to take the purse out of my pocket and disappear.

But the moment never came. It was a small house, and everywhere I went I practically stepped on someone's head. Finally, I went home with the intention of coming up with a plan in the morning. I'd find an opportunity to return the lost purse and calm my hysterical friend. I had many intentions ... but none of them bore any fruit. The money was not returned.

You are doubtless surprised. You are wondering what can be so difficult about finding a second when no one is looking, to throw the purse into some hidden corner and be done with the whole foolish affair. Evidently, I was already in the grip of the evil inclination, although I wasn't aware of it yet. The next day, I walked into my friend's house again, to "comfort him." To my shock, I found several people there, banging on the table and shouting at him. "Liar! Give us our money! You made up this whole thing just to get out of paying what you owe us. Give us back our money!"

The men who had loaned him the money to buy merchandise for his trip had been whispering secretly among themselves. Slowly, their suspicions grew louder. They suspected that the whole story of the vanishing purse was nothing but a fabrication that had only one goal: to arouse the lenders' compassion and free him of his debt. They had come to his house, where I came upon them heaping blame on his head. I, and only I, knew that the blame was my own.

Had I been more courageous, I would have taken out the purse and exposed the truth at once. But a different truth — a hard one — hit me: It's easy enough to perform a prank, but difficult indeed to repair the damage it causes! I was weak, a coward. I didn't dare reveal that the missing purse was no fabrication, but a childish antic that had been blown up to monster proportions.

The lenders thumped their fists on the table, shouting at poor Menachem Dovid, who kept murmuring with a downcast face, "I'm not guilty. I promise to repay the loans as soon as I find what was lost."

After they had vented their anger on my friend, the men got up and left. I escaped as well. I didn't know what to do.

Several days passed. The uproar began to die down. Now my *yetzer hara* began to whisper persuasively in my ear. "Look, you can't return the money in any case. Menachem Dovid is walking around again, not lying with his face to the ground. Those are round coins. They roll from person to person. Tomorrow his luck will turn and he'll find some other money. Why not enjoy this cash?"

At first, I recoiled, stunned by the *yetzer hara's* incredible chutzpah. What nerve — to try and persuade me to become a thief! I didn't understand that this is the very nature of the evil inclination. Chutzpah and brazen nerve are the tools of its trade. I pushed it away, saying, "You foul thing, get away from me! Don't persuade me to take money that is not mine!"

But that wily old king laughed in my face. "Look who's talking! ... I'm persuading you to take somebody's money? It was you, and no one else, who already took the money. Without the slightest hesitation, you stuck your hand into that cupboard and took money that was not yours. Did you really believe you'd return it? Well, now you can't. Listen to me, friend. Why should that money lie around like an old, moss-covered stone? Go out to the marketplace, buy and sell, do some business, make a few bucks, and then return the purse to its place. That way, you turn a profit and he loses nothing."

I had no defense against these slick arguments. Thinking it over, I decided that his words made a certain amount of sense. I could do it. I'd go down to the marketplace, set up business with my friend's money, make a quick profit, and then return the money at once.

After a little more consideration, however, I realized that the matter was not that simple. People are not stupid. If I went down to the market, bought merchandise, and got rich, people would ask questions. It would not take much calculating before they would come upon the only possible solution: "Menachem Dovid had money, and that money disappeared. His next-door neighbor had no money, and now he has some. Judging by what our eyes can see, it's clear as the noonday sun that one took the other's money!"

In light of this, the *yetzer hara* began hurling a new volley of poisoned arrows at me, with fresh thoughts of sin:

"Forget your naive plans to return the money. That business is over and done with forever! You can't return it without arousing everyone's anger. Leave this place, Berel. Go to a distant city, and start a business there with your friend's money. Buy and sell and prosper!"

I let myself be persuaded. I was deep in the *yetzer hara's* clutches.

I began making my preparations. First I would leave on my own, so that no one would suspect anything. Afterwards, when I had succeeded in launching my business and had set myself up in my new place, I would call for my wife and children to follow. In a distant city, where no one knows me, no one would ask embarrassing questions. No one would hear that I had grown rich overnight. And even if they heard and talked about me, what did I care? In a faraway place, I could do whatever I pleased.

That's how it went. I progressed from bad to worse, with one *aveirah* dragging another in its wake. I personally witnessed the way one needs to crack open only a tiny entrance for that wicked one, and he'll drag you after him into the depths. He, too, knows how to say, "Open up to the width of a needle's eye ..."

I took the money and set out. Here I came, to this city where I planned to settle down and build a rosy new future for myself.

And then, as I walked along, I saw your rebbe approaching me. He had never seen me before, but he came over and whispered in my ear:

"Listen to me, my friend. Go back home, and return the stolen money to your friend. I promise you faithfully that I, personally, will appear at the *beis din* in your hometown to testify on your behalf that you had no evil intentions when you took the money."

That's what he told me — words that pierced me like a sharp sword. I saw that all that is hidden lies revealed to that holy man. We had never in our lives even laid eyes on one another before today!

Berel breathed deeply, sighing from the depths of his heart. To the band of disciples, he said, "I feel an indescribable sense of relief ... as though a millstone has rolled off my neck. With Hashem's help, I'm going to do as your rebbe said. I've repented of my evil intentions. I'll go home at once and return the money to my poor friend. He will take me to court and expose me as a thief — but I am certain that your holy rebbe will keep his promise and come testify that I had no evil intention when I took the purse. I believe that it will all come out right in the end."

"Greetings, Heavenly Court!"

L UBLIN WAS THE HOME OF THAT GIANT AMONG MEN, THE holy *gaon*, R' Shlomo Luria, known as the Maharshal of Lublin and author of the *Yam Shel Shlomo*. One of his most outstanding students was a young man by the name of Nachum who came from Leivnitza, a small town on the outskirts of Lublin.

Even as a young child, Nachum's cleverness and beauty drew all eyes to him. At his bar mitzvah, he dazzled everyone with a complex Torah sermon. His face shone like the sun and his eyes sparkled with the light of Torah as pearls of wisdom issued from his mouth. One of those present at the bar mitzvah *seudah* was the blacksmith, Meir Meirim. Few were aware that Meir Meirim was one of the generation's thirty-six hidden *tzaddikim*, who used his blacksmith's role as camouflage.

Meir Meirim had been invited to the *seudah* by Nachum's father, Menashe the butcher, who was a close friend of the blacksmith and knew of his hidden qualities. Upon hearing the amazing Torah insights from the bar mitzvah boy, Meir was struck by inspiration. The next day, he proposed to his friend Menashe that they make a match between their children. Nachum, destined for greatness, would become engaged to Meir's modest daughter, Esther.

Menashe's joy knew no bounds. He knew very well who and what the "blacksmith" really was. Those who were in the know in Leivnitza claimed that Menashe was a "butcher" the way Meir was a "black-smith" — that he, too, was one of the generation's hidden *tzaddikim* who, between selling one cut of meat and the next, concerned himself with the most exalted and elevated of subjects.

The engagement was contracted. The *kallah*, who was only 12, continued to help her mother with the housework and in caring for her younger brothers, while the *chasan* continued to learn diligently, growing great in Torah and piety.

When Nachum reached the age of 17, he was at the peak of his youthful growth. His smooth cheeks were rosy and his blue eyes shone with the glow of youth and the light of Torah. His parents decided that this was the proper time for Nachum to be married. The *kallah's* parents agreed. Their daughter was 16 now, healthy, strong, and mature enough to take on the responsibilities of marriage. Before long, the happy couple stood together beneath the *chupah*.

After the week of *sheva berachos*, Nachum told his wife, Esther, that he had decided to leave their little village and move to the big city of Lublin. He had heard tales of R' Shlomo Luria's great yeshivah, and yearned to hear the Rosh Yeshivah's incisive lectures. The new bride, wishing to help her husband grow to greatness in Torah and piety, and never one to place any obstacle in his path, agreed at once — despite the fact that she was an only daughter and deeply attached to her mother. Without delay, the couple moved to Lublin.

Nachum was tested by the Maharshal and accepted as a student. He immediately excelled and rapidly moved upward, and soon was one of the foremost students of the Maharshal.

⌘

At first, Esther was happy in Lublin. Though homesick for her family, she overcame her feelings in order to help her husband grow to his maximum potential in Torah. She undertook to support herself and Nachum by hiring herself out as a washerwoman in the homes of the rich. For long hours at a stretch she would bend over wooden washboards filled with soiled clothes and sudsy water, scrubbing until her fingers were raw and her back ached. The wealthy women were pleased with her work and praised her heartily. The shirts that Esther washed sparkled with whiteness, and the children's trousers, stained with mud and grease, looked new after her devoted ministrations. The payment she received was paltry when compared to the quality of her work, and she knew that her employers were taking advantage of her. But her zeal and hard work never slackened. All that mattered to her was that Nachum be able to sit and learn in peace.

During their first year in Lublin, the only thing that marred Esther's contentment was her longing for her mother, in particular, and for the rest of her family in general. From time to time, when the feelings would overwhelm her, she would wipe the tears from her eyes and ease her pain by listening to the latest *divrei Torah* her husband brought back from yeshivah.

In the second year of her marriage, a new worm began to gnaw at Esther's heart. Unexamined fears ran through her, along with vague, fluttering anxieties. A quiet depression took hold of her, though she did not know why. Finally, one day, the thought formulated itself clearly in her mind:

"It's been two years since the wedding, and we still have no children!"

There was a certain relief in understanding what the vague anxiety had been about, and to have her fear out in the open. Now she knew why she had been feeling so troubled. She began to worry why she had not yet merited having a baby, like all her friends and neighbors. Every young couple around her was caring for a child or two, while she wandered about alone, a barren woman.

She knew that it was still early. Two years was actually a short period of time. No need to panic. But emotion does not easily bow to logic. Her mind told her one thing, and her heart told her another

— and it was usually logic that went down, defeated. For many nights she lay sleepless, torn by fear and anxiety. Day followed day and month chased month. All her neighbors' homes were filled with the happy sounds of babies and children. Only their home, Esther and Nachum's, remained desolate and empty.

Immersed in Torah, Nachum had no time to sense that something wasn't right — and Esther zealously guarded his peace of mind. An inner purity left its radiant mark on his countenance. Torah brought him joy and engaged every waking thought, leaving no part of his mind free for worry or depression to find a foothold. Esther, on the other hand, alone in her empty world, was constantly tortured by her stormy thoughts, which robbed her of all joy in life. Worst of all was the secret fear that she might die without ever having embraced a child of her own.

This terror would bring on bouts of choked weeping. Esther tried with all her might to hide the tears from Nachum, to spare him his share of her agony.

Another bitter year passed in this way, and then a fourth. She was still young — only 20 — with "her whole life ahead of her." She tried to remember this, and to calm her tortured spirit. But nothing helped. The thoughts continued to grow in strength until she was afraid she would simply explode.

At last, one day, Esther gathered her courage and said, "Nachum, it's been four years since we were married."

"Yes," he nodded, lifting his eyes from his *sefer*. "May Hashem help us to continue living in peace and harmony until one hundred and twenty."

"Amen," Esther said automatically — just before the tears spurted forcefully from her eyes. She sobbed into her hands.

"Why are you crying?" Nachum asked in distress. "Aren't you happy with me?"

"I'm v-very happy," she gulped through her sobs. "But our house is empty. I want to hold a little baby, to carry it near my heart, to hug and kiss it the way all my friends do. Why have I not merited a child?"

Nachum occasionally suffered from feelings of sadness or frustration, but he always managed to bury himself in his learning until his heart was at peace again. Now he suddenly realized that, while he found his consolation in Torah, his wife was contending alone with a profound sorrow too great for her to bear. Tears glistened in his own eyes as he shared in her pain.

"We must *daven* to Hashem. Surely He will send us salvation," he told his weeping wife.

Both of them prayed fervently for a child. Esther offered her help to mothers burdened with many youngsters, in the hope that, in return, Heaven's compassion would be aroused for her.

But it was not to be. Year followed year, until a full decade filled with pain and distress had left its stony stamp on Esther's heart.

One day, she felt too ill to work. She lay in bed, wracked by illness. Sensing the way the disease was taking over her body, bit by bit, she knew that her end was near. In the intervals when the pain gave her some respite, she would brood over the future — the time to come after her death.

Nachum was still a young man, only 27 years old, a formidable scholar and a pious individual with an excellent reputation. There would surely be no shortage of marriage offers for him. He would not remain a widower for long. Within months he would undoubtedly be remarried, and when a year had passed he would be embracing his child. Why not? Was every woman in the world cursed with barrenness, as she had been? Nachum would mourn her for a month or two, and then lose himself in his Torah. He would find comfort, he would remarry, he would start a new family — and he would forget that she had ever existed!

"There will be no reminder of me," Esther thought. "I leave nothing behind. Soon, now, my body will lie in the grave, rotting, and he will forget me."

The idea was simply unbearable. She had resigned herself to dying, but was even Nachum not to remember her? This was something to which she could not resign herself.

"Nachum," she called weakly, her voice choked with tears.

Nachum approached the sickbed where his wife lay. His eyes were swollen from hours of weeping. "Shall I get you something warm to drink?" he asked.

"No!" she said, her expression agonized. "My decaying body doesn't need anything anymore. I have only one request to make of you, my dear Nachum."

"Whatever you want, it won't be hard for me to do," Nachum replied, his voice trembling.

"Are you prepared to promise me anything?"

"Anything!"

⚜

"I'm going to die," Esther said, the tears beginning to flow again.

"Is that any way to talk?" her husband scolded. "Is Hashem incapable of sending you a speedy recovery?"

A sea of pain was evident in Esther's eyes. "Stop. The decree has already been made. It has been sealed, and there's no changing it. I know that my end is near. I sense clearly that, in just a few minutes, my Creator will gather me to Him. I can only hope that a few of the good deeds I've done in my life will serve as my defenders on the Judgment Day."

Here she burst into a fresh bout of tears. Nachum wept along with her, his tears flowing even more copiously than hers.

"What will happen after I die?" asked Esther, sobbing. "Will you marry a new wife and forget me entirely? You'll be happy, you'll live and flourish, while I rot in the grave, forgotten by everyone. Even the husband with whom I shared my life for ten years will rejoice with his new wife and children, and forget that he ever had a wife named Esther."

Nachum's face grew white. He had never given the future a thought. He had not wanted to believe that the worst could happen ... and here was Esther, speaking of what was to come. Was she not correct? In all probability, what she had described would take place. The agonizing thought filled him until he felt as though he were choking. How could he ever forget her? How was such a thing possible?

Without thinking twice, he burst out, "Esther, I promise that I will never marry another woman. I will remain faithful to you forever!"

"You promise?" Esther asked, hardly believing her ears.

"With all my heart."

"I'd like you to swear," the dying woman requested.

To satisfy his poor wife, Nachum swore.

A happy smile crossed Esther's ravaged face. She closed her eyes and fell into her final sleep.

Nachum mourned his wife deeply and bitterly. Caverns of pain and sorrow filled his heart. There were moments when he wished he could have died along with her. The world would never be the same without her. The sun would never shine again.

His friends came to console him during the week of *shivah*, making sure he was never alone. They attended to all his needs, providing food and drink. They spoke gently with him, attempting to ease his pain.

When the week was over, Nachum returned to the *beis midrash*. He drowned his sorrow in the edifice of Torah and in composing novellae. As the months passed, his friends began to notice a curious fact. The passage of time, instead of easing the widower's pain, seemed to do the opposite. From day to day he sank into a deeper gloom, withdrawn from everyone. He seldom spoke and never smiled. Nachum's friends were surprised, because they knew that the words of our Sages apply to all, and they had stated that the dead gradually *do* depart from our hearts, whether it be the wife of one's youth or an elderly spouse. Time, like dust, eventually covers everything. In that case, why was Nachum refusing to leave his circle of grief? Why was he so detached from the world, enveloped in a bubble of sorrow?

They beseeched him until he finally revealed his secret: On his wife's deathbed, he had promised her — sworn to her — that he would never marry again. Now he regretted the oath. He wished to establish a Jewish home, but could not. He was trapped.

Nachum's friends, at a loss as to how to extricate him from his predicament, turned to their rebbe, R' Shlomo Luria.

The Maharshal immediately summoned his dear student and asked, "Is this true?"

Nachum confirmed the story, and related to his rebbe exactly how events had unfolded.

The Maharshal stood up and said forcefully, "Your vow is null and void. It has no existence. Though it is a mitzvah to fulfill a dying person's request, this holds true when the request does not contradict the Torah. In this case, a vow was extracted from you which you cannot fulfill, and which stands in opposition to our holy Torah's command to 'be fruitful and multiply.' You must remarry and bring a new and blessed generation into the world."

"But how can I ignore my promise?" Nachum asked fearfully.

Rabbeinu Shlomo placed an affectionate hand on his student's shoulder. "That is on my head. This very day, I will speak to matchmakers on your behalf, and ask them to seek a proper match."

For the first time in a very long while, the light returned to the young widower's eyes. A faint smile showed upon his pale face.

That same day, the Maharshal spoke to the elderly *gabbai* of the shul, who had made numerous matches in his time. The *gabbai* promised to search for a proper wife for Nachum the widower.

The moment the Maharshal left his home, the matchmaker began to think. The names of all the people in town were etched in his mind, and he went through them carefully. His face lit up. Taking his stick, he went to the home of Chayah Perel, a divorced woman. This, he believed, was a match made in heaven.

Chayah Perel, too, thought it a fitting match. The matter progressed smoothly, until there was nothing left to do but announce the engagement.

And then, on the morning of the appointed day, terrible news spread through the city. Nachum was dead. He fell down, and with no discernible reason, died!

"His first wife must have summoned him to the Heavenly Court," the people whispered with fear. "Nachum broke his vow and was about to announce his engagement to another woman."

In tears, the *shamash* of the shul brought the tragic news to the Maharshal. "We wanted to help the unfortunate fellow, and look what's happened now!"

Rabbeinu Shlomo's expression remained calm. He instructed the old *shamash*, "Tell the *Chevrah Kaddisha* to handle him in the normal fashion and to perform the *taharah*. But when you are in the cemetery, about to perform the burial, please send for me. I want to be there."

∽∾∾

A large crowd had come to pay their last respects to the deceased. Numerous Jews, having heard of the tragedy, flocked to his house.

When the funeral procession neared the cemetery, the Maharshal approached the bier where the dead man lay. Before Nachum's body could be lowered into the grave, the Maharshal placed a slip of paper into Nachum's hand. On the paper were the following words:

"Greetings, Heavenly Court. How is this possible? Doesn't an '*asei*' (a positive commandment) take precedence over a '*lo sa'aseh*' (a negative commandment) in the Torah? I decree with the authority of the Torah that you return this young man!"

The body was lowered into the grave and covered with dirt. The crowd dispersed. Whispers passed from mouth to ear, telling of the mysterious note that had been placed in the young man's hand. Those with some knowledge explained its contents: The positive commandment of *"peru u'revu"* (be fruitful and multiply) took precedence over the negative commandment of breaking a vow.

A short time later, shocking news began to spread like wildfire through the community: The dead Nachum had risen from his grave! Still dressed in his shrouds, he was walking through the city as though nothing had happened.

Lublin was in an uproar. The man newly risen from the dead threw a pall of fear over everyone he met, making them flee to the safety of their homes. Everyone waited with bated breath to see what would happen next. As for Nachum himself, he did not seem overly excited by the turn of events. He went to the Maharshal's home and said simply, "Rebbe, they returned me to life."

"I knew they would," replied his rebbe. "But you cannot walk around among the living wearing a dead man's shrouds. Go home, take them off, and put on your old clothes."

Nachum did as he was told, and returned to his home. By the time a week had gone by, the furor had died down. People peeked fearfully at the man who had returned from the dead, and were afraid to come too near to him. It goes without saying that no woman, single, divorced or widowed, would listen to his name as a possible match. "Marry a man who was once dead?" they exclaimed with a shudder. "No!"

Nachum saw that he would be forced, against his will, to live by the oath he had sworn to his first wife. He went to his rebbe and poured out his woes. He would never live this down. The label "dead-alive" stuck to him like glue.

"Have no worry," Rabbeinu Shlomo said. "There is a solution to this as well."

After Nachum left the house, the Maharshal stood up and decreed with the authority of the Torah that the Angel of Forgetfulness erase the memory of the entire episode from the hearts of Lublin's populace.

Astonishingly, that is exactly what happened. Every Jew in Lublin forgot the whole story, as though it had never happened. Nachum was just like anybody else. He married a pious women and raised a fine family. It was only years later that the memory of what had happened began to return to the people. In order that the story not be lost again, they wrote it down in the archives of the Chevrah Kaddisha of Lublin, in eternal memory.

The Gerrer Rebbe, author of the *Imrei Emes*, read this story in the archives of the Lublin *Chevrah Kaddisha*, and it was he who told it to the public. Whenever he told the tale, he would add:

"The fact that the Maharshal was able to revive the dead is no news. But the decree that he placed on the Angel of Forgetfulness, making all of Lublin forget such a powerful story — now, that is something new!"

An Honest Mistake

T HE FIRST EDITION OF THE TAZ'S *MAGEN DOVID* ON *SHULCHAN Aruch Orach Chaim* includes the following comment regarding the laws of making *Kiddush*: Although the *Shulchan Aruch* rules that, where wine is unavailable, it is acceptable to make *Kiddush* over beer since it is a *chamar medinah*, a respectable beverage, the people of the city of Potolich may not make *Kiddush* over beer or whiskey, because they despise sharp drinks.

This interesting comment can be found only in those few isolated extant copies of the first-edition *Taz*. Beginning with the second edition, the comment was omitted, though no one knows why. Why was the comment written, and why was it erased?

Between the first edition and the second lies a fascinating story, which was set down in the community archives of Potolich.

When the "Bach" — R' Yoel Sirkis — was appointed rabbi of the city of Mezhibozh, he founded a large yeshivah there. Boys from every corner of Poland flocked to the yeshivah. Among them was an especially talented youth by the name of Dovid Halevi Segal, son of a respected member of the Jewish community of Ludmir. Youngest of all the students — he had yet to reach the age of bar mitzvah — Dovid, who was later to be known as the "Taz," quickly outshone all his classmates with his brilliance, breadth of knowledge, and humility.

When he was ready for marriage, his rebbe chose him for his youngest daughter, the clever Rivkah, and promised the young couple several years' support in his home. Some time afterward, however, the Bach grew poor, and was no longer capable of providing his son-in-law with the daily meat meal he had promised. As a substitute, he served him liver — whereupon the Taz summoned his father-in-law to a *din Torah* for violating the terms of the nuptial agreement. The Bach responded by writing several halachic treatises proving that liver falls into the category of meat, and that it is questionable whether a person who has vowed to abstain from meat is permitted to consume liver.

Asked why he had taken his illustrious father-in-law to court over this matter, the Taz replied simply that, from the time he had begun eating liver, he had grown weak, unable to learn at his usual pace or to think up Torah novellae at his full strength. The Heavenly Court, said the Taz, had raised a complaint against the Bach because of this.

"That's why I called my father-in-law to a *beis din*," explained the Taz. "When there is a court case below, there is none above! And not only that, but once the Bach succeeded in proving that liver falls into the category of meat, the *beis din* ruled in his favor — and the Heavenly Court always rules in consonance with the earthly one."

With the passage of time, the Bach grew so destitute that he was unable to support his son-in-law and daughter at all. The Taz was forced to seek a source of livelihood. Though averse to the burdens of the rabbinate, he believed that only in that role could he learn Torah day and night with peace of mind. He sought a position, and heard that the small town of Potolich was seeking a rav. The Taz offered himself for the job, and was accepted.

Potolich was a rustic place, its inhabitants mostly laborers with little knowledge of the Torah. In light of this, it comes as no surprise that they lacked an appreciation for the awesome stature of their new rabbi, who was worthy of serving much larger cities and resembled, in that provincial little town, a beautiful pearl that has fallen into the hands of salt merchants.

As soon as he arrived in Potolich, the Taz went out to take stock of the town. Discovering the nature of the townspeople, he despaired of teaching them and immersed himself instead in Torah. For their part, the people of Potolich undertook with great zeal to fulfill the igno- rant Jew's "commandment" to hate the *talmid chacham*. They turned against the young rav at every opportunity, treating him with scorn. Because they did not recognize his greatness in Torah, they paid him a salary so paltry as to be laughable. But the rav and his family weren't laughing. The few pennies he earned were not enough to supply even their most basic needs. It is no exaggeration to say that the rav and his family were close to starvation.

Trying to ignore his hunger pangs, the Taz sat and learned night and day. It was winter, and the cold overpowered even his hunger. The house was frozen. The big oven built into the kitchen wall was cold, since there was no money for even a few sticks of kindling.

R' Dovid took advantage of the quiet nighttime to flourish in Torah. Deep into the night the young rabbi sat, while the cold penetrated his very bones. Because he had hardly eaten that day, he was overcome with a sudden weakness, and nearly fainted. Had it been only hunger that he had to contend with, he could have conquered his discomfort. If it had been only the freezing cold that he was forced to fight, he might have been able to continue. But with both these things attacking his frail form at once, R' Dovid was finding it difficult to learn. With the last of his strength he plowed on, attempting to concentrate on his *sefer* while wrapped in a thick coat against the cold.

After a prolonged struggle, he felt as though he were about to expire. In distress, he sought a solution to both problems, the cold and his hunger — a solution that would enable him to continue learning by candlelight. It occurred to him that whiskey would warm him, and would also chase away a bit of the emptiness inside.

There was one place that was open into the late hours of the night, where it was possible to obtain whiskey. The tavern was not far from his home. After brief consideration, the Taz left his house and went over to the tavern to save his life.

In his humility, and because his total absorption in Torah had left him detached from wordly matters, he thought that the tavern was a liquor shop and nothing else. It never entered his mind that there might be a diminishment of honor in the rav's entering such a place. His weak legs plowed through the deep snow toward the lit-up tavern.

A blast of warmth greeted him as he walked inside. As opposed to the stove in his own home, the one in this tavern blazed merrily, with a pleasant crackle of logs. R' Dovid's lips moved with difficulty as he ordered a drink.

"Beer or brandy?" the tavern-keeper asked laconically.

"Beer does not satisfy or warm the body," the Taz answered. "Give me a glass of brandy. But I must reveal the truth: I don't have a penny in my pocket. Could you sell it to me on credit?"

"Certainly," smiled the tavern-keeper. He pointed to the wall behind him. "See there? They're all buying on credit."

R' Dovid was too weak to grasp the man's meaning. He recited the *Shehakol* blessing with fervor and then, closing his eyes, cautiously sipped the drink.

The tavern-keeper stared at him in surprise. This customer's refined behavior was in glaring contrast to his usual clientele.

A pleasant warmth spread through R' Dovid's body. The brandy was, indeed, refreshing his weak heart. With renewed vigor, he walked home and learned happily until morning.

Seeing that the drink had enabled him to learn with added diligence, he went back to the tavern on the following night, to order another glass of brandy. The Sages who came before him had stated that brandy was sometimes mentioned in a positive light and sometimes spoken of with disfavor. R' Dovid saw it only in a positive light ... This magical drink helped him to learn Torah, and that was all that mattered to him.

On this second night, too, he ordered the drink on credit. Again, the tavern-keeper drew the customer's attention to the scarred wall behind him. Only then did R' Dovid lift his eyes and see that the entire wall was covered with words and figures that the tavern-keeper had written there in charcoal. So-and-so had taken this many bottles of whiskey and wine, and owed such-and-such a sum. So-and-so had drunk this many glasses of whiskey, and his debt was such-and-such ... and so on. Among the names listed there was a new one: R' Dovid Halevi Segal, town rabbi, had taken two glasses of brandy on credit, and owed a certain sum of pennies.

"And what happens when I'm able to pay what I owe?" asked R' Dovid.

With a grin, the tavern-keeper pointed to a dirty rag. "I use this to erase the debt in an instant."

Because his salary did not increase in the following days, and since he and his family were hungry for bread and shivering with cold, R' Dovid had nothing left over with which to pay what he owed. Having no other option, he continued to buy brandy on credit, so that it might allay some of his hunger and warm him in the terrible cold.

One night, a group of local townspeople entered the tavern together. As they waited to be served, they glanced idly at the list on the wall. Suddenly, one of them caught sight of a new line that said that the rabbi, R' Dovid Halevi Segal, owed the tavern-keeper for a certain number of glasses of brandy that he had drunk.

"Do you see what I see, or am I just imagining it?" the man asked his friend, nudging him in the ribs. The friend read the line, as did all the rest. They shouted, "What, does the rabbi like a little drink? We're only simple folk, but he's a refined yeshivah man. Look how he's been fooling us!"

The outcry soon reached the rest of the town. Gossipers spread the news everywhere, until the community leaders — who already despised the rav — called a hurried meeting in which they voted to dismiss him from his post and from the town.

That same afternoon, they placed the rav and his family on the garbage wagon and drove them out of Potolich.

The downfall was Hashem's handiwork, and was necessary for the ensuing ascension to take place. In truth, the road to finding the peace he craved was now open to R' Dovid. Immediately after leaving Potolich, he served as the unofficial rav of Posen and was then invited to serve as rabbi of the city of Ostroh, home of the Maharsha — a place where there were always Torah scholars and a yeshivah, and where even the householders were refined people who loved the Torah and knew how to venerate their new rav as he deserved.

It was here, among the people of Ostroh, that the Taz wrote his famous work, the *Magen Dovid* on the *Shulchan Aruch*. Because his salary was now sufficient for his needs, he even had the money with which to print the *sefer*.

When he reached the section on what one may use for *Kiddush* when wine is unavailable, he added the comment about whiskey with reference to his first rabbinical post, Potolich. Ignorant of the ways of the world, the Taz knew nothing about the true nature of the tavern situated just steps from his door. His eyes never strayed, so that he never saw the drunkards spending their days and nights drinking in the tavern, growing intoxicated and wild, and ending up under the table. Seeking a reason for the local populace's rage against him — a fury that had led them to the extreme move of chasing him out of their midst — he decided that the reason must be that they hated intoxicating drinks and therefore could not tolerate a person who drank them!

The truth, of course, was exactly the opposite. The people of Potolich did not hate whiskey; they loved it! In fact, a large portion of the town's residents earned a living through the production of beer and whiskey.

No sooner had the Taz's work been published than it was eagerly embraced by Torah scholars everywhere. His thoughts were discussed in *batei midrash,* and the generation for which original Torah thoughts were like food and drink praised the Taz as a pillar of Israel.

Along with the rest of his wonderful work, the Torah community noticed the curious reference to the people of Potolich who, according to the Taz, could not fulfill their *Kiddush* obligation with whiskey because they could not tolerate strong drink. Within a short time, word spread everywhere that the people of Potolich hated whiskey! All the liquor merchants who dealt with them regularly and bought their products were certain that the people of Potolich had a change of heart — that they now despised alcoholic drinks and were no longer producing them! Before long, none of the merchants came to Potolich anymore. The source of the town's livelihood quickly dried up.

Their former rabbi, R' Dovid Halevi Segal, whom they had run out of town in disgrace, had turned out to be a towering edifice of Torah, one of the generation's great men, praised everywhere, and petitioned for halachic rulings from every corner of the world. Because he had written that they hated whiskey, he had changed reality. Unintentionally, he had chased away all the merchants with whom the town had done business in the past.

Bit by bit, they pieced together the entire story. They spoke to the tavern-keeper, who revealed that because of their intransigent attitude toward the righteous rav they had afforded him such a paltry salary that he was forced into the tavern, to warm his frozen bones and allay his gnawing hunger after days of fasting. On learning this, the townspeople were struck with remorse, and angry with themselves for their mistaken attitude toward the great rabbi whom they had not known how to revere properly. Even more, they were pained at the financial loss they had sustained. The town decided to send a delegation of respected community members to apologize to R' Dovid, and plead with him to erase from his *sefer* the reference that was causing them such serious damage.

R' Dovid and his family were sitting at home when there came the sound of heavy footsteps approaching.

"That is a delegation from Potolich," R' Dovid said.

His family was astonished. "How do you know? Is this *ruach hakodesh*? How can you identify someone before you have even seen him?"

The Taz smiled. "The heavy, awkward footsteps belong to the people of Potolich, who wear heavy, awkward shoes. What business brings them to Ostroh? They must be coming to see me."

Indeed, just moments later the delegation entered the house.

The people of Potolich were earthy, but they were not stupid. Clumsy, yes — but also seasoned businessmen. First, they announced that they had come to beg the rav's pardon on behalf of their entire town, for their attitude toward him when he had served as their rabbi, and especially for the humiliating manner in which they had sent him away. The Taz forgave them immediately, adding that Hashem had directed these events for his benefit, as now he was surrounded by Torah scholars like himself. Once the atmosphere had thawed, he asked his rebbetzin to serve his guests some refreshments.

The rebbetzin hurried to the kitchen, and returned with a tray laden with various kinds of cakes and biscuits. The visitors sat chatting with the rav, but did not touch the tray.

"Why won't you taste anything?" asked the Taz.

The merchants exchanged a glance. "Is this what you call refreshment? The main thing is the whiskey, along with which one may eat some cake to accompany the drink and make it taste even better."

The Taz was surprised. "But you detest alcohol!"

This was the moment which the Potolich delegation had been waiting for. Here was their chance to correct the rav's false impression and set things right. "On the contrary — that's our primary drink, and we make our living from it. All our livelihood comes from the production of alcoholic beverages."

The Taz ordered some whiskey brought to the table.

A short time later, when the Taz printed the second edition of his work, he deleted the line relating to the people of Potolich, which had been written in error. Almost at once, the town's economy again began to thrive.

The Lvov community archives state that "Rabbeinu Taz was *Av Beis Din* of Potolich, near Rawa, when his father-in-law, the Bach, was *Av Beis Din* in Belz ... Before the Bach went to serve as *Av Beis Din* in Cracow, he went to visit his son-in-law, the Taz, and his daughter, in Potolich, to see to their welfare before his departure. I heard from the great and brilliant *gaon*, R' Naftali Hertz, that he saw the Bach's handwritten letter in the home of the *gaon* R' Efraim Zalman Margulies, author of the *Beis Efraim*. The Bach had written to his son-in-law as follows:

" 'When I was at your home in Potolich, I witnessed your poverty and was very distressed at the fact that you cannot sit over your Torah in peace. But I hope that Hashem will broaden my horizons so I may send you a gift.'

   "Indeed, afterwards he sent him a gift, along with his hearty compliments."

~๑๛~

[My thanks and blessings to my dear friend, R' Shmuel Honig, who brought this unusual story, found in an old and rare source work, to my attention.]

The Man Who Died Twice

THE HOLY *GAON*, R' NAFTALI HAKOHEN KATZ, AUTHOR OF THE *Semichas Chachamim*, who left this world on the 24th of Teves 5479 (1719), and was buried with honor in Istanbul, was "the greatest man of his generation, over and above all the wise men of our time," according to the sages of his own day. His name was spoken with awe by his contemporaries and by those who came after him. His Torah novellae, his stories, and the prayers he composed have been a source of light and inspiration to many.

There are authors, and there are authors. There are those whose work outstrips them, and those who far outstrip their work. This giant of his time, author of the *Semichas Chachamim*, was such a towering and awesome figure that he was far greater than anything he wrote. Though his writings were great, they were dwarfed by their author. His writings did not fully express the essence of his brilliance, which embraced numerous worlds. In the words of one of his students, R' Naftali was "among the greatest men whom Israel has seen in recent generations."

When still very young, he served as rav and rosh yeshivah in the great Torah center of Pozna, in Western Poland. One day, a covered coach drawn by four mighty horses pulled up in the street fronting the yeshivah. From the ornate carriage descended Herschel Magnus, the moneychanger — or, as the job was called in those days, the "coin supplier." Herschel Magnus, known for his outstanding wealth, had come in search of a Torah scholar to wed his daughter.

He spoke with the Rosh Yeshivah, R' Naftali Katz. "I have an excellent daughter at home," said Herschel Magnus. "I'd like an exceptional young man from your yeshivah, someone upright and pious, and well-accomplished in Torah, to be my son-in-law."

The Rosh Yeshivah thought for a moment, then said, "I can suggest Yosef of Koritz, one of my best students, outstanding in Torah and piety, and crowned with fine *middos*."

Without hesitation, the moneychanger summoned the *bachur* and proposed the match. "I'll clothe you like a rich and honored man. I've also set aside a large dowry for my daughter, as well as support in my home — "kest" — for five years. Are you willing?"

The wedding took place a short time later. Yosef of Koritz married Taibel, daughter of the wealthy moneychanger, in a lavish ceremony as befitted the daughter of such a rich man. The young couple made their home in her parents' house and were supported by them, as promised.

It soon became all too clear to the moneychanger and his daughter, however, that while money may buy a *chasan*, it can't necessarily buy a husband.

For some reason, Yosef took a dislike to his wife, and spent his days away from the house, learning in the *beis midrash* from morning to night.

Young Taibel sat home all day long, waiting for him, and taking consolation in her mother's company. At first, she thought that Yosef had simply not yet adjusted to married life. But as more time passed without any change in his behavior, she began to question and pester him, asking why he was making her suffer by staying away. Yosef remained silent, offering no answer — and there was no change at all in his inexplicable behavior. He left the house early in the morning and returned late at night, when the household was asleep. At last, Taibel complained to his friends in the *beis midrash*, pouring her heart out to them.

Yosef's friends tried to reason with him. "What did your wife do that was so bad?" they asked. But he would not answer them. He refused to divulge his secret, feeling that the match had been forced on him from the start, and that Taibel did not please him at all. Nevertheless, after his friends' scolding he changed his habits slightly and began to stay home at times. But his company was far from pleasant: He sat there like one of his father-in-law's beautiful pieces of furniture — silent and still.

Taibel tried to draw him out of his shell. She told him stories of things that had happened the day before, and the day before that — who said what to whom and who went where. But how long could she talk to the walls? He would not be engaged in conversation with her. After several fruitless days of this, she realized that he had no desire to speak with her at all. She decided to force him to speak. She began to say things to annoy him — insulting, provoking words. Perhaps he would grow angry and say something, anything. She would break his silence!

These tactics did not work, either. Yosef just met them with more of the same: silence. In her anger and pain, Taibel began to revile and abuse him at every turn.

Her behavior finally produced results — in the opposite direction. Yosef found himself unable to bear the tense atmosphere at home, and equally unable to live peaceably with her. One day he left, as usual, early in the morning. This time, a small sack was slung over his shoulder. It was the last time he would leave that house.

He did not return that evening, and was gone all the next day. Taibel wondered if he could no longer tolerate living at home, and preferred sleeping in the *beis midrash*. After he had been missing for three days, she began to repent of her behavior and went in search of her husband, intending to apologize.

To her shock, Yosef's friends informed her that they had not seen him at all for the last three days. Taibel trudged home, where she waited — in vain — for her husband's return.

A month passed, and then two. At last, a full year had gone by since her husband's disappearance. Another year was added to that. They searched everywhere for him, but it was as though the earth had swallowed him up, leaving no sign of him.

For thirteen years Taibel remained an *agunah* — a deserted wife. She hated her life — a life without children and family, without purpose or satisfaction. To her parents, she would sob, "I prefer death to a life like this!"

Her father, Herschel the moneychanger, could no longer stand his daughter's pain, and asked his friends' advice. "What do you think I should do? How can I help free my daughter from the chains of her prison?"

One of them replied simply, "Go back to the *shadchan* (matchmaker)."

Herschel laughed bitterly. "Do matchmakers offer a guarantee for the *shidduchim* they make?"

But his friends persisted in all seriousness. "The *shadchan* was the holy R' Naftali, who lives in the city of Pozna. He has a reputation for having *ruach hakodesh*. We think you need him now. Perhaps his luminous eyes will be able to locate your lost son-in-law."

Herschel did not dawdle in carrying out his friends' suggestion. He had his carriage hitched up at once and traveled to Pozna. There he fell at R' Naftali's feet, weeping. When he had calmed himself, he related what had happened to his daughter after marrying R' Naftali's student.

"I have not come here to complain to you, Heaven forbid," the father cried bitterly. "I have only one request. Please, let the Rebbe, with his *ruach hakodesh*, tell me where the missing husband is living."

Sparks seemed to fly from R' Naftali's eyes. "*Hasachas Elokim ano-chi*?" he quoted. "It is said of *HaKadosh Baruch Hu* that His eyes see everything. Who am I? I am a mere mortal, born of woman to exist for a short while!"

The distraught father left even more downcast than when he had arrived. The next day, he returned to plead again, "Rebbe, take pity on me. I can not bear it any longer."

Once again, R' Naftali sent him away empty-handed. Herschel, in his despair, became a regular nuisance. R' Naftali would send him away and he would return; R' Naftali would reject him and he would come back for more. It seemed as though the rebbe would never tell him where his son-in-law was to be found.

Finally, an acquaintance of Hershel's who frequented R' Naftali's household, told him, "Two are better than one. Let us go to see him together."

On the following day, the two went to R' Naftali's home, taking the *agunah*, Taibel, along with them. Herschel fell to the floor, sobbing and pleading for the rebbe to take pity on him and his daughter, who desired death because her life was no life.

R' Naftali's compassion overcame him. "Take your daughter outside," he told the rich man. "I will see what I can do."

The moment the father and daughter had left the room, the rebbe told his students, "This is an unsavory matter. The two of them are very unfortunate. For thirteen years she has been an *agunah*, and she may very well stay that way until her dying day!"

The students trembled to hear him speak so strongly. R' Naftali continued, "I do not see the missing husband in this world at all. I do not know where he is. But I will now make a mighty effort to discover where the man went and where he is now. Perhaps I will find him somewhere."

He turned to his students. "Listen carefully," he warned. "I am going to sit in my chair, and a great sleep will come over me. Watch me every second. When you see my face changing, call out loudly, 'Rebbe, Rebbe!' until I wake up. Then I will sleep again, and you will do the same thing. Do not take your eyes off me, and when my face changes you will call out again, 'Rebbe, Rebbe!' as loudly as you can, until I awaken once more. Sleep will overtake me a third time. When you see that I am nearly spent, do everything in your power to wake me. If I do not wake, know that I am in great distress, and make every effort to rouse me, for if you do not wake me that third time, I will not return."

He finished speaking, sat in his chair, and fell at once into a deep sleep. His face turned red as flames. This lasted approximately half an hour. Suddenly, his face altered completely and his features became frighteningly different.

Alarmed, the students did as they had been instructed. In loud voices, they cried, "Rebbe, Rebbe!" until he woke from his sleep.

R' Naftali opened his eyes a crack, looked at them, and immediately fell asleep again. Hearts pounding, his students watched him. Before their very eyes they saw his features change again, until his face no longer resembled his own.

They understood that they had to wake up R' Naftali again. Standing up, they screamed, "Rebbe! Rebbe!" at the top of their voices.

R' Naftali did not wake up.

The more practical of the students took action. They seized their rebbe's hands and waved them energetically around. This did the trick. R' Naftali did wake up, though with tremendous difficulty. His eyes opened slightly, dazed and empty. "Rebbe's not really here with us, in this world," the students whispered to one another. This was no ordinary sleep. R' Naftali's soul had gone to a different world.

As they whispered, a profoundly deep sleep overcame R' Naftali once again.

If his face had changed the first two times, now the change was so dramatic that, had they not been forewarned, they would not have believed that a person's face could alter to such an extent. Had another student wandered into the room at that moment and been asked who the man in the chair was, he would not have known that it was his own rebbe.

R' Naftali had spoken about this moment. It seemed that his soul had taken flight, with only a frail stem linking it to the body sitting in the room. In just a moment, the stem would snap ...

Bellowing for all they were worth, the students tried to rouse their rebbe. Some grasped his hands and waved them even more forcefully than before, but R' Naftali did not wake up. He was still in another, very distant, place.

With quaking hearts, the students recalled their rebbe's warning. If they were not successful in waking him, that meant he would not come back. Still, they did not give way to hysteria. While several cried out loud to him, others tugged at his hands and shook him the way the wind shakes the trees on a stormy day.

Suddenly, R' Naftali's eyes flew open. He looked as though he longed to leave again. But his students did not permit this to happen. They called to him, reminding him that he was still alive, and must return to this world.

R' Naftali shook his head. Slowly, he rose from his chair and began to look more like himself. Turning to his students with great joy, he exclaimed, "I found him!"

The students stood transfixed.

"What is the matter? Have you all fallen asleep?" R' Naftali chided good-naturedly. "Hurry and call the *agunah* and her father. Tell them to come here at once."

The students left the room, returning almost immediately with the moneychanger and his daughter.

"I've found your missing son-in-law," announced R' Naftali, without preamble. "If you wish to free your daughter from being an *agunah* forever, this is the time."

Herschel fell to his knees and burst into tears of happiness.

"This is no time to cry!" R' Naftali urged. "You have to act now. Go to all three *dayanim* (judges) of the city, and ask them, in my name, to go with you. Take along the scribe, too, with all the tools of his trade, parchment, ink, and quill. You will need two kosher witnesses as well. The whole entourage must travel quickly, not stopping night or day. About two miles outside of Vienna, you will find a large inn. Enter that inn. By some long tables you will see three army officers. Two of them will be seated on either side of the third; you will have no occasion to speak to them. But the third, seated between them in the center, is your missing son-in-law — Yosef, from the city of Koritz — though he looks very different today from the way he looked when he learned in my yeshivah.

"When the middle officer sees your daughter, he will recognize her and call her by name. He will tell his friend, 'That is my first wife, whom I left years ago.'

"When you hear this," continued R' Naftali to his spellbound audience, "you must scold him: 'How does a Jewish man leave his wife an *agunah* for thirteen years?' Tell him that you are not asking him for anything except to give her a divorce, so that she may rebuild her life and establish a righteous new generation."

R' Naftali unwound the future as though it were the past. "He will refuse. You will offer a great deal of money as a bribe, to induce him to give the *get* (divorce). If he persists in his refusal even then, send a messenger to his superior officer, the most senior general in Vienna, asking him to force your son-in-law to divorce her."

∽∾

Matters unfolded exactly the way R' Naftali had described them, detail after detail: the inn outside Vienna, the three officers, the middle officer who recognized his wife, the outcry and recriminations, the refusal to grant her a divorce, the hefty bribe, the repeated refusal, the messenger sent galloping away on a speedy horse to the general in Vienna.

A few hours later, the messenger returned bearing a sealed note from the general. The note ordered Yosef to divorce his wife. To everyone's shock, Yosef said insolently, "I do not take orders from that general. He is as the dust beneath my feet."

Turning to the woman, standing there with tears on her cheeks, he jeered, "I hated you from the moment I saw you. I decided to make you an *agunah* for the rest of your life. I would not give you a divorce for all the money in the world. Not even a command from the king himself would change my mind."

"What is that you are saying?" his two fellow officers exclaimed furiously. "Would you speak that way even to the king?"

"Big heroes," Yosef scoffed. "Have you ever seen battle or shed blood at the front? From the houses where you sat snugly, like cowards, you sent your soldiers to the front — where they fought valiantly, to their last drop of blood ..."

His words inflamed the two officers. He had hardly finished his mocking words, when the two soldiers drew their swords and — almost as though they had planned the move ahead of time — cut off Yosef's head.

"Now you have your life and your freedom back," they told the stunned wife. "Now you do not need a divorce!"

The *dayanim* said shakily, "Please, let us bury the dead officer. He is a Jew, one of ours."

The officers refused. "A man who scorns the king is not worthy of burial."

They left the inn, taking the body with them.

On their return to Pozna, Herschel related to R' Naftali the entire story of how Taibel's freedom had been won — not through a divorce, but rather through her husband's death, in front of many eyewitnesses.

The rebbe smiled mysteriously. "The man you saw, Yosef of Koritz, has not been in this world for many years already. I raised him from the bottommost level of the grave because he was needed.

"When he fled from his wife," R' Naftali continued to his stunned listeners, "he was attacked by a gang of thieves. Seeing that he had no money, they wanted to kill him. In his desire to save himself, he proposed that he join their gang and help them. He became one of them. At first, he refrained from taking part in their evil deeds, but as he grew used to them, he changed, and became like them — a thief and a murderer.

"One day, the gang heard about a very rich man who was transporting all his wealth along the king's road. It required a sharp mind to plan the heist. The former yeshivah *bachur* undertook the task, and he did it well. With careful thought he planned the robbery, down to the last detail. The job was succesfully pulled off.

"When the time came to divide up the loot, a quarrel broke out among the thieves. Yosef claimed that, if not for his careful planning, there would have been no loot to divide, and therefore he deserved a larger share than the rest. His cohorts argued that the division ought to be equal. Forgetting whom he was dealing with, Yosef stubbornly clung to his position. Tempers flared, a sharpened axe appeared from somewhere, and the former yeshivah student's body slumped to the ground, missing its head.

"On his arrival in the Next World," R' Naftali said, "his actions were weighed. I need not tell you that he was lowered to the deepest level.

"When you came to me, I was overcome with pity for the *agunah*. I wanted to have the dead man raised from his grave. To do this, I had to pass through the three gates of Gehinnom.

"The first gate agreed to my request at once. The second did not wish to release him, but finally agreed. The third gate was hardest of all. It refused to release him, even for a short time. Only after I exerted tremendous effort to show them the *agunah's* pain as she waited outside the door of my room, telling them that she was likely to wallow in anguish for the rest of her life, did they agree, at last, to release him briefly. They insisted on sending along two destructive angels, in the guise of high army officers, who would return him the moment our business was done. They were to kill him exactly the way he was killed before, to relive the deed and add what was missing the first time: kosher witnesses to testify that he was dead, so that the *agunah* might be released from her bondage and freed to marry again."

"Look at the Semichas Chachamim's power," one of the *tzaddikim* of his day said, after telling this tale. "He was prepared to enter Gehinnom, to bargain with its three gates with tremendous self-sacrifice, in order to bring a criminal back to this world, have him once again garbed in a body, and bring about that entire episode — in order to rescue a Jewish daughter from the pain of being an *agunah*."

The Power of
a Bas-Kol

WOLF THE FARMER SURVEYED HIS FARM WITH A satisfied air. As far as the eye could see were fields, golden with ripe wheat. In just a few days' time, the harvest would begin. His hands would be filled with the work of cutting down all of that wheat. His heart swelled with joy when he thought of his storehouses, filled to the brim with turnips, cabbages, and potatoes.

Wolf was a farmer to the core. He knew nothing except the soil and its bounty. All his days were spent in manual labor, as they had been from the moment his father — also a farmer — had taken him out to the fields as a young boy. Ever since, he had worked hard, expanded his property, and become a man of means.

Ignorant and uneducated, Wolf did not even know the Hebrew alphabet. He had no idea how to read from a *siddur*, praying from memory what he had absorbed during his lifetime. There was no shul in his district, so he always *davened* alone. Only for the holidays did he travel to the nearest town to pray with a *minyan*.

Wolf was different from his father, though. While his father had neglected Wolf's education, Wolf was anxious for his own two sons to learn. He decided to hire a tutor for them, as his ardent desire was for his boys to grow up to be Torah scholars.

Unfortunately, Wolf and his family lived in a remote village in the wilds of the Ukraine. So remote, in fact, that no tutor was prepared to completely abandon civilization and travel to a place where there was no shul and no Jewish community.

Instead, Wolf took his sons to the home of a teacher in a distant city. He paid a high tuition for the boys' education, room, and board.

Hashem blessed this endeavor with success. From their earliest childhood, the boys had witnessed their father's distress over his own ignorance, and they knew how earnestly he desired to have them taste the flavor of Torah. They did not disappoint him. Devoting themselves to their studies, they turned into outstanding, diligent students — and, eventually, into noted *talmidei chachamim*. At the right time, they each married girls from wonderful homes. Their father's *nachas* knew no bounds.

Not content with their spectacular progress in Torah study, the farmer's two sons seached for someone to guide them in *avodas Hashem*. They heard about an individual who passed through their area from time to time — an amazing man with many disciples who was known as R' Yisrael Ba'al Shem Tov. From the first moment they began to learn from him, their hearts became his. Day and night, they studied ways to elevate themselves and made every attempt to stay close to their teacher. From the Ba'al Shem Tov they learned about Chassidus and fear of Heaven, and they grew tremendously in holiness.

Their attempts to explain to their father about this *tzaddik* and his Chassidus, however, were unsuccessful. Wolf the farmer knew that apart from the craft of his labor, there was only one other wisdom, and that was Torah. He knew that his sons had elevated themselves to a much higher plane than he ever could, and that they were smarter than he was — but why were they always traveling to Mezhibozh, time after time? That he did not understand.

"What is it about that man that makes you waste your time on these trips?" Wolf asked his sons.

The sons knew it was useless to try to describe the holiness and greatness of their rebbe. Instead, they tried to tell their father something that he would accept. "There is an outstanding wise man who lives in Mezhibozh," they said. "We are trying to absorb what we can of his wisdom."

"Wise man, wise man," muttered the father. In his book, there was no wisdom higher than the art of working the land. "Does he understand plowing, planting, harvesting?"

"Yes, Father. Certainly."

The farmer glanced sharply at his sons to see whether they were making fun of him. "Is he able to tell you when is the best time to plant onions, and what kind of soil is best for growing fine beets?"

The sons believed that there was nothing their holy rebbe did not know or understand. They ventured to reply in the affirmative to their father's question. Could a person to whom Divine secrets stood revealed not know the secrets of working the land? "Of course," they replied. "He can advise you about anything you wish."

The sons' aim was to help their father refine his own self a bit — to help him rise a little from his sunken spiritual plane.

Hearing that the wise man of Mezhibozh was well-versed in farming lore, Wolf decided to visit him. He chose the best produce of his fields and gardens to bring along with him.

The sight of a simple villager bearing the fruit of his land to the Ba'al Shem Tov was not an unusual one in Mezhibozh. Even young children knew enough to point out the familiar house of the great sage.

Wolf arrived at the Ba'al Shem Tov's home laden with baskets filled with all manner of excellent things. He requested permission to bring the baskets into the house, and to ask a few questions.

His request was granted. Wolf found himself standing in front of a man of radiant countenance — but his own nature was so coarse and material that he was not awed by the holy man. At once, with no sign of hesitation or fear, he began to ask his questions.

"My sons tell me that Your Honor is a wise man, who is well-versed in the art of farming the land, and a wonderful expert in all village matters. Is this true?"

The Ba'al Shem Tov answered simply, "Yes. Ask, my son, ask. But before you ask your questions, let me tell you something."

The Ba'al Shem Tov began to describe Wolf's fields. He stated their dimensions, their fertility, and what was growing in each one. He mentioned the yield of that year's crop, and those of the year before. Before the farmer could so much as open his mouth, the "wise man" had drawn an accurate sketch of Wolf's fields, dating back twenty years and up to the present day.

Wolf listened intently, bobbing his head to indicate that he agreed with every word. This wise man had met with his approval from the first moment. His sons were not mistaken. Yes! This man knew what he was talking about. Wolf had never met anyone like him — a person who could tell him, at first meeting, every detail about his fields and crops as though he had learned them from Wolf himself. Even more, the "wise man" went on to describe all of Wolf's own actions, in his fields and at home!

Yes, this is a very special man, Wolf thought.

Never having heard of *ruach hakodesh*, when he encountered it in so blatant a fashion he did not know how to categorize it — except as "wisdom."

"Today I have heard things that I have never heard from anyone else," he said earnestly. "I would like to ask your advice with regard to a few matters in my fields."

Wolf began to throw question after question at his host, and the Ba'al Shem Tov answered with great patience, instructing him as to what was worth planting, and how, and in which field, on which day, and even where to buy the best seeds.

Wolf left Mezhibozh and went directly home. He did everything the Ba'al Shem Tov had suggested — including several matters about which his own farmer's wisdom told him to do the opposite.

The blessing was quick to follow. The next year, his fields were bursting with crops such as he had never seen before. The quantity was outstanding, and the quality truly superlative.

Still, Wolf did not acknowledge the holiness of the Ba'al Shem Tov — not through any rebelliousness of spirit, but because he did not recognize the very concept of a great and holy man. Witnessing the fulfillment of the blessing with his own eyes, his conclusion was clear: The man's wisdom had proven itself. It was no wonder that the crops had grown so beautifully. After all, the suggestions had been clever and well thought out. It all made perfect sense, within the framework of Nature!

Before the next planting season, there was no longer any need for his sons to persuade him to visit their rebbe. Wolf did so on his own initiative. The results of his previous visit certainly justified the expenditure.

If he had been well-off before, now that he had begun to ask advice of the holy man, blessing followed everything he undertook.

Wolf's wealth increased by leaps and bounds. He purchased additional fields, and his crops attained such a fine reputation that he was able to sell them at twice the going price. From then on, he did not do anything, large or small, without first consulting the Ba'al Shem Tov.

Little by little, over the course of his periodic visits to Mezhibozh, the hoped-for change began to occur. He was no longer the coarse villager who saw everything through the eyes of a laborer of the soil. His frequent trips did their job. Slowly, without Wolf realizing it, he became more refined. He prayed with more feeling. He learned Torah from his sons and began to be more scrupulous in his observance of the mitzvos.

Several years later, Wolf brought a new and complicated question to Mezhibozh. His daughter had reached marriageable age, and a large number of young men were vying for her hand. She had a great deal going for her: her own personal qualities, her father's wealth, and her two brothers, who were known everywhere as fine Torah scholars and pious chassidim.

Wolf was utterly at a loss. He brought with him to Mezhibozh a long list, bearing the names of twenty excellent young men who had been suggested as a match for his daughter. If only he had had twenty daughters, and could win all twenty young men as sons-in-law! Each had a special quality that raised him over and above the others. One was talented, another was clever. One was knowledgeable and another incisive. One came from prestigious stock and another was the scion of a wealthy family. One was handsome and one was tall. The single thing they all shared in common was their excellence. They were all outstanding young men and worthy contenders for his daughter's hand.

Being accustomed to having the Ba'al Shem Tov resolve all his difficulties, and because he did not know which of the young men was the right match for his daughter, he decided to present the Ba'al Shem Tov with the list and let him choose the best *chasan*.

The Ba'al Shem Tov perused the long list. After scrutinizing each name, a surprised expression crossed his face. "I do not see your daughter's *ben zug* (partner) here," he told Wolf.

"How can that be?" exclaimed Wolf. "Twenty boys, and not even one is appropriate?"

With a smile, the Ba'al Shem Tov explained to the naive farmer that it was not the list's length that was the essential thing, but whether a certain name appeared on it — the name of the true partner destined for his dear and estimable daughter. At any rate, the name did not appear on this impressive list. His name had not yet been suggested to Wolf as a match for his daughter.

"Where am I to find him?" asked Wolf. "What do I do now?"

"When you get home, send me your two sons," said the Ba'al Shem Tov.

The farmer went home, and sent his sons to Mezhibozh as instructed.

When Wolf sons arrived, the Ba'al Shem Tov sent his servant, Alexei, to harness his wagon. Together they all set out on a journey.

The group of four traveled for several days before reaching a distant city. There they stayed as the guests of a respected member of the city's Jewish community. The host prepared a meal for his honored visitor, and sent for his friends, rabbis, and community leaders to join them.

As the Ba'al Shem Tov sat at the table with the rabbis and leaders, he told them, "I have come here in order to find a *chasan* for the sister of these two fine young men." He pointed at Wolf's sons. "I know that the sister's match resides in this city. His name is So-and-So, son of So-and-So ..."

The invited guests began to whisper among themselves, asking one another whether anyone recognized the name. No one, however, knew of a young man whose own name and those of his parents fit the Ba'al Shem Tov's specifications. Not even the community elders, who knew every Jew in the place, could think of whom he meant. Knowing, however, of the effort the Ba'al Shem Tov had put into making the long trip to their city — in the belief that this was where he would find the proper partner for the sister of the two outstanding young men seated beside him — they strained their minds.

Everyone came up blank.

The Ba'al Shem Tov was insistent. "There is someone in this city whose name is So-and-So, and he — specifically he — is the true and proper match for the girl."

The meal ended without results. The sought-after *chasan* was not to be found.

The Ba'al Shem Tov was loath to leave the city before he had achieved his goal.

Days passed, and soon it was Rosh Chodesh.

It was that community's custom to hold a big Rosh Chodesh feast in their largest shul for all the city's Jews. This was a very fine feast, with all kinds of delicious foods and dishes. It was a golden opportunity for the city's destitute and downtrodden to satisfy their hunger one day a month with a proper meal, without any attendant embarrassment.

Everyone was sitting at this feast, enjoying the good food, when there suddenly entered a wild-haired young man with dirty clothes. He seized a loaf of bread from the table and ran back outside.

A community member, who had worked to prepare the meal, ran after him and called to him to enter and eat with the rest — not to grab food like a dog. He called the young man by his name, and those of his parents.

Many of those present caught their breaths. The name that the man had called out was exactly the name the Ba'al Shem Tov had spoken a few days earlier. They knew the young man well. He came from a poor, low-class family that lived at the edge of the forest — a family with which no one desired to cultivate an acquaintance. The boy himself was so coarse and wild that no one had thought of him when searching for the name's owner. It was not possible that the Ba'al Shem Tov had meant him!

Nevertheless, to dismiss all doubt, they approached the Ba'al Shem Tov and told him what had just happened — not forgetting to mention several times, quite forcefully, that they were referring to a family of low-class folk with whom no one wished to ally themselves in marriage.

To their astonishment, the Ba'al Shem Tov's face lit up with joy. "Bring him here!"

"Rebbe, that boy knows nothing! A person as ignorant and uneducated as he comes along only once in a generation! Is this the one to be chosen?"

"Go to him at once. Cut his hair, wash him, dress him in silks and linens, and bring him here to the feast," ordered the Ba'al Shem Tov. His tone left no room for argument.

Out of respect for their honored guest, the people went after the young man who had snatched the bread. He had not gone far, and upon seeing that he was being pursued he thought the others intended to punish him for stealing the loaf. Frightened, he began to run like a deer. The men gave chase. With tremendous effort, they managed to catch him, and with even greater difficulty persuaded him to go along with them. They barbered and bathed him and changed his clothes, then brought him to the feast, which was reaching its height.

When the young man walked inside, he was almost unrecognizable. His long hair had been shorn, his soiled clothes had disappeared, and his face shone with a grace that had never been glimpsed before. The Ba'al Shem Tov welcomed him warmly, seated the boy beside him, and ordered him to eat of all the delicious food. The young man washed his hands and ate in a polite, refined manner. The Ba'al Shem Tov waited until he was finished. Then he passed his handkerchief in front of the young man's face, and said, "Speak Torah."

The young man opened his mouth and began to address his stunned audience. He spoke pearls and gems of wisdom, original thoughts, and nuggets of Torah so profound and incisive that even Wolf's two learned sons — themselves outstanding *talmidei chachamim* — barely managed to understand even a portion of what was being said.

"Well? Will he do?" asked the Ba'al Shem Tov with a twinkle in his eye.

"Very much so!" answered the brothers, enchanted.

"Go to your father at once with this *bachur*, and set up the *chupah*," the Ba'al Shem Tov ordered.

The matter was accomplished amid great rejoicing. During the *sheva berachos* after the wedding, the *chasan* spoke brilliantly, leaving his listeners open-mouthed with wonder. The family's happiness knew no bounds. Happiest of all were the two brothers. They had merited a shining diamond that had been hidden in mud.

After the week of *sheva berachos*, however, came disillusionment. The mud returned ... The *chasan's* brothers-in-law had the custom of rising each night to recite the *Tikkun Chatzos,* and were certain that the outstanding newcomer to the family did the same. To their surprise, they learned that he was not an early riser. They barely managed to wake him at a late hour of the morning from a slumber as deep as that of a bear in the woods. When he did wake up, he did not wash his hands or recite *Modeh Ani.* Looking at them bleary-eyed, he turned over and went back to sleep.

The brothers understood that this was no meaningless event. Clearly, an *ayin hara* (evil eye) had affected the *chasan.* They traveled to see the Ba'al Shem Tov and poured out their hearts to him about the terrible curse that had befallen their brother-in-law, the brilliant *chasan*, with no warning.

The Ba'al Shem Tov did not appear surprised. Evidently, he had anticipated this eventuality long before the brothers' arrival. He said, "Forty days before a baby is born, a *bas kol* announces that 'this girl will marry that boy.' That, however, is the end of the process — the conclusion of a big discussion. Just as there are matchmakers here below, in this world, there are matchmakers in the upper world as well, whose job is to match each girl with the right boy.

"When they matched your sister to this *bachur*, those on the good side protested that the match should not take place. That the daughter of a rich man, whose sons were outstanding *talmidei chachamim,* should marry a completely uneducated young man from a very low-class family was in their opinion, not an appropriate *shidduch.* Those on the other side retorted, 'So what? Let the girl be born defective, so that no one will want to marry her. That way, she will end up wedded to an *am ha'aretz* (ignorant one).'

"The good side said: 'The girl's father will be very wealthy, and will be able to "buy" an excellent *chasan* for his daughter even if she does have a defect. He will not want just any boy.'

"The other side replied: 'That can be solved, too. Her father will die, and she will be orphaned and defective, so that she will be forced to marry him.'

"I entered into the middle of the debate," said the Ba'al Shem Tov, "and stated that I do not consent to have any harm done to either the girl or her father. I undertook to influence the *bachur* with an outpouring of Torah, so that her brothers would agree to take him for their sister. Normally, my influence should have lasted his whole life, but because his nature is so coarse and earthy, it was only with difficulty that I managed to give him enough Torah to last through the week of *sheva berachos*.

"Now he has returned to his nature. But he is your sister's true *zivug*, no argument about that. If you teach him Torah, he will absorb it and achieve at least some level of Torah."

With no choice, the brothers undertook to follow the Ba'al Shem Tov's instructions. They taught their brother-in-law much Torah, until he began to absorb some of it. After a number of years, he was able to learn on his own, and eventually achieved a good level of Torah learning.

[The source of this story is my friend, R' Shmuel Honig, grandson of R' Shmuel Gafner *zt"l*, of Jerusalem. R' Shmuel heard the tale from his rebbe, who was an Apter chassid, who had heard it passed down from the holy rebbe, R' Avraham Yehoshua Heschel of Apta, who personally told this story. Upon its completion, he would add, "Some of the chassidim who surround me are children born of that marriage."]

The Promise

A TERRIBLE TRAGEDY HAPPENED SOME 300 HUNDRED years ago, on Thursday, 3 Kislev 5463 (1702), in the city of Lemberg (Lvov) in the Western Ukraine, then under Polish dominion.

The city was tranquil, its borders secure. In the Jewish quarter, nothing seemed out of the ordinary. Little sunlight was able to penetrate its narrow streets. Because of government restrictions to contain the Jewish population inside the ghetto, the tall houses had been built very close together. The city clock stood at an hour before noon. Merchants hawked their wares in the marketplace. People walked the streets and greeted one another; babies gurgled in their carriages. Small children played in their homes.

From the upper story of one house — a house which was the focus of much public attention — there came the sweet sounds of Torah learning. The city's young rabbi, *hagaon* R' Yaakov Yehoshua Falk, later to become known by the work he was to write, the *P'nei Yehoshua*, was sitting in a large room, teaching his students. Numerous young men sat listening to their rebbe's words, seeing how the whole Torah was spread out before him like a bolt of cloth.

In the adjoining rooms, members of the household were busy with their various tasks. There was Leah, the young rebbetzin; their only daughter, Gittel; the rebbetzin's mother, Raizel; and even the rebbetzin's grandfather — her mother's father — R' Shmerel Katz, who sat to the side of the large room and listened with pleasure to his grandson's Torah.

The sound of Torah study was the only one to be heard. No one dreamed that everything could change in an instant.

Suddenly, a defeaning explosion sounded — and then another — and then a third and a fourth. The series of booms put an instant end to the peace and tranquility.

Not far away stood a military warehouse, filled with barrels of gunpowder, intended for filling cannons and making bullets. The reason for the explosion remains unclear, but the results are well-known. One of the exploding barrels began a terrible chain reaction that blew up all the others in turn — with a cataclysmic impact that destroyed adjacent buildings and razed them to the ground.

The rabbi's house was not spared. Just a moment before, R' Yaakov Yehoshua Falk had been sitting among his beloved students, his mouth flowing with jewels of Torah and wisdom. Then the entire house crumpled and fell inward like a pile of cards. Everyone was hurled from the upper floors down to the ground.

Gunpower is highly flammable. An inferno began to rage through the Jewish quarter, completing the destruction not finished off by the explosion. Houses blazed in a huge bonfire.

In all, thirty-six Jewish souls perished in the catastrophe. Among them were the family members of the P'nei Yehoshua; his wife, Rebbetzin Leah; his beloved only daughter, Gittel; his mother-in-law, Raizel; and her father, R' Shmerel Katz — all were killed.

R' Yaakov Yehoshua himself was thrown from the top of the house down to the ground, where the whole structure collapsed and covered him.

Enormous beams of wood surrounded R' Yaakov Yehoshua on every side, pressing in on him like pincers. He could not move so much as his little finger. He felt all his bones shattering beneath the weight of the heavy beams and the fragments of broken wall that covered him. The young rabbi was buried alive.

Even if he had been able to move an arm or leg, he was afraid that the slightest movement might bring the walls tumbling down on him and finish him off. The great beams hanging over his head looked like hands reaching out to end his life. All too soon, he believed, he would undergo all four deaths of *beis din*: *sekilah* (stoning), *sereifah* (burning), *hereg* (stabbing), and *chenek* (choking). Indeed, he had already suffered all four versions in a partial sense. He had undergone *sekilah* when he fell from the upper floor to the ground; he had been burned, *sereifah*, by the flames that had licked his wounded body; every limb had been pierced by sharp stones, nails, and fragments of wall, which was *hereg*. As for choking, *chenek*, a beam was pressing on his throat and making him struggle for every breath. Was that not tatamount to *chenek*?

He lay for some time under the rubble. Clouds of dust and smoke still surrounded him, but the flames had died. Lemberg's Jews ran about trying to save who and what could be rescued. Not ten people came, or a hundred, but "thousands and tens of thousands," as R' Yaakov Yehoshua later put it in his sorrowful introduction to the *P'nei Yehoshua*. Anyone who had heard the blast, and the cries and shrieks that followed, ran out into the streets. For a time, the flames made it impossible to help anyone. Only when the fire had been extinguished did the rescuers come to the aid of those trapped in the rubble. Unfortunately, the huge number of rescuers proved a curse rather than a blessing. Many of the trapped and injured victims were trampled to death by the numerous eager feet.

The P'nei Yehoshua lay beneath the rubble of his house, praying for salvation. Then, seeing the enormous damage that the horde of "rescuers" was causing, he understood that it was not they who would save him.

The young rabbi's life hung in the balance. He was only a small step away from certain death. Beams of incredible weight pressed against his entire body, leaving only his head free of their deadly threat.

From the depths of his tomb, R' Yaakov Yehoshua cried out to his Creator. He was so young, and yet had accomplished so much in his 22 short years. He had been born to R' Tzvi Hirsch and Miriam, daughter of the renowned R' Avraham Halevi, who was son-in-law to the *gaon* R' Yehoshua, author of the *Maginei Shlomo*. In his youth, R' Yaakov Yehoshua had learned Torah from

R' Gavriel, rabbi of Nikolsburg, then residing in Cracow, R' Yaakov Yehoshua's birthplace. He later moved to Lemberg, where one of the community leaders, R' Meir Shlomo Segal Landau, chose him as husband for his daughter, Leah.

At the start, he was appointed supervisor of the city's Talmud Torah schools, and he became a community activist. Before long, he had risen to the position of "head activist." When his brilliance and clarity of mind were recognized, however, he was not permitted to continue in posts that did not resonate with his stature and character, but was appointed to the position of disseminator of Torah. Hundreds of students began to flock to his doors to hear his brilliant *shiurim*. And that had been the state of affairs to this very day — until a few short minutes before, when his world was turned to rubble in an instant.

As he lay there, he saw the image of his great-grandfather, his mother's grandfather, the *gaon* R' Yehoshua, *Av Beis Din* of Cracow and author of a volume of responsa — the original *P'nei Yehoshua* — as well as the *Maginei Shlomo*, composed in order to resolve difficulties among the Ba'alei HaTosafos on Rashi. In every instance where the Ba'alei HaTosafos ask questions on Rashi's interpretation, or leave their questions unresolved with the word "*Timah*," R' Yehoshua would resolve the difficulty.

His great-grandfather's *sefer* created a furor in the Torah world. Generations of scholars have studied it to learn answers to the very difficult questions of the Ba'alei HaTosafos on Rashi.

R' Yehoshua of Cracow, himself a holy man, revealed to his students that when he completed his *sefer*, Rashi himself had appeared to him, face wreathed in joy. "Happy are you in this world, and it will be good for you in the next," said Rashi, "because you have saved me from the mighty lions ... the Ba'alei HaTosafos."

Rashi promised R' Yehoshua of Cracow that when the time came for him to depart this world and enter eternal life, he, Rashi, along with all his students, would personally come to welcome him!

Indeed, when the author of the *Maginei Shlomo* was on his deathbed, Cracow's leading Torah lights surrounded his bed as his soul prepared to depart his body. Suddenly, R' Yehoshua had addressed

the group: "Make room! Rabbeinu, light of our eyes, the *gaon* R'
Shlomo Yitzchaki, has come to me along with all his holy ones, and
has joyously welcomed me, to show me the living way — because I
always stood by him to resolve the Tosafos' questions."

R' Yaakov Yehoshua remembered all this about his great-grandfather as he lay amid the rubble. He began to pray: "If Hashem
will be with me and remove me from this trap in safety, and if He
allows me to build a faithful Jewish home and broaden my horizons
with students, I will never leave the walls of the *beis midrash*. I will
diligently study *Shas* and the commentaries, delve into the depths
of halachah, and follow in the footsteps of my grandfather, author
of the *Maginei Shlomo*. I will write a *sefer* dealing in depth with
concepts in *Shas*."

He was still immersed in prayer when the miracle occurred!
Beyond the mighty beams and the debris which had all but completely buried him, R' Yaakov Yehoshua saw an opening, and the weighty
beams seemed to give way of their own accord, allowing him the
opportunity to escape!

Healthy and whole, he extricated himself from the rubble that
just moments earlier had been ready to bury him alive, and stepped
outside unscathed. None of the rescuers had been able to lift a finger to help him. It was impossible to reach the place where he had
been buried, but, by Hashem's command, those tons of rocks and
timber made way for R' Yaakov Yehoshua to leave unharmed.

Shaken, he stood contemplating the miracle that had just been
wrought for his sake. With his own eyes he had witnessed the Hand
of Hashem, sent to pluck him out of the morass. His heart pained him
grievously when he learned of the personal tragedy of his beloved
family's deaths, including his wife and only child. After he had
mourned them bitterly for seven days, and then another thirty, he
began to devote all his time to the study of Torah.

He would sit in the *beis midrash* and learn for 18 hours at
a stretch. One frigid winter day, his students failed to arrive for

their morning *shiur*. He sat alone in the *beis midrash* until noon, wrapped in his *tallis* and crowned with his *tefillin*, waiting in vain for his students to arrive. At midday they trooped in, covered with slivers of ice.

"Where have you been?" asked their rebbe.

"We could not come because of the cold."

He wanted to rise and cross to the window, to see how cold it was outside. He could not do so, for his beard was stuck to the table. As he had pored over his *sefer,* the breath he exhaled had frozen in the icy air of the *beis midrash*, causing the hairs of his beard to stick to the table. It became necessary to bring a bowl of hot water to thaw his frozen beard.

"I suppose it is quite cold," he remarked with a smile.

He studied Torah with tremendous self-sacrifice. He completed all of *Shas* a total of thirty-six times (the number of victims taken in the tragedy), before writing his great work, the *P'nei Yehoshua* on *Shas*. From the time he started writing, he did not stop until he had completed the work and published it, volume after volume, to fulfill the promise he had made in his hour of need.

The *sefer*, conceived under such dire circumstances and written amid the flames of *mesiras nefesh* and neglect of all worldly considerations, was immediately embraced by the Jewish world with tremendous enthusiasm and admiration. Only few works have merited such widespread acceptance. The Chasam Sofer remarked that, "Since the work of the Rashba, there has been no work like the *P'nei Yehoshua*." The Sanzer Rebbe, author of the *Divrei Chaim*, declared that he was called upon to correct an error in a chassidic tradition which stated that the Ba'al Shem Tov had received a heavenly order to serve the *gadol hador*, author of the *Tevuos Shor*. In actuality, claimed the Sanzer, the Ba'al Shem Tov had journeyed to serve the P'nei Yehoshua!

[Incidentally, while R' Yaakov Yehoshua still held the post of rav of Lemberg, the Ba'al Shem Tov sent him word by special messenger about a certain *shochet* in the city who was a member of the heretical Frankists sect. After having his *shechitah* knife inspected by the rabbi, the *shochet* would then create a flaw with his coat button, in order to cause the populace to eat nonkosher meat. After looking into the matter, the P'nei Yehoshua removed the man from his position.]

In a later generation, the *gaon* R' Yechezkel Benet sighed: "When I come to *Shamayim* they will ask me, 'Yechezkel, you engaged in and taught Torah and *emunah* — why didn't you also learn all of the *P'nei Yehoshua*?" The Heavenly Court may lodge a complaint against anyone who studies *Gemara* without looking into the *P'nei Yehoshua*!

R' Chida, on a visit to the community of Frankfurt, stayed as a guest in R' Yaakov Yehoshua's home. He wrote in his *sefer*, "Young as I was, I merited greeting the face of the *Shechinah* for several days. His appearance is that of an angel of G-d."

R' Yaakov Yehoshua also began a *sefer* about Jewish customs, in which he set out to demonstrate that all of *Chazal's* customs are alluded to in the Torah. He wrote thirty pages, until *Parashas Noach*. At that point, however, he stopped writing. Before his passing, he revealed that Heaven had stayed his hand from completing the book. Had he continued writing it, he would have thereby hastened the coming of the Mashiach!

[I express my gratitude to my dear friend, R' Yechiel Goldheber, for his help with this story.]

The P'nei Yehoshua's Glasses

"MAZAL TOV!" EXCLAIMED THE MIDWIFE, HOLDING OUT the squalling newborn. "It's a boy!" The new mother, exhausted and spent, reached for the child with hands that trembled slightly. She threw a timid look at the baby's crumpled face, and the mouth that was emitting a sharp wail. Gazing into the blue eyes that seemed so filled with expression, she burst into emotional tears — the aftermath of tension.

The midwife smiled understandingly. Taking back the infant, she placed him in a wooden cradle near the mother's bed. Both beds were canopied, the mother's in rich burgundy and the cradle in ivory silk. In Lvov (Lemberg), an important city in its time, and for many years the capital of Galicia, every self-respecting new mother rested under an almost royal canopy.

In the first weeks after the baby's birth, the mother was content. As the days passed, however, she began to feel anxious. All the other infants her son's age had begun to follow moving objects with their eyes, but her Baruch did not seem to see at all. His eyes did not gaze at her as she tended to him. Something seemed wrong with his empty stare.

When Baruch was 6 months old, his parents knew with certainty that their son was totally blind. He could not, and would never, see. They took him to experts and eye specialists, doctors who, after a thorough examination, told the downcast parents that there was nothing to be done. The child had not been blessed with the gift of vision. While his eyes were perfect in their structure, with all of the usual components accounted for, the Divine spark that turns an eye from a mere orb of flesh into an organ to transmit all the world's sights to the brain and the soul was missing. Only the Hand of G-d could provide that spark.

When the parents realized that even the greatest experts were unable to help their son, they were scarcely able to bear the anguish. Little Baruch would never see colors. He would never be moved by the beauty of a sunrise or sunset, or gaze with pleasure at the sky's delicate blue. He would never taste food as a seeing person does, because the sense of taste is influenced by the sense of sight. But all this was dwarfed in comparison to the essential tragedy: For the rest of his life, Baruch would never be able to learn Torah from a *sefer!* His eyes would not see the letters of the Torah. He, whose name meant "blessed,"would be unable to recite the blessing, *"Baruch poke'ach ivrim"* ("Blessed is He Who gives sight to the blind").

They wept bitterly over the plight of their small son, whose fate was to live in darkness all his life. Grief tore at their minds until they nearly went mad. At long last, they began to accept that this was Heaven's decree. This was their ordeal and that of their son, and they must bless for the bad as well as for the good. They thanked Hashem for the sons and daughters who was born after him, all of them with the wonderful blessing of normal vision.

As Baruch grew, he was not sent to the *melamed* like the other boys. He stayed at home and learned from his father. The child's questions were sensible and clever, and his father answered them all, teaching him the stories in the Written Torah. He told of Adam HaRishon, the Patriarchs and the twelve tribes of Israel, of Moshe Rabbeinu and *Bnei Yisrael*, the ten plagues and the splitting of the Red Sea. With increasing age, Baruch learned the Oral Torah as well, as far as he was capable of understanding — a bit of *Mishnah* and *Gemara*, a smattering of *Midrash*, and anecdotes of *Chazal*.

Each time his father would read him something from a *sefer*, Baruch would finger the pages, his face glowing with endless love. Because books in those days were printed on antiquated machines, with leaden hammers that hit the paper and stamped the letters onto it with black ink, the letters stood out from the page. Little Baruch would feel them with all the pleasure of a child eating candy.

He groped his way through the house, walking carefully from room to room, sometimes stumbling and falling over pieces of furniture until he learned to avoid them. He remembered where every object was placed, learning its shape through feel, so that when he needed to use that object he could do so without anybody's help. But he knew nothing of the world outside his front door. When he needed to go out into the street, he was liable to fall into holes and injure himself on obstacles. His father hired a boy to be his guide and accompany him wherever he needed to go.

Seeing the way Baruch was drawn to the holy *sefarim*, his father sent him to the *beis midrash* for long hours at a time. Within its walls, the boy grew; soon he was a teenager. He would attend long *shiurim* in *Mishnah* and *Gemara*, enjoy the rabbi's stories and parables on the weekly Torah portion, and listen avidly to the sermons of traveling *maggidim* who passed through the city from time to time. Baruch's memory was remarkable and, if vision had been denied his eyes, his ears were many times sharper than the ordinary, able to catch the slightest sound.

Though blind, Baruch was not behind others his age in Torah learning. He knew all the daily *tefillos* by heart, word for word, and was scrupulous about *davening* with a *minyan* morning, noon, and night, raising his sweet voice in prayer. Through paying careful attention in the *beis medrish*, he was well-versed in *Mishnah* and *Aggadah*. And because he loved *sefarim* so much, he treated them with enormous respect. Studying them was denied him because of his blindness, so he demonstrated his love in other ways. After a *shiur* in the *beis midrash*, he would return the *sefarim* to their places, showing amazing discernment based on the book's height and width. He would stroke the *sefer* lovingly, moving his fingers over the pages, straightening each creases and unfolding the corners.

One day, he passed a shul where he was not accustomed to *davening*. Because the hour was advanced and it was time to *daven Minchah*, he asked his companion to help him into the shul. Entering, he realized that he was early; the place was still empty. While waiting for others to arrive, he decided to pass the time with his beloved *sefarim*. He went immediately to the bookcase and began to lovingly finger the books.

His hand came across a large, thick, old volume, bound in wood. With rising excitement he removed it from the shelf, placed it on a table, and began to feel the pages as usual. His fingers touched something caught in the paper. Removing it with care, he felt a small object that seemed to him to be in the shape of eyeglasses. After fingering the object for a few moments, he placed the glasses on his eyes.

He was bathed in a sudden, intense light ...

Baruch did not understand what was happening to him. Suddenly, he was able to see everything around him. In an instant, he had gone from darkness to light! He saw tables and chairs, shelves groaning with books, and the heavy *sefer* from which he had taken the glasses.

So intense a transition was unbearable. Badly shaken, he hurriedly removed the glasses — and the darkness descended again. Slipping the glasses into his pocket, he lost himself in thought.

For a long time he sat immobile as a stone. Men gathered for *Minchah*, but he was not aware of them. They *davened Minchah* and then *Maariv*, but Baruch neither knew nor heard. His mind was entirely caught up in the eyeglasses that had come into his possession, and the miracle they had wrought. Not even after the worshipers had dispersed to their homes was his mind settled. He was thoroughly thunderstruck, and consumed with terror.

"It is time to go home." His guide was speaking.

Baruch stood up as though waking from a dream, patting his pocket to be sure that the glasses were still there. In total silence he followed the other boy out of the shul.

He did not tell his parents what had happened, but they sensed that he was different from before. Impatiently, he declined the evening meal his mother offered. This was not the first time that something had occurred to cast his spirits down . At such times, his parents and siblings tactfully stayed out of his way, waiting for the dark mood to pass.

Baruch did not sleep the entire night. He was afraid it had been nothing but a dream — a sweet dream from which one wakes to a cold, hard reality. Perhaps the entire episode had been only a figment of his imagination. How was it possible for his blind eyes to open in a single instant, giving him vision like anyone else? The miracle was beyond his understanding, and filled him with terror at the thought of losing it again.

At dawn, he got out of bed, washed his hands, and reached into his pocket. Slowly, he lifted the glasses to his face and put them on.

It had not been a dream! His blind eyes had become seeing eyes. Everything stood out with crystal clarity. His bed, his bowl of water ... There was no need to grope in the dark, no need to stumble over the dozens of objects standing in his way. He went to the window and threw open the shutters.

His heart soared at the sight of the rising sun. For the first time in his life, he saw his Creator's world. Heart pounding, he saw the sky slowly turning blue as the remnant of starlight faded. He stared at the pale strip of light expanding in the east, then closed his eyes and fervently thanked Hashem for the incredible miracle that had happened to him.

"I can see!" he wanted to shout from the rooftops. "I can see!"

But, despite the almost overwhelming joy that suffused him at that moment, he conquered his happiness with all his might, and did not say a word. An enormous kindness had been bestowed upon him — an open miracle. Blessing does not rest except on that which is concealed; if the matter became general knowledge, someone might cast an evil eye on his good fortune. He continued to wear the glasses, but behaved as though he were still completely blind.

His family awoke to the sight of Baruch wearing an old pair of glasses on his nose. When they asked him about it, he replied evasively. They believed it was only a passing fancy — that he had found a pair of glasses and decided to put it on.

To everyone's surprise, Baruch insisted on wearing the glasses outside. He was waiting for everyone to grow accustomed to seeing him in them. Before long, he began to let his behavior drop clues as to what was really transpiring. At first it was his parents and siblings who noticed — and their joy knew no bounds. Then it was his neighbors, and in their wake the remainder of his acquaintances. Suddenly, everyone realized that Baruch was no longer blind. A miracle had happened. Baruch now had the same vision as other people!

The boy who served as his guide was sent home. Baruch walked the streets of Lvov as though he had always been able to see.

～の～

All Lvov was talking about it. Blind-from-birth Baruch was suddenly able to see! How had the miracle occurred? The people speculated endlessly. Who had ever heard of such a thing? A person who had been blind from birth, suddenly regaining his vision — without benefit of complicated and difficult surgery.

Those who were closest to him ventured to ask him about it. Baruch was evasive: "Is anything impossible for Hashem?" To those who pressed him, he would add, "Hashem blinds one person and opens another's eyes." To the real nuisances who persisted in their questions, he would quote from *Tehillim*: "*Im yotzer ayin halo yabit?*" ("Shall He Who created the eye not give sight?") Was it for naught that *Chazal* included in the morning blessings one that says, "*Baruch poke'ach ivrim*" ("Blessed is He Who grants sight to the blind")?

But the nuisances would not accept these evasive answers. They drove him nearly mad with their persistent questions, until at last he yielded and told them how it had happened.

The people began to wonder about those amazing glasses. Who had made them, and where had they come from? They went to the shul where Baruch had found them and began to investigate. The trail led to an elderly Jew who *davened* there every day. He had merited the privilege of knowing the *gaon*, the P'nei Yehoshua, who had lived in Lvov many years previously.

The old man's memory was extremely lucid, and he clearly recalled the old volume with the wooden binding. "The glasses belonged to the P'nei Yehoshua," he stated with certainty. "During the time R' Yaakov Yehoshua lived in Lvov, he would *daven* in this shul. His custom was to linger after *davening* every day. He would sit alone, wrapped in his *tallis* and *tefillin*, learning a regular *seder* in the Torah's hidden secrets."

The people hurried to the *sefer*, and discovered that it did, indeed, contain mystical content. Moreover, it was inscribed with R' Yaakov Yehoshua's name.

The old man nodded, his long white beard swaying with satisfaction. "Did you think I was making it up? R' Yaakov Yehoshua used to learn this *sefer* with his glasses on, and then would place them between the pages and the wooden binding. Sometimes he left our city to travel to the cities of Germany. The *sefer* from which he learned his regular mystical *seder* remained in its place in the bookcase, and no one ever looked inside, as it contains very deep secrets of Kabbalah."

This story raised the P'nei Yehoshua's reputation to even greater heights. He now stood revealed not only as a brilliant *gaon*, but also as a holy and exalted figure and one of the *tzaddikim* upon whom the generation rested. If the implement that he used had such powers, what could be said of the man himself?

Baruch himself was especially shaken when he realized that the date on which he had found the glasses — 14 Shevat — was the P'nei Yehoshua's *yahrtzeit*! He undertook to hold a *seudas hoda'ah* (thanksgiving feast) on that day each year, to thank Hashem and to relate the miracle that He had wrought for him.

When Baruch was blind, he had not been able to recognize letters except by feeling them with his fingers. Now that his eyes had been opened, he could finally see the way the letters looked. His fathered hired a tutor to teach him the *aleph-beis*. Baruch proved to be a diligent student. Like a small child, he joyfully studied and reviewed his letters. In two or three weeks he was able to link them up into words, and soon he was able to read from a *siddur*. His family happily celebrated this milestone.

Baruch advanced on to *Chumash* with *Rashi* and moved quickly on to *Gemara*, with which he was familiar from his oral study. Through earnest and diligent study he became a genuine *talmid chacham*, and took special pains to learn from the texts. Because he owed a debt of gratitude to the P'nei Yehoshua, whose glasses had rescued him from darkness, he constantly studied the *sefer* until he was extremely well-versed in every section.

Later, he married, and tried his hand at a business in order to support his wife and children. He grew very prosperous, with fleets of ships that sailed the seas carrying goods from shore to shore. But his first and most precious "business" was Torah; he spent every spare hour poring over a *Gemara*, with a volume of the *P'nei Yehoshua* always open nearby.

Each year, on the 14th day of Shevat, he would conduct a *siyum* in which he held forth on the original thoughts of the P'nei Yehoshua. Then he would relate the way he had been completely blind from birth until the age of 17, when a huge miracle happened and the P'nei Yehoshua's glasses fell into his hands. From that day on he began to see with his eyes, as though he had never been blind at all.

Hashem blessed Baruch. He was a well-to-do businessman, as well as a *talmid chacham,* who learned in all his spare time, and always with a renewed vigor. The first seventeen years of his life had been spent in darkness, and he never forgot a day of them. Till his old age, he would recite the blessing "*Baruch poke'ach ivrim*" with great fervor and tremendous joy, and a special feeling of gratitude to the Creator Who had opened his eyes. He thanked Hashem for the past and asked that the light never be extinguished for him in the future. The glasses never left him. He guarded them zealously, for without them he was compared to a dead man.

Baruch lived a long life, filled with peace and *nachas*, sons and daughters. When the time came for him to depart this world, at a venerable age, his entire family was present at his bedside.

On their return from the cemetery, his children sat to observe the *shivah,* but before the week was even over, a quarrel broke out over the disposition of the inheritance. Their father, a very wealthy man, had left behind a great deal of money — but all the money in the world was nothing compared to that wondrous pair of glasses! The children viewed the glasses as not only the souvenir of a miracle, but also as a kind of talisman for good luck in life. Each of them wove strategies for getting the precious glasses into their own possession.

They debated the matter at length. Each wanted the glasses for himself. As the argument intensified, the brothers tried to wrest the glasses from one another's hands. Suddenly, the glasses fell to the ground, where they shattered into fragments.

For seventy years, their father had managed to protect those spectacles and safeguard them from all harm. The moment he was dead and buried, the glasses were broken ...

Everyone crouched down and began to gather the tiny shards, in order to put them in a safe place as a relic for future generations, to learn of their father's miracle.

To this day — so goes a bit of old family lore — R' Baruch's descendants bear the name of "Brill," which means glasses, in memory of the miracle that happened to their ancestor — R' Baruch "of the glasses."

False Witness

THE CITY OF AMTZISLAV, IN RUSSIA'S MOHILEV REGION, boasted a large Jewish community. Most of its members were scrupulous in their mitzvah observance — but even the rosiest apple will have its worm. Among the Jewish population of Amtzislav dwelled a man by the name of Aryeh Briskin. A quarrelsome fellow, he did not take pleasure in his *Yiddishkeit* or live on peaceful terms with his fellow Jews. The weakness in his roots eventually toppled the entire trunk, and Aryeh converted to Christianity. The other Jews of Amtzislav could not forgive his apostasy, and hardly managed to say a civil word to him. As for the children, they shouted out insults and called him names that enraged him.

Had it been within his power to do so, Aryeh Briskin would have burned down the entire Jewish community with a single word — that was how far his hatred extended. As his words did not have the power to start that kind of conflagration, he bided his time, waiting for the right moment to sink his poisoned fangs into living flesh.

The moment was not long in coming.

On that black day, a division of army troops burst into the town, searching every Jewish shop for contraband merchandise. It was a well-known fact that these searches were conducted on the basis of prior information, and the widespread nature of the operation was only camouflage. By the time they were through, the soldiers had narrowed their focus on the workshop of Raphael the tinsmith, behind whose shop, they believed, smuggled goods were being sold.

Raphael was surrounded by three armed soldiers, his soot-blackened face white as chalk. With terrified eyes he watched the soldiers begin to confiscate his valuable merchandise.

The street quickly filled with Jews intent on helping the tinsmith. Berel and Pinchas, two stalwart butchers, formed a barrier between Raphael and the soldiers, enabling him to make his escape. Furious, the soldiers began raining blows on the butchers, who fought back valiantly. The shop was soon filled with Jews determined to protect the tinsmith's possessions. They argued vociferously with the soldiers. On all sides, voices were raised in tumultuous shouts.

Suddenly, there came the sound of a single gunshot.

One of the officers clutched his chest. He crumpled and fell. Rushing to his aid, his fellow soldiers realized that there was nothing they could do. He was dead.

"You killed him!" bellowed the group's superior officer in a towering rage. "You will all be punished. You murdered an appointed officer of the Czar in the fulfillment of his duty."

"We did not touch him," the Jews protested. "We do not have any guns. It was a bullet from a Russian rifle that killed him."

The soldiers picked up the body, along with the confiscated goods, and left. A report was soon sent to the local authorities, who passed it on to those above them. Finally, the affair reached the city of St. Petersburg, home of Czar Nikolai of Russia.

The Czar could never have been accused of being overly fond of the Jews. Still, to maintain a proper appearance, he ordered an investigation into the events that had transpired in the tinsmith's shop. The Jews were claiming that one of the Czar's soldiers had inadvertently discharged his own rifle, letting loose the bullet that had killed his comrade. For their part, the soldiers said that one of the Jews in the shop had seized the rifle from a soldier's hand and fired it.

The situation remained unresolved — until Aryeh Briskin stepped forward to testify. The apostate's moment had arrived. He stated that he had personally witnessed the Jew, Moshe Rabinowitz, grab a rifle and shoot the soldier.

Briskin's account tilted the scales. He was summoned to testify under oath before the judges of the local court, where he became a tool in the hands of the anti-Semites. With vengeful joy, Briskin performed the lowest act of all: He offered testimony against his fellow Jews, leaving them open for retribution.

Czar Nikolai accepted the results of the inquiry, which stated that the Jews of Amtzislav were disloyal to the regime and had dared to shoot and kill a Russian soldier.

His orders were not long in following, and they were wicked and cruel as only the Czar's orders could be:

Every Jew in Amtzislav, young and old, was to line up in the street. Every tenth person would be conscripted into the army, whether he was a boy of 3 or an old man of 80. Every fifth person would undergo twenty-five lashes by enthusiastic soldiers. Also, a military guard would keep a close watch on the Jewish homes in the city for a period of half a year.

A decree of destruction had fallen on Amtzislav's Jewish community.

The decree arrived on Taanis Esther, as the Jews were packed into the shuls, praying. Upon hearing the news, there was a great wailing.

Apart from the Czar's public decree, a quieter order was whispered as well. In the dead of night, several of the Jewish community's most respected citizens were arrested and taken to the prison, where they underwent a series of degradations and beatings.

After stealthy negotiations, a substantial sum of money was handed over to the authorities to buy several weeks' respite for the Jews before Nikolai's order was to be carried out.

Dire danger hung suspended over the Jews of Amtzislav.

R' Yitzchak "Itzele" Zalkin was a leading member of Smolensk's Jewish community. Though not a learned scholar, he was a pious man and a devoted follower of the Vilna Gaon's students. The Jews of Smolensk loved him because he was dedicated, heart and soul, to their welfare.

R' Yitzchak's fortune was legendary. With the ruble being a currency of high value, R' Yitzchak employed five accountants, each of whom was responsible for a fifth of his fortune — 400,000 rubles. He was the owner, in other words, of the staggering sum of two million rubles.

His wealth did not turn his head, though his home was admittedly suited to his great worth. Food was served only on gold or silver plates, and there were those who claimed that even the cleaning utensils and chamberpots were made of pure gold. A well-equipped stable occupied a corner of the courtyard. When R' Yitzchak needed to travel, his servants hitched his fine carriage to a pair or two of excellent horses, which drew him through the streets like one of the country's highest ministers.

Still, his wealth did not make him haughty or unreachable. R' Itzele dealt simply with his fellow Jews and gave charity with a lavish hand. He especially enjoyed giving to those who learned Torah, and provided dozens of Torah scholars and their families — both in his own town and in others — with financial support each month.

R' Yitzchak was even better known, however, as an activist. Whenever any new trouble struck at the Jews in Russia, Lithuania, Latvia, or other trouble spots in the region, everyone knew the right address to turn to for help. R' Yitzchak was prepared to pass through fire and water to help a Jew in trouble — let alone an entire community of Jews threatened with terrible danger.

That night, as R' Yitzchak and his entire household lay asleep, there came a pounding on one of the doors of his mansion. The commotion woke his servants, throwing them into confusion and panic. One of them ran to open the door.

A tall, bearded Jew stood in the doorway. He wore a fur hat on his head. The look on his face spoke of age and weariness.

"Are you the servant?" he asked.

"Yes, sir."

"Please wake your master at once, and tell him that the lives of an entire community are in danger. There is not a moment to be lost!"

The stranger's noble demeanor underlined the urgency of the situation. The servant invited him in, then went to R' Itzele's room and respectfully woke him.

R' Itzele dressed hurriedly and went out to greet his visitor. He blurted in surprise, "Welcome, R' Avraham Simchah! How are you?"

"I feel fine — but my *kehillah* is in grave danger," the rabbi replied.

He was R' Avraham Simchah, author of the volume of responsa entitled *Binyan Shel Simchah*. He was also a nephew of the holy R' Chaim of Volozhin. Renowned throughout Lithuania as a *gaon* and a *tzaddik*, R' Avraham was a wise and scholarly individual. Happiness always radiated from his countenance — except on this occasion, when sorrow and anxiety peered from his eyes instead.

R' Itzele wanted to pour his guest a cup of hot tea, but R' Avraham did not want to partake of anything until he had told his story. They sat together at the heavy antique table, illuminated by the glow of a small taper. He related the chain of events, ending with a plea: "Do something — before tragedy strikes the Jewish *kehillah* of Amtzislav!"

R' Itzele closed his eyes and reflected, swaying to and fro as though in prayer. One foot tapped absently on the hardwood floor. He cupped his gray beard as though to help him think.

At last, he opened his eyes. "My dear and illustrious rav," he said. "I am prepared to go out and do whatever is necessary, right this minute. But I must insist on one condition first."

"And that is ...?" R' Avraham Simchah questioned anxiously.

R' Itzele gazed deeply into the rabbi's eyes. "I am prepared to do everything within my power on your behalf — but first, you must promise me that this is a false accusation, cobbled together by haters of Israel. Are you absolutely certain that no Jew killed that Russian soldier?"

R' Avraham replied without hesitation. "I am absolutely certain. Let us consider the question logically. Do Jews carry firearms? Do they even know how to pull a trigger? Do you really consider it feasible that, under those circumstances, a Jew would manage to grab a soldier's gun and successfully shoot him?"

"Logic is on our side, this time," conceded R' Itzele. "But we are opposed by a bloodthirsty apostate who has managed to get the Czar to act against us. I must tread on sure ground here. Are you ready to swear to me that no Jewish hand spilled that blood?"

The rabbi rose to his feet and looked around him. R' Itzele, understanding, took him into a nearby room that served as a shul in his mansion. He went to the *aron kodesh* and removed a *Sefer Torah*, on which R' Avraham Simchah swore that the Jews' hands were innocent of the slain soldier's blood.

R' Itzele waited no longer. Summoning his head groom, he ordered four of his finest horses to be hitched at once to his most ornate carriage.

That same night, the rabbi and the rich man set out for St. Petersburg. Hidden deep inside their luggage, among their clothes, were white shrouds.

They were prepared to go the full length — even to the point of self-sacrifice!

The considerable distance between Smolensk and St. Petersburg was easily swallowed beneath the peerless horses' galloping legs. With only brief stops, they reached the outskirts of the Czar's capital in only three days' time.

While the older, exhausted rabbi rested in an inn, R' Itzele did not waste a moment. He set off at once to see the Russian Minister of the Interior, a man by the name of Kukarin.

The minister welcomed his old acquaintance with honor. Inviting him in, he listened to the Jewish version of the Amtzislav incident. R' Itzele watched him tensely, awaiting his reply.

Kukarin nodded his head and compressed his thin lips. "It pains me to disappoint you, my dear and loyal friend. This time, I am unable to help. The Czar becomes enraged whenever anyone mentions what happened in Amtzislav. He views it as a spark of rebellion. Jews, with the audacity to shoot a Russian soldier? The notion makes him very obstinate, and determined to teach the Jewish community a lesson it will never forget."

Another man would have thrown up his hands in defeat at this news. Not R' Itzele!

"My dear Minister Kukarin, I cannot accept that. You know as well as I that here in Russia, nothing is impossible ... If you wished, you could help us change the Czar's mind even in this apparently hopeless matter."

He gazed directly into the interior minister's eyes, adding emotionally, "If you succeed, I will be in your debt for the rest of my life. And you know that, with a millionaire like myself as your debtor, you won't lose from it."

The minister flushed with pleasure. The Jewish activist knew exactly how to win him over. Rising with alacrity from the plush crimson sofa, he energetically crossed the ornate room. R' Itzele's eyes never left him.

At last, Kukarin turned. "The only one who can help you now is the Crown Prince and heir to the throne, Alexander II. Unlike the Czar, he does not hate the Jews. It may be possible for me to change his mind."

That evening, when the rav of Amtzislav and R' Itzele were in their room at the inn, they were surprised by a visit from his honor, the Minister of the Interior, in person.

"Itzik," exclaimed Kukarin. "You have a compassionate Father in Heaven. I spoke with the Crown Prince, and he is prepared to talk to the Czar and recommend mercy on your behalf. Before that, however, he wants to meet with you. At 3 o'clock tomorrow afternoon, come to my office at the Ministry. I will take you to the royal palace, where I will introduce you to him."

It was impossible to sleep a wink that night. The two Jews stood in fervent prayer for long hours, pleading with Hashem for the success of their mission. They *davened Shacharis* at first light, refrained from breaking their fast with a morning meal, and dressed, putting on under their clothing the shrouds they had brought with them. At the appointed hour they rode to the Ministry, from which they were escorted at once to the palace.

On the way, Minister Kukarin instructed them in proper behavior before the Crown Prince — the second most powerful man in all of Russia. The Jews were consumed with tension. As they rounded the last bend and saw the palace looming imposingly ahead of them, both men broke out in sweat and trembling. R' Itzele's tongue stuck to his dry palate, and his eyes felt frozen.

Kukarin led them to the spacious hall in front of the Crown Prince's chamber. The hall was filled with people — noblemen, generals, and government ministers — all waiting silently for their turn to meet with the prince. In front of the doors stood a pair of severe-looking soldiers, drawn swords in hand. Terror overcame R' Itzele. The blood drained from his face, and his heart drummed so loudly that he felt close to collapse. Glancing over at the rabbi, he was stunned to see the difference between them. R' Avraham stood erect, his face pale, but tranquil. His eyes shone with joy and excitement and his lips moved in a whisper.

"Are you reciting the *Viduy*?" R' Itzele asked fearfully.

The rabbi nodded.

The time for self-sacrifice had arrived. The shrouds on their bodies were ready to do their job. R' Itzele joined the rabbi in whispering the words of the *Viduy* — the confession before death.

Without warning, the door to the Crown Prince's chamber opened. Alexander II stepped out and approached them. It seemed to R' Itzele that he was garbed in gold. Coming closer, the prince fixed them with a piercing gaze. R' Itzele's breathing stopped. Dark spots swam before his eyes.

Gathering his strength, he recited the blessing, "Blessed is He Who has shared His honor with mortal men."

Then he fell to the floor in a dead faint.

Upon waking, R' Itzele found himself lying on a clean white bed in a well-appointed room. Nearby sat a doctor, who fed him bitter medicine to restore his strength.

He was confused at first — until he remembered the circumstances that had brought him here. Unable to contain himself, R' Itzele burst into tears. A curse on his weakness! Why did he have to be such a coward in front of a mere creature of flesh and blood? "I lost my chance to speak with the Crown Prince," he thought bitterly through his tears. "An entire community is in grave danger because of an overabundance of improper emotion!"

He was still weeping and silently berating himself when Minister Kukarin walked into the room. Approaching the bed, he scolded, "Why are you crying, Itzik? Your G-d is with you in everything you do! The Crown Prince was shaken to see a Jew fainting at the mere sight of him, and he told the Czar about it. The Czar reacted with the words, "A person who faints at the sight of the Crown Prince is no liar. Bring him to me!" When you regain your strength, Itzik, I will accompany you to the Czar and you can tell him everything that is on your mind."

R' Itzele nearly fainted a second time. Now the mighty Czar himself wished to see him!

He spent the next two days in bed, imbibing strenghtening potions. His companion, R' Avraham Simchah, became overexcited at the prospect of a face-to-face meeting with the Czar, and fell ill as well.

On the third day, Kukarin took R' Yitzchak Zalkin to the palace and presented him to the Czar. With Heaven's help, he managed not to faint this time, though he was even more shaken by the encounter with royalty than he had been the first time around.

The moment Nikolai laid eyes on him, he bellowed, "How dare you Jews kill a Russian soldier?"

R' Itzele drew a deep breath, and answered politely but firmly. "It was not we who killed him. Our enemies have slandered us."

"According to the information passed along to me by my loyal workers, the Jews killed him!"

"But, Your Majesty, your men are mortal, and therefore may fall into error. If it should please the Czar, let him send a senior military officer, someone incorruptible, to investigate the matter. I am confident that he will arrive at the truth."

Nikolai sat lost in thought for several moments, turning over the Jew's suggestion. Suddenly, he rose from his gilded throne and approached R' Itzele. He stared piercingly into the Jew's eyes, until R' Itzele felt his blood freeze in his veins.

"Tell me," the Czar asked in a soft, menacing tone. "What will you do if the senior officer I send also discovers that it was the Jews who killed a soldier. What will you say about the fact that you deceived your king?"

R' Itzele's heart thudded wildly. His head spun with fear — until he remembered R' Avraham's oath on the *Sefer Torah*.

"Your Majesty, Czar of all Russia. If it turns out that it was the Jews who killed that soldier, and that I deceived Your Majesty, Heaven forbid, I will accept this punishment: Let the two million rubles that the good L-rd has given me be turned over to the royal treasury. G-d has granted me seven sons — let them all be taken for military service. As for myself, let me be sent away to Siberia, to serve a life sentence of hard labor."

The courageous reply pleased the Czar. He accepted R' Itzele's proposal and appointed an independent commission of inquiry, which came to Amtzislav to investigate the matter in depth. The apostate Briskin's defamy was exposed when an interrogation of the soldiers brought to light the fact that it had been an accidental discharge from one of their own rifles that had ended their comrade's life.

The Jews of Amtzislav were able to breathe again. The danger was lifted from their heads. And the story of the devoted R' Itzele Zalkin was told everywhere, with reverent gratitude, as the epitome of dedication and self-sacrifice.

It's Never Too Late ...

THE RUMBLE OF A COACH'S WHEELS AND THE CLIP-CLOP OF horses' hooves broke the silence of the street outside. In the dim room, rosy light filtered through the curtains. Rivkah, the woman of the house, put down her ball of yarn and went to look out the window.

"It is nearly sunset!" she cried in distress. "The sun is going down, and I have not *davened Minchah* yet!"

Setting down her long knitting needles on the embroidered tablecloth that covered the heavy wooden table, she quickly washed her hands in the basin that sat in one corner of the room. She closed her eyes and *davened Minchah* from memory, the way her mother, Bluma, had taught her. In Cracow in the year 5295 (1535), there were no *siddurim* yet. Jewish women who knew how to *daven* did so from memory. The teachers in those days were the mothers, who taught their daughters what prayers they knew.

Rivkah prayed fervently, eyes closed, pronouncing each word slowly. Unaware, tears began to trickle from her eyes. From a general prayer she moved to a private one, which bubbled up from the depths of her anguished heart:

"Master of the Universe, see my pain! Fifteen years have passed since I married my husband, R' Yosef, may he live and be well. I am not complaining; I know that You run Your world with kindness and great compassion. Everything that You give us is a gift. In terms of my deeds, I am certainly undeserving of anything. But — please! Give me a gift. Give me a son! A son who will be the light and joy of my life. One son ... One soul from Your infinite treasury of souls. Please!"

This was the kind of prayer Rivkah invoked when the pain overflowed her aching heart, when she felt as though her very soul was being torn to bits through sheer longing for the child she had never had. When she had married at the age of 17, like all her friends in Cracow, she had been hardly more than a child herself. The future had seemed rose-colored and certain. Who could have imagined that, a decade and a half later, her friends would be in over their heads caring for children, some of them mothers of large families — while she herself remained barren.

Each year, in the *Minchah* of Tishah B'Av, when Rivkah *davened* the special *Nachem* prayer and reached the words comparing Jerusalem to a barren woman, her heart would break afresh and the bitter tears would flow. She would be ashamed, afterwards, for having mingled her personal sorrow with the great, general one — yet the same scene repeated itself, year after year.

Once, she had wished for ten children. Now she would be satisfied with just one. A single cradle would be enough to rescue the house from its terrible desolation. It would be enough to change everything.

The hot tears that rose from her broken heart as evening fell joined the reservoir of tears that had preceded them. Her prayers were accepted on high. But in order for her wish to come true, she would first have to undergo a complete personal upheaval.

Her husband, R' Yosef, was a successful businessman and a man of great personal charm. He traveled throughout Cracow and outside it, buying and selling. Respected in his own town, he was also held in great esteem by the area's *pritzim*, or noblemen, who prized his integrity in their dealings with him.

There were times when R' Yosef was away from home all week long, arriving back on Friday afternoon just as Shabbos was approaching. He was always traveling. He, too, suffered the anguish of childlessness, and distracted himself from the pain by keeping his thoughts busy, day and night. In his vest pocket he carried his thick account book, filled with lines and tiny numbers which occupied his mind so that he could not think of his pain.

His wife, in contrast, sat at home knitting baby clothes. She did not need to do this in terms of earning a livelihood; R' Yosef's income was more than sufficient to support even a large family in comfort. Rivkah distributed the exquisite, handmade garments to poverty-stricken mothers. One of Cracow's leading rabbis had suggested this to her, as a means of rousing Heaven's mercy to grant her a child of her own.

Free of workaday cares, Rivkah had the leisure to fill herself up with the sight of babies — laughing, crying, gurgling, yawning, smiling. Longing filled her to the breaking point. She yearned to knit a tiny garment for a baby of her own, who would smile at her as she cradled it in her arms. Sitting alone with these long-unfulfilled dreams, she felt as though her heart would shatter from the sheer weight of her sorrow. That was when her eyes would turn into a pair of spigots, pouring out the tears that streamed heedlessly down her face. Her bitter weeping would fill the house, until even the neighbors heard, and felt their own hearts constrict with sympathy.

But the gates of tears are never closed ...

That day, R' Yosef concluded a successful business deal with one of the local noblemen who lived near Cracow. The *poritz*, well pleased, added an unexpected bonus to the agreed-on price.

R' Yosef left the *poritz's* house with a heavy bundle of money, which — for fear of vandals — he made haste to hide in a dark corner of his carriage.

He had good reason for this fear. The two gentile coachmen, seated up front behind the horses, saw the heavy bundle and coveted that money. They exchanged a meaningful wink.

The following morning, while their master was immersed in his morning prayers, one of the coachmen slipped away through the trees, deep into the forest. He returned a short while later, before R' Yosef had finished *davening*, and whispered to his friend, "I spoke to the gang. They are waiting for us."

"Excellent."

R' Yosef completed his prayers, folded his *tallis*, and sat at ease in the coach. Despite his continued childlessness, he felt optimistic. One must never despair. He would be blessed with children yet, and then he would be the happiest of men!

Many are the thoughts in man's heart — but only Hashem's plan will endure ...

The carriage drove deep into the heart of the forest. Suddenly, it was surrounded by a gang of armed robbers. The two traitorous coachmen joined them. R' Yosef was murdered in cold blood and his money stolen. Later, the carriage would be found overturned, the horses freed of their harness. Beneath the carriage lay the body of poor R' Yosef.

All of Cracow was plunged into mourning at the tragedy that had befallen their beloved brother. R' Yosef's death was a grievous loss to the community, and to his friends. The hardest blow of all, of course, was felt by his wife, Rivkah, left a widow in the prime of life. She wept day and night and would not be comforted. The only crumb of consolation came in the discovery of his body, without which she would have been left an *agunah*.

Because R' Yosef had left this world without bearing offspring, it was necessary for Rivkah to undergo the *Chalitzah* ceremony with R' Yosef's brother. The custom is to conduct this ceremony publicly, and a large crowd came to the *beis din* at the appointed hour. After the rite had been performed, the judges blessed Rivkah, wishing her a happy second marriage and the merit of bringing children into the world. The crowd answered, "*Amen*." When the last echo had died away, it was time for the second ceremony.

The old *shamash*, R' Yaakov Yukel Segal, emerged from his corner, walking on shaky legs. He straightened his back before the honored *dayanim*, cleared his throat importantly, and announced in a clear, loud voice:

"In the name of the rabbis and judges of this holy city of Cracow, I hereby announce that anyone who wishes to marry the *chalutzah*, Rivkah, should step forward before the *beis din* and receive the blessing of the *rabbanim* seated here."

The crowd held its breath. Everyone hoped that someone would come forward for the young widow, so that she might now end her life of loneliness and merit seeing some happiness and consolation after fifteen years of pain that had ended in such tragedy. But, in that large crowd, there was not one person who stepped forward.

The following days, as well, saw no one offering himself as a candidate for her hand — neither a *bachur*, nor a widower, nor a divorced man.

Six long, heartbroken months passed for the widow, with no sliver of hope on the horizon ...

Thirty years before the events described above, when Rivkah was only a little girl, 2 years old, a man came to live in Cracow. His age appeared to be about 50 and his name was R' Yosef Yospa. Even in Cracow, a city filled with scholars, R' Yosef drew every eye. People began to imitate his ways and to whisper wondrous stories about him. He was involved in Torah and *avodah* all day long, detached from worldly concerns. From morning to night he sat in the shul, where he learned a regular schedule of subjects. Rumor had it that he possessed an awesome breadth of knowledge and was familiar with the entire Torah. No one had ever seen him engaged in idle speech. No one had ever heard him speak in anger. Immured in his corner of the shul, a huge pile of *sefarim* before him, he chanted quietly as he learned. It was not long before people began to refer to him as a holy *tzaddik*.

His appearance seemed to confirm this label. As the years passed, his countenance grew more refined and filled with holiness, until he seemed almost angelic. His beard lengthened and turned white and his face reflected a noble sensitivity. His eyes shone like a pair of lanterns and his high forehead gave him the appearance of a mighty thinker.

R' Yosef Yospa had never married. Like Ben Azzai in his day, R' Yosef desired nothing but Torah. In order to facilitate his ability to learn, he had never taken a wife and experienced the distractions of raising a family. On his arrival in Cracow, the matchmakers came out in hordes — some of them sent by important rabbis — to try and interest him in various widows and divorcees. At first, not knowing him, the matchmakers thought it had been sheer bad luck that had kept him from marrying. Surely, if they only suggested a suitable widow, or a divorced woman of childbearing age, he would leap at the chance.

But R' Yosef Yospa would not listen to any of these proposals. He lifted his eyes from his *sefer*, smiled apologetically beneath his whitening mustache, and pointed to the *sefarim* waiting for him to reach them. It was as though he were saying, "Because of these, I have no time to marry."

The matchmakers, understanding the situation, tried to tempt him with even better offers. But R' Yosef only smiled his apologetic smile so sweetly that all complaints dried up at once. The matchmakers knew when they had been defeated.

Despite his complete detachment from Cracow's affairs — or perhaps because of it — R' Yosef was held in universal appreciation in the city. He lived his life quietly and in peace, learned Torah and served Hashem in holiness, year after year. He grew older, and passed his 80th year. Decades of laboring in the service of Hashem had purified his countenance until it shone like the noonday sun. All who saw him believed that there was nothing left for him to do but eventually rise up to Heaven, like Eliyahu HaNavi. What did an angel like this, who had reached old age in such purity, have to do with our frail world? Let him live out the remainder of his years, rising ever higher, until he turned into an actual angel!

And then the day came that showed all of Jewish Cracow that there is no limit to the surprising things that can happen ...

The *shamash* of the *beis din* stepped back respectfully before R' Yosef Yospa's shining visage. R' Yosef stood in the doorway and kissed the *mezuzah*.

"Please, come in, holy rabbi," the *shamash* cried. What, he wondered, had brought this *tzaddik* to the *beis din*? It was inconceivable that he had come to arrange a *din Torah* over some dispute with another member of the community. Or ... perhaps he had? Had someone cheated him? Before he could complete the thought, R' Yosef had walked up to the table at which the *dayanim* sat. Instinctively, the judges rose to their feet out of respect for the sage.

"What is His Honor's business here? How may we help you?"

The answer took their breaths away.

"Half a year ago, this *beis din* performed a *Chalitzah* ceremony for the widow of R' Yosef, the businessman. Afterwards, the *shamash* announced that anyone who wished to marry the widow should come to the *beis din* to recieve the rabbis' blessing. I have thought it over, and I have come to propose myself. I wish to marry the widow, Rivkah, if she will have me, of course."

The judges were rendered speechless.

Delicately, the *Av Beis Din* asked, "Is Your Honor not concerned about his advanced age?"

Standing like a student before his rebbe, R' Yosef Yospa replied humbly, "I am 80 years old today. A person's life span is meted out by *HaKadosh Baruch Hu*. My heart tells me that I still have many years of life ahead of me."

The *Av Beis Din* remembered that he was talking with no ordinary man. At once, he sent a messenger to summon the widow, Rivkah.

Rivkah entered the courtroom. Her questioning gaze fell on R' Yosef Yospa, standing with eyes downcast. Before a word was spoken, she burst into a great weeping that shook all who heard it.

"Why are you crying?" the *Av Beis Din* asked compassionately.

Regaining her composure with difficulty, the widow answered, "I had a strange dream, several times now. At first I thought it was nothing, but when it recurred again and again, it began to weigh upon me and has given me no rest. I am embarrassed to relate it here, in public, yet I cannot get it out of my mind."

"On the contrary — speak," urged the *Av Beis Din*. "It will make you feel better. Let the weight that is pressing on you roll away. Come, let us step aside, where no one will be able to hear."

At the *shamash's* command, everyone but the members of the tribunal moved to the other side of the big room. Now Rivkah could reveal her distressing dream:

"In the dream," she began, "I saw my father, may he rest in peace. He was dressed in his Shabbos clothes. I became very excited and thought he was alive. 'Father!' I cried out joyfully. 'How are you?'

"My father corrected my error. 'Have you forgotten, my dear daughter, that I am no longer among the living? I have come to instruct you to marry the holy *tzaddik*, R' Yosef Yospa. Tomorrow morning, send him a messenger saying that you wish to marry him.'

"I was thunderstruck. 'Father!' I shrieked. 'I am a young woman, and he is 80 years old. Must I become a widow again so soon? Once was enough. I wish to marry a young man.'

"But my father would not back down. Again and again he repeated his words. I awoke trembling — and realized that it had been a dream. I decided not to think about it. But the following night, Father returned to me and scolded, 'Why have you not sent a messenger to the *tzaddik*, R' Yosef Yospa?' I awoke, shaken to the core. On the successive nights, too, my father came back, again and again. Then I understood that this was no idle dream. Since then, I have known no rest."

The *Av Beis Din* beamed. "But it was for that very reason that we summoned you here! R' Yosef Yospa has come to ask you to consent to be his wife."

He called over his fellow *dayanim*, to whom Rivkah repeated her amazing dream. The *beis din* decided unanimously that it was the truth.

R' Yosef was informed that the widow, Rivkah, had given her consent to the marriage.

All of Cracow joined in the joyous occasion of the widow Rivkah's marriage to R' Yosef Yospa. A strange feeling surrounded the event — as though someone were whispering in the guests' ears, telling them that this was no ordinary marriage, no routine event, but something extraordinary, outside the bounds of nature, whose secret was known only to He Who dwells on high. All the city's Kohanim came to bless the couple with the traditional *Birkas Kohanim,* and every person present, young and old, wished the couple a life of happiness and the blessing of righteous offspring.

The joy multiplied astronomically when, a year later, a son was born to them. They named him Eliyahu, after Eliyahu HaNavi.

When Eliyahu turned 2, his father (now 83 years old!) began to teach him Torah. All through his own remarkable old age, R' Yosef continued to teach and guide his son. As Eliyahu neared bar mitzvah age, he was already beginning to be recognized as a holy *tzaddik* in his own right.

Two weeks before Eliyahu's bar mitzvah, R' Yosef told his wife, Rivkah, "The time has come for me to leave this world. Do not cry over me too much, for I have lived a long life, praise Hashem, and am today 94 years old. Let our son, Eliyahu, continue to work according to his own understanding. Do not interfere with him, for his path in Torah and *avodah* is already laid out before him. He knows what his job is in this world."

Two days after he had celebrated him son's bar mitzvah, R' Yosef Yospa's soul left his body, at a ripe old age. His wife, Rivkah, obeyed his instructions to the letter. She merited seeing tremendous *nachas* from her only son, who rose higher from day to day and went on to become the great and holy *tzaddik* known to all as "Rebbe Eliyahu Ba'al Shem." He lived in the city of Worms, where he taught Torah to numerous students who, in their turn, went on to illuminate the Torah to future generations of Jews.

Heavenly Strength

THIS STORY TOOK PLACE ABOUT 400 YEARS AGO, IN THE CITY of Ragusa, Italy — home of the *gaon* R' Aharon HaKohen of Ragusa, author of *Zekan Aharon*.

Ragusa was a small city that boasted only a few score of Jewish families living among a Christian community many times its size.

On the first day of Succos, the daughter of a Chrisitan businessman disappeared. A frantic search was launched, and toward evening word spread that the lost girl had been found, healthy and safe. The news reached a circle of people that included the girl's father and several of his friends. One of them was a Jew.

"You Jews are in luck today," one of the Christians told the Jewish man. "If we had not found her, it would have been obvious that you Jews killed her for your holiday needs."

"Ach! You are a fool," the Jew said with a burst of laughter. "This is our festival of Succos, not Pesach! You people create blood libels for us at Pesach."

The Christian bit his lip, mortified.

It was not long, however, before it became known that the joy had been premature. The lost girl had *not* been found at all. Ragusa boiled. When night fell, the father and the city guardsmen continued to search for her in every corner of the city. When she was not found, they extended the search to the towns outside the city, going from house to house.

The searchers arrived at the home of a Christian woman who was known for her wicked tendencies. Suddenly, they spied a bundle of old rags beneath her bed. The bundle aroused their worst suspicions. Sure enough, when they opened the bundle, they found the lifeless body of the lost girl.

"Why did you do it?" screamed the heartbroken father. He advanced menacingly on the murderess, intent on exacting his revenge. The guards had a struggle on their hands to prevent him from ending the woman's life on the spot.

"There are judges in this country," they told the father, trying to calm him. "You cannot take the law into your own hands."

The woman was handcuffed and placed under house arrest until morning. With first light, her friends and neighbors began to come to the house, filled with righteous indignation.

"Why did you do it?" they asked, spitting at her. Silently, she bowed her head in fear and shame. But it was not long before a new culprit was found. Naturally, it was the Jews.

A sly gentile who could not bear the sight of the humiliation being heaped on the Christian woman's head, approaching her and asked, "Perhaps it was the Jews who ordered you to kill the child, in order to use her blood for some religious purposes of their own?"

As she listened in silence, he continued, "Of course! That must have been the way it happened. When they bring you up before the judge, tell him what I am telling you to say."

The murderess absorbed his message. When, several hours later, she was taken to court and asked for her motivation behind the killing, she thought a moment and then answered in a hesitant voice, "A Jew by the name of Yitzchak Yeshurun forced me to do it."

Yitzchak Yeshurun was the only Jew the woman knew. She had once borrowed a small sum of money from him, and had left him her winter coat as collateral. She now made an evil return for the favor he had done her. His name had floated up through her consciousness, in a wicked twisting of their fates.

A troop of Italian soldiers descended on Ragusa's Jewish ghetto. With a terrifying clamor they burst into Yitzchak Yeshurun's home and dragged him off to court with no explanation.

Yitzchak was confused and frightened when they confronted him with the gentile murderess.

"This woman says you know her. She says that you persuaded her to kill a young Christian girl."

Yitzchak's eyes darted fearfully around the crowded room. He had never before found himself in a situation even remotely resembling this one. It was true that he was acquainted with the woman and had innocently lent her some money, but that was the extent of their relationship. The brazen accusation confused him, and made him say the wrong thing. Had he stated that he did know her as someone to whom he had loaned money, they might have believed him. Bewildered by and afraid of this life-threatening accusation, he decided to deny everything.

"I do not know her!" he cried. "I have never seen her before in my life. I do not even speak her language."

This constituted serious perjury. The court indicated that they had several witnesses who had seen him speaking to the woman in her own language! He was dragged off to prison, where he underwent a series of interrogations at odd and unexpected hours. After a few days, the order was given to torture him until he confessed to inciting the woman to murder.

On the third day after his arrest, Yitzchak Yeshurun was brought to the city square, to undergo public torture.

A bloodthirsty crowd of spectators was on hand to watch. They were eager for the smell of Jewish flesh. A tall, burly Italian, with the red face characteristic of those who drink too much hard whiskey, stood facing the crowd. He announced, "The Jew, Yitzchak Yeshurun, has been sentenced by the judges to public torture until he confesses his guilt."

Yitzchak was white as a sheet. Looking at the huge wooden poles, his heart quailed. "How will I ever live through this torture? *Oy*, Father in Heaven, give me the strength to endure, and not to confess to something I did not do!"

He feared for his own life, for he knew that to admit to the murder was to sentence himself to death. His fear came also from a profound sense of responsibility toward all his fellow Jews. If the crowd heard that a Jew had instructed a gentile to murder another gentile, they would fall on the Jewish ghetto and pitilessly massacre every Jew in Ragusa.

He was still lost in thought, his lips moving in silent prayer, when he was brought before the torture instruments. His hands were manacled behind his back and then tied with ropes to the tall poles. He was forced to dangle by his manacled hands for an entire hour.

The pain was horrific. He felt as though his bones were being torn asunder, as if his arms were being ripped from his shoulders.

When an hour had passed, Yitzchak was lowered to the ground. If he had thought the torture session was over, however, he was mistaken. The "main course" was yet to come.

He was hauled by rope to a height of 20 meters in the air, with his hands still tied behind his back. Suddenly, he was dropped nearly to the ground, and abruptly stopped.

The crowd roared at the sight of the falling Jew. Yitzchak was certain that his life was over. Every limb seemed to be pulling away from his body, but, to his amazement, he still lived. He was raised again and then dropped in the same manner. Three times he underwent the torture, and after each time his interrogators screamed at him, "Do you confess?"

"No! No!" Yitzchak cried through foaming lips. "I cannot confess to something I did not do!"

Bruised and broken, Yitzchak was returned to his tiny prison cell. No medical treatment was provided after the excruciating tortures he had undergone. He lay on the hard floor, groaning with pain. No one heard him.

The judges made up their minds to break Yitzchak, once and for all. The following week, they would put him through the entire, hour-long torture again. Before that, however, they shaved all the hair from the prisoner's head. The judges believed that Yitzchak practiced magical arts whose source was to be found in his hair. Only magic could have given him the strength to withstand the terrible agonies he had undergone.

He was chained again to the thick poles, hands secured behind his back. His screaming and crying were to no avail. His body, still aching from the previous week's torture, began a second round.

Yitzchak did not confess.

The judges conferred. "Only an innocent man would not confess after such pain," some of them said.

The matter was moved up to a higher court. Twelve judges discussed the case, weighing it from every angle. Their decision: Yitzchak must be tortured yet again, even more severely than before.

Once again, he survived the ordeal without confessing. He incorporated his agonized cries in *tefillos* to Hashem. His torturers scoffed cruelly, "Why are you praying to your G-d? Dirty Jew, everyone knows that you got that woman to kill the girl. Why will you not confess?"

"I — am — innocent," Yitzchak gasped. "I will see you before the Heavenly Court, if I die under your torturing hands."

They laughed at the Jew's "threat."

The fourth round of torture stunned the judges. This Jew was not human! Why was he not dead yet? By Italian law, in such a situation they were required to stop the torture. They arrested the gentile woman who had been accused at the outset, and submitted her to the same torture. She hung by her hands for an hour. But a wicked person, even when poised at the gates of Gehinnom, does not repent.

The women screamed that the Jew was guilty, and that he had induced her to murder the girl.

To a gentile, another gentile's pain hurts more than that of a Jew. The judges, with their delicate sensibilities, could not bear her suffering. They decided to return their attention to their Jewish prisoner instead, and to submit him to a torture that no one, in the natural order of things, could possibly survive.

There is nature, and there is something that is above nature. Yitzchak underwent a horrible series of bitter tortures, calculated to break his spirit and force him to confess to the crime he did not commit. His body was stretched in a manner perfected in Medieval dungeons, to the point where he was broken and torn inside, but Hashem miraculously helped him to remain alive.

The crowd whispered excitedly. "He is a sorcerer. He is a wizard!" Fingers pointed accusingly at the tortured man. The judges' hearts remained hard as stone, undiluted by the tiniest drop of compassion. They ordered the torture redoubled. But they did not take into account the Master of the Universe.

By this time, Yitzchak was ready to confess. He was ready to do anything to put a stop to the agony. But *HaKadosh Baruch Hu* invested him with extraordinary strength to withstand the torture, to the point where he hardly felt the pain anymore. On the contrary: He grew stronger. He began to shout at the judges, "Do you think *I* have the power to withstand this kind of suffering? G-d has sent His angel to me, the way he sent an angel to Daniel in the lions' den!"

Like Pharaoh in his time, the judges hardened their hearts. They continued the torture for a long time, but fresh strength flowed miraculously into the prisoner's body, helping him survive the searing pain.

When he was finally released from the torture device, he stood on his own two legs, unsupported, like a healthly man newly risen from his bed instead of one who had just undergone an ordeal of grotesque, inhuman torture.

"He is a mighty wizard," the judges declared, in an attempt to explain the inexplicable.

They tried again to extract the truth from the gentile woman who had been accused of the murder. The court sentenced her to death. In her final confession to the priest before her execution, he asked her to admit that she had concocted a slander against the Jew. The wicked woman already had one foot in Gehinnom's fiery pit, but she would not repent.

"The Jew made me do it," she said.

And she died.

The judges were furious. They passed the case to the highest court in the land, known as the "*Prigai.*" That court decided that the first order of business was to get rid of the Jew's magical powers.

Yitzchak was "treated" to remove his powers. All his hair, from head to toe, was shaved off. His fingernails and toenails were cut and his clothes exchanged for those of a gentile. He was transferred to a different prison, where he was forced to drink something that made him vomit. His body was cleaned thoroughly, in the manner of corpses. Priests came to see him each day, bearing incense and muttering all sorts of incantations to expel the magic. The last indignity was hardest of all: The food he was now served came directly from the prison's own kitchen — nonkosher meat — for fear that the kosher food he had been eating carried some secret strength for him.

But his real secret was prayer.

Prayer and fasting and weeping to Heaven, by all his Jewish brethren throughout Ragusa.

Each time Yitzchak was taken out to be tortured, there was a terrible fear not only for his life, but also that he would "confess" and thus expose the entire community to genocide. The Jews of the town gathered in the shuls, *davening* and crying out as they pleaded with Hashem to free Yitzchak, and until then, strengthen his spirit and grant him the ability to withstand the torture. Words of prayer did not leave their lips until the torture had ended.

The Christian judges did not know — or did not want to know — that it was Hashem Who had invested the feeble Jew with the spiritual and physical fortitude to withstand his ordeal.

After the "magic" was removed, the torture was resumed. Yitzchak heroically survived this round as well.

There no longer existed any legal grounds for continuing the Jew's torture. Moreover, among the largely wicked judges were a few who possessed a conscience, and who defended him. They claimed that the court had lost all sense of proportion in the case.

In a last attempt to shake up the Jewish community, several other Jews were arrested, interrogated and tortured, among them, the local rav. With Hashem's mercy, all came through the ordeal, and were released.

At last the case was routed to the highest authority in the land: the high court in Rome.

That court decided to exact its revenge against Yitzchak for withstanding the torture. They sentenced him to twenty years of imprisonment in a cave.

No sooner was the sentence handed down, than Yitzchak was taken from his holding cell and led into a dark, deep cave, and its entrance was secured.

Yitzchak was a broken man. His bones were literally shattered and his entire body was covered with wounds and bruises. But his hands were worst of all. They had been nearly torn off his arms. He had lost all sensation in them, as if they were paralyzed. The Jewish community hired a gentile to feed him mashed-up food and tiny quantities of water through a straw.

The cell was inaccessible except to the man who fed him. It reeked with a foul odor, and Yitzchak's body was soon crawling with lice. He seemed to have reached the end of his road.

But even here, Hashem's compassion did not abandon him. A simple cat turned out to be his salvation.

One day, Yitzchak found a cat at his feet. He trained the animal to lie on his arms, where its constant kneading gradually restored circulation to the paralyzed limbs. Within a month, feeling had returned to his arms.

Incredibly, his entire broken body eventually healed itself — without benefit of a single medication.

＊＊＊

Ragusa's Jewish community was in crisis. Grave danger had appeared on the horizon. The city's Jews had not escaped untouched from Yitzchak's sentence: They were now forbidden to leave the city limits without the mayor's authorization. The inflamed gentiles believed the Jews thirsted after Christian blood — if not for religious rituals, then for the purposes of their "magic." If Yitzchak Yeshurun was found guilty, they decided, then all the Jews would deserve death. Special guards were posted to ensure than no Jew in Ragusa escaped.

It took time, but the wheel began to turn the other way. The Jews debated the matter with their gentile neighbors, demonstrating the misguided nature of the blood libel until they succeeded in convincing them. Their best argument was Yitzchak's supernatural ability — though he was not an especially strong individual — to endure tortures that would have broken most men many times stronger than he. This was surely proof that Hashem had protected him, and lent heavenly strength to his weak and broken body.

And then there was the series of mysterious deaths that befell Yitzchak's judges and torturers. Within a year, nearly all of them were gone.

"It is the Finger of G-d," the people — even the now-frightened remaining judges — whispered fearfully.

At the year's end, the case was judged again by the high court in Rome. This time, it concluded with a full acquittal for Yitzchak Yeshurun.

Yitzchak was released from his prison. A large crowd was present to watch, disbelievingly, as he got out of his pit. He had recovered completely and was able to walk upright. His body was healthy and whole; the agonies he had suffered had left no mark, except for a scar on the little finger of his left hand.

The small Jewish community celebrated Yitzchak's release with jubilation. With their own eyes, the gentiles had witnessed the way Hashem protects His beloved children even in the direst of cirumstances, imbuing them with the strength to endure whatever suffering has been decreed for them.

A Valuable Coin

R' YUDEL LIVED IN A SMALL VILLAGE OUTSIDE THE CITY OF Zlatopol. A friendly and well-liked man, he rented the tavern and restaurant from the Count who owned the village. This brought insufficient income to support his family, so he also rented from the Count, at a good price, several inns (known as *kretchmers*) in which travelers could pass the night. These he rented out, in turn, to a few of the village Jews.

If R' Yudel thought this would be a way of increasing his income, he was mistaken.

R' Yudel was blessed with a truly righteous wife, who was known by the entire village as Fraydel the *Tzaddekes,* and with good reason. She was as pious as she was kind-hearted. Everyone who saw her was moved by her modesty and fine *middos.* Most admiring of all, however, were the innkeepers who rented the *kretchmers* from her husband. They could testify, firsthand, to her unparalleled generosity of spirit.

Living at poverty's edge, the small income the villagers earned by renting out rooms was barely enough to feed their families. When the rent was due, there was not so much as a penny left over with which to pay R' Yudel.

To their surprise, Fraydel came to their homes on the day before payment was due. She conferred privately with each of their wives, then took her leave. The women all emerged from the conference beaming with joy.

Fraydel knew that the renters would be unable to pay. Therefore, she had taken money secretly and given it to the innkeepers' wives to use in paying her own husband. R' Yudel never knew that one of his hands was placing money into his pocket, money that had been taken out of his second pocket by his other hand ... that is, the hand of his good wife, Fraydel the *Tzaddekes*.

This state of affairs went on for a considerable time. R' Yudel was at a loss to understand why his budget seemed to have a hole in it, so that no matter how assiduously he calculated the numbers, he could not figure out where the money was going.

But it is in the nature of secrets to become revealed eventually. The proverbial cat longs to leap out of its bag and into the light. And so, one day, it did. R' Yudel discovered the truth. But the way in which this transpired was such that he would have preferred to have his wife continue supporting the innkeepers indefinitely, if only she would live.

Fraydel fell ill. Without warning, she took to her bed with a headache and mounting fever. She quickly became incoherent. When R' Yudel returned from shul that evening, he was shocked and horrified to find his wife lying in bed, with a gray pallor and still as a stone.

"Chananyah, Duvid'l, Hershel!" he called to his three oldest sons. "Come here and watch over your mother. I am running over to the doctor's house."

He returned a short time later with the doctor, a gentile professional by the name of Dr. Sasha. A brief examination was enough to tell the medical man that Fraydel's condition was grave. Her hours in this world were numbered!

R' Yudel burst into bitter tears. "Is there no hope? Is it so bad?" He grasped the hem of the doctor's coat as though it were a straw and he a drowning man.

Dr. Sasha spread his hands, sighed, and was silent. His silence frightened R' Yudel more than any words could have done. His heart froze.

Long minutes passed as he stood with head bowed and shoulders heaving with the force of his sobbing. He pleaded with his Creator to spare Fraydel's life and not deprive him of his wife. Then, having regained at least a bit of his composure, he began to think about what else could be done in this difficult situation.

Summoning the *Chevrah Kaddisha* would be premature. That need be done only in the end, when the worst had happened. Right now, though, his wife was still alive and breathing. There was still something he could do. He could *daven*!

Like a storm wind, he burst out of the house and began to run in the direction of the shul.

"R' Yudel, what happened?"

The speaker was a short, round man whose face always wore a smile — Akiva, the innkeeper. He never had more than a penny or two in his pocket, but his financial state and his emotional state were two things that maintained separate existences and never met. Akiva always had a comforting word to uplift and encourage those who had not been blessed with his own happy nature. Seeing R' Yudel racing down the street, pale and distraught, the innkeeper found his own smile wavering for a moment.

R' Yudel stopped running and gulped some air into his starved lungs. "My dear Akiva," he said in a quavering voice, "I am in terrible distress. My wife is dying! Come along with me to the shul. I want to get a *minyan* together to say *Tehillim* for her."

Akiva stood as though thunderstruck. "Mrs. Fraydel is dying?" he asked incredulously.

"Yes!"

"*Oy, oy*," wailed Akiva. "A *tzaddekes* like her has to die? She deserves to live a very long life. Do you hear, R' Yudel? Your wife should get better right away, and live a long, good life!"

"*Amen, kein yehi ratzon.* May it be Hashem's will," answered R' Yudel fervently. "Meanwhile, we have to do something!"

"Of course we do," Akiva said. "Don't worry, R' Yudel. I'm going to call all my fellow innkeepers. *Oy, oy,* we are with you in your pain, R' Yudel. If Fraydel dies, where will we get the money to pay your rent?"

"What?" Yudel blinked incomprehendingly.

"Uh — er — I spoke without thinking. It was nothing," Akiva retreated. "I am running to fetch the others." He ran off, leaving a confused and broken R' Yudel behind.

Akiva went from house to house among his friends, telling everyone the terrible news. They received it with sinking hearts. Should R' Yudel's wife die, they could say good-bye to their inns within a very short time. After all, it was only because of the amazingly kind-hearted Fraydel that they had managed to hold onto their source of livelihood without paying rent, and thanks to her that the meager profits were theirs, free and clear, to help feed their families. Unless a miracle occurred, their own futures looked gloomy indeed.

"We have to do something quickly," one of them said.

"What can we do? She is dying, poor woman."

"There is still a Master of the Universe," a third declared. This was the chassid among them, a man by the name of Shaul'ke. "I am going to Zlatopol."

In nearby Zlatopol lived a holy man, renowned throughout the land, by the name of Rebbe Nachman of Breslov.

Shaul'ke wasted no time carrying out his plan. He ran to the shul at once, where he found a frantic R' Yudel pulling volumes of *Tehillim* off the shelves. By the size of the pile he was preparing, he was obviously hoping for the company of hundreds of Jews to join him in prayer. But apart from his two oldest sons, Chananyah and Duvid'l (Hershel had stayed home with his mother), and two neighbors who took pity on R' Yudel, no one had come.

When R' Yudel saw Shaul'ke, his eyes lit up. He asked the innkeeper to join in a *minyan* in reciting *Tehillim* for his wife.

Shaul'ke, however, had something else on his mind. He told R' Yudel of his intention to travel to Zlatopol to ask the holy Breslover Rebbe to intercede for the sick woman. He asked R' Yudel for money for the redemption of Fraydel's life.

R' Yudel was no chassid in general, and had little sympathy for the Breslover chassidim in particular. But even he had heard wondrous tales about the Breslover Rebbe. He acceded immediately to Shaul'ke's request, giving him a *rendel*, a respectable donation, for the sake of his sick wife's recovery.

"I am leaving at once," Shaul'ke said, hurrying to the door. "Every minute is precious to your wife right now. The sooner I reach the rebbe's house, the better."

Shaul'ke was afraid lest Fraydel breathe her last before he reached Zlatopol. He urged the wagon-driver repeatedly to speed his horses on the paved road that would lead him to Rebbe Nachman.

Shaul'ke approached the rebbe with quaking knees. R' Nachman's appearance inspired awe. All the deprivations the great sage had suffered since childhood had left their mark, leaving him like something that had form but no content. His material body was nearly nullified by his giant soul, transforming it into a thing of the spirit thinly covered with rarified flesh and blood.

With awe and trembling, Shaul'ke related to the rebbe the reason for his visit. He told of R' Yudel's ailing wife who lay near death's door, mentioning both her name and that of her mother. Then he laid R' Yudel's *rendel* on the table.

The rebbe picked up the coin, held it in his hand for a moment as though weighing it, and then said, "This *rendel* is no good. Its weight is short."

Stunned, Shaul'ke offered to run out into the street to find someone who would exchange the coin for him. He quickly suited word to action. Outside, he scurried about searching for someone who would agree to exchange coins with him. He returned to the rebbe soon afterwards, the substitute *rendel* in hand.

Once again, the rebbe held the coin as though weighing it, and was dissatisfied. "This *rendel*, too, is not up to its proper weight. It is missing a little."

Shaul'ke returned to the street. The same scene repeated itself three more times. Each time, Shaul'ke searched for someone to switch coins with him — and each time, the rebbe expressed his dissatisfaction with the new coin's weight, saying, "This coin is not up to its full weight."

On the verge of despair, Shaul'ke was suddenly struck by inspiration. Running back outside, he soon returned with a moneychanger, who carried a box filled with bills and coins as well as a small set of scales with which to weigh the coins.

"Here is the solution," announced Shaul'ke happily. "This is a suitable fellow to give the rebbe whatever he wishes. Among his scores of coins he surely has one good one. Besides, he has a set of scales and can use it to determine whether or not the coin's weight is true."

A pleased expression settled over the rebbe's face at the sight of the moneychanger and his scales. From the look of deep satisfaction, it seemed clear to Shaul'ke that the rebbe had intended all along to prod him in this direction.

The moneychanger began to search among his coins for a good *rendel*. He held one out to R' Nachman. "It seems to me that this *rendel* is the exact weight."

"Are you sure?" asked the rebbe.

The moneychanger smiled modestly. "After so many years of handling coins, I can feel the weight in my fingertips. I only carry around the scales to be absolutely certain."

"Nevertheless, bring me the scales."

The moneychanger handed the scales to R' Nachman, who placed the *rendel* on it. He weighed it carefully once, twice, and then a third time.

"True enough," he answered with satisfaction. "You are right. This is a *rendel* of the correct weight."

The rebbe turned to Shaul'ke. "You can go home now. I received the coin for the redemption of the sick woman's life. She is already on the road to recovery."

All the way back from Zlatopol to the village, Shaul'ke's head spun. Something had happened just now! Something amazing! First the rebbe had declined a number of *rendels*, claiming that they were coins of diminished weight. This had led to Shaul'ke's bringing in the moneychanger, and the weighing of the coin on a scale, and finally, the rebbe's statement that the woman would recover.

Still, despite his excitement, he had his reservations. He needed to check the situation and see for himself.

The coach entered the village and made with all speed for R' Yudel's house.

There were dozens of people gathered together in front of the house. For a moment, Shaul'ke nearly froze in panic. It looked like he had come directly to the funeral.

A closer look, however, discerned the expressions of joy on the people's faces. He breathed a sigh of relief and plunged into the crowd.

"Well, what do you think of that?" someone asked him excitedly. "Fraydel woke up!"

With hammering heart he listened to the whole story.

After his departure for Zlatopol, the patient's condition had taken a turn for the worse. Matters reached the point where the *Chevrah Kaddisha* surrounded her bed as, by all indications, the soul departed her body. They were waiting the halachically prescribed number of minutes before they could place the body on the ground, when the "corpse" suddenly opened her eyes and asked for a drink of water!

Fraydel's condition gradually improved, until she was able to exchange a few words with her husband before falling into a deep sleep. Dr. Sasha was thunderstruck. Never in all his born days, he had declared, had he witnessed anything like this.

Beaming, Shaul'ke took great pleasure in the story. This was the outcome, but the other side of the picture had taken place in Zlatopol.

"Do you want to hear what happened in Zlatopol?" he asked those standing around him.

"Of course!"

He told them about the *rendel* that the rebbe had weighed on the scale until he was satisfied, and his guarantee that the sick woman had returned to life.

Within a few days, Fraydel had recovered sufficiently to get out of bed and walk briefly in the yard. Her gray pallor was replaced by the rosy hue of good health, and her footsteps were steady. Neverthless, from time to time she was overcome by an attack of weeping. She would hide her face in her hands and sob uncontrollably.

Her friends and children begged her to tell them what was troubling her. At last, she agreed.

"I was already over there," Fraydel said, pointing upward. "I stood before the Heavenly Court. If not for that holy man, I would have remained there." Once again, she burst into choking sobs.

"Please," the others begged. "Tell us the whole story!"

Fraydel took a deep breath, and began.

"You should know this: I was indeed dead. My soul left my body and soared up to the Heavenly Court. There, judges conferred amongst themselves and decided that my time had come to die, because the weight of my sins was greater than those of my good deeds!

"I wept and pleaded for my life, but in vain. 'I cannot leave behind little orphans,' I begged. But they explained to me that the father of my orphans could also care for them! I gave up. I was getting ready to remain there and face the great judgment, when a holy man appeared before the Court."

Here, Fraydel proceeded to render an exact description of R' Nachman of Breslov.

"There was a clamor in the Court. The man approached the scales and threw something onto them. I saw that it was a coin — a *rendel*. The coin tipped the scales of merit downward, and an acquittal was pronounced. It was decreed that I return to life.

"I awoke at once and found myself covered in sweat and my throat parched. So I asked for a drink of water."

R' Yudel and Shaul'ke synchronized their timetables. At the precise moment when R' Nachman was weighing the *rendels* on the scale, the woman had seen a vision of the Heavenly Court. The rebbe had tossed a coin in this world — and the scales had tipped in the next one!

Deeply moved, and elated at his wife's amazing recovery, R' Yudel stood up on a table and announced merrily to the group of innkeepers: "I believe that Hashem repaid my wife for her generosity and the good deed she performed each month — at my expense. He did not forget it when her time came."

The innkeepers exchanged a wondering look. Where was R' Yudel headed with this?

"Therefore," R' Yudel went on, "from this day forward, I am hereby absolving each and every one of you from paying me rent! Until now, this was taking place without my knowledge. From today on, there will be no reason to go behind my back.

"And," R' Yudel said, "if you ask what I will live on, the answer is simple: I will live exactly the way my family and I have lived all these years, when Fraydel would take the money without my knowledge and give it to you to pay my rent. The One Who supported me all those years will continue to support me and my family for a long and good life."

Like a Slap in the Shechinah's Face

"He who slaps another Jew's face is as one who slaps the Shechinah's face" (Sanhedrin 58b)

"**L**ET ME IN TO SEE THE REBBE."

"Absolutely not."

"Please, let me see the rebbe," pleaded the newcomer with tears in his eyes. "I am in great distress and must receive the rebbe's blessing!"

"I have already told you," the *gabbai* said, hardening his heart. "I cannot let you in under any circumstances. The rebbe himself has severely forbidden me to allow you into his room."

"But — why?" asked the man in shock.

"I do not know why," replied R' Aryeh, the well-known *gabbai* of R' Meir of Premishlan. "But this I do know: The rebbe's words burn like coals, and I will not cross them."

An important visitor was present in the rebbe's room just then and overheard what was going on outside the rebbe's office. He was another rebbe, R' Tzvi Hirsch of Liska, known by his work, *Ach Pri Tevuah*. R' Hershe'le of Liska often visited Premishlan. For his part, R' Meir would say that he placed the "key to Hungary" in the hands of R' Hershe'le of Liska.

Hearing the argument that was taking place between the *gabbai* and the other man, R' Hershe'le was astounded. Why was the troubled fellow not allowed in?

The argument was not over yet. As the two rebbes conversed, the voices from outside continued to penetrate the inner room. The man wept bitterly, explaining in a choked voice that he was in a terrible crisis and asking how it was possible to ignore his plight.

R' Hershe'le's heart constricted with pity. He could not bear the man's suffering. He broke off in the middle of his talk with R' Meir to ask humbly, "Permit me to ask: Why is that man, who seems to be suffering so badly, not being permitted entrance?"

"Meir'l knows what he is doing," replied R' Meir shortly, and continued the conversation as though nothing had occurred to interrupt it.

Just a few minutes later, the man's agonized cry echoed through the house. "Help me! Let me in to see the rebbe! Help me, I have lost everything. Why are you being so cruel to me?"

R' Aryeh, the *gabbai*, responded just as firmly: "I am acting on the rebbe's instructions. He has forbidden it."

R' Hershe'le of Liska could not bear it. Once again, he broke into his discussion with the rebbe to beg him to let the man in to pour out his woes.

"You want to know why Meir'l will not let that man come in to see him?" asked R' Meir. "Let me tell you a story that happened recently, and you will understand everything."

In a village in the Ukrainian wilderness, Wolf lived a prosperous life. His two-story inn was made of fine wood, inside and out. It was surrounded by a spacious courtyard that held stables, barns, and coops for hens and geese. The rooms were large, as were the windows. Each bedroom was equipped with several beds so that many visitors could find a good night's rest there.

To make the situation absolutely clear, let us begin by saying that, although his inn was fully equipped for any number of guests, Wolf did not have a single one!

How can this be?

Wolf was prepared to house any visitor, Jew or gentile, rich or poor, on one condition: full payment for lodging.

Many a poor traveler chanced upon the inn without a penny in his pocket. Wolf would chase them away without a moment's hesitation.

"Charity?" he would snap, when anyone dared ask for a free night's lodging, or a bowl of hot soup on a cold winter night. "Go to the poorhouse, or to the home of some compassionate rich man. I have to support my family, and this place is my primary source of income. It is open only for those who can pay."

So consistent was Wolf in his policy that he earned a reputation in the region as a hard, cruel man. His heart, they said, was made of stone, and there was no use expecting a speck of compassion from him even in the most extreme of circumstances.

It was that way on a stormy night, when the powerfully gusting wind persuaded even stray dogs and cats to seek shelter. A poor man knocked at the door of Wolf's inn, asking for shelter and a bit of food. Wolf chased him away into the swirling snow. At that moment, an outcry was raised in heaven. The prosecuting angels demanded that Wolf be punished immediately.

"A Jew becomes an innkeeper on a main road so that he can perform kindness with his brothers. *That* one opens his doors only to those who can pay. What is the point of letting him continue being prosperous? Let his property be taken from him," they argued.

"The Heavenly Court nearly determined to take Wolf's possessions away from him," R' Meir told his guest. "But then Meir'l got involved. I told the Court: 'Is it possible? The prosecutor says something, and you rush to punish?' I argued that the man be given a chance to correct his actions. He should be put to a repeat of the test. If he met the challenge properly, he would remain a rich man. If he failed, he would lose everything.

"The Court accepted my argument. It decided to put Wolf to the test of *hachnasas orchim,* welcoming guests. Now a new question was raised: Who should be sent to test him?

"Eliyahu HaNavi volunteered at once. He asked that he be sent to Wolf in some physical guise. The Court rejected the idea: 'Eliyahu HaNavi is overly merciful. He will submit Wolf to an ordeal that is too easy.'

"Next to volunteer was the Satan himself. Once again, the Court was against the idea: 'The Satan is too hard and cruel. He will offer a test that is too hard, one that Wolf will certainly fail.'

"In the end, the decision was made to send them both, representing holiness and its opposite, working hand-in-hand to accomplish the mission."

Wolf was curled up in bed, covered from head to toe with a soft, goose-down quilt. Outside, the wind shrieked and the wind-driven snow beat insistently against the shutters. How sweet it was to lie in a warm bed and listen to the wailing wind. If only no traveler stopped at the inn tonight …

Someone stopped.

There was a pounding at the door. Though not overly loud, the knocks were clear and impossible to miss. As though to make certain, a voice called out, "Take pity and open up, before I freeze to death!"

Faithful to the principle of "as long as you can make a profit — do so," Wolf heaved himself out of bed, threw on his robe, and went to the door.

The blood rushed to his head when he opened it and saw an itinerant beggar. As if that were not enough, the man explained that he hoped to spend the night at the inn for free, because he did not have a penny to his name.

"Go to the poorhouse, you hear?" Wolf berated the unfortunate fellow. "And do not dare show your face around here without money in your pocket!"

"The poorhouse is very far off. I do not need a thing," pleaded the beggar in a trembling voice. "I will not even ask you for food, not even a hot drink to revive me. Just a small corner where I can lay my weary body — a few hours' shelter until the snowstorm ends."

The traveler's face was drawn with fatigue. Lines were etched into his forehead and cheeks, as if to underscore the terrible suffering that was his lot. His dark eyes were sunken and flakes of snow covered his silvery hair. But the sight did not soften Wolf's heart a bit. Taking the man by one ragged sleeve, he sternly pointed out the path leading down through the snow. "Get out of here. How dare you disturb my sleep after a hard day's work!" he shouted.

Wolf stepped back into the house and brushed off the snow that had settled on his shoulders. He had been awakened for nothing. For money, he would have been prepared to tear himself away from sweet slumber — but for nothing?

He returned to bed and burrowed beneath the thick quilt, where he attempted to recover the lost threads of sleep.

It was, it seemed, a night for all the troublemakers to be out. No sooner had the innkeeper drifted into a doze when a fresh bout of knocking reached his ears. This was no gentle flurry of knocks, but a powerful pounding accompanied by coarse shouts. "Open the door this minute, Jew, if you want to stay alive!"

Wolf was out of bed in a twinkling. Leaving off his robe, he raced breathlessly to the door. In the doorway stood a tall *poritz*, or nobleman. He wore an expensive coat and his eyes flashed fire.

"Let me in, Jew!" he roared. "You should have opened the door at once!"

"I came as soon as I woke up," Wolf apologized. His stern demeanor had melted at the sight of a person stronger than himself. He shook all over, both from the cold and from fear. "What can I offer Your Honor?"

"A hot meal and some whiskey," demanded the *poritz*. "And afterwards, a good bed."

Wolf and his family toiled to feed the hungry nobleman and to warm his frozen bones. They offered course after course of meat and other deliacies, and poured him one drink after another. So busy were they that they never noticed the first traveler, the poor Jew, who had slipped secretly into the house seeking escape from the bitter cold outside. He curled up in a corner of the long hall, near the front entrance, trying to remain invisible. Snow fell off his clothes and melted on the floor, eventually forming a puddle that trickled down the length of the hall.

The *poritz*, having feasted his fill, wiped his thick moustache and asked, "So where is my bed?"

"I will take you at once to a heated room with a clean, comfortable bed," Wolf said hastily. He was disturbed by a thought. Had he remembered to lock the front door after the nobleman's entrance? "I will just be a minute, sir. I need to lock the door."

A flickering candle in hand, he hurried to the door. His jaw dropped at the sight of the puddle disfiguring the front hall. Lifting the candle to see better, he spied a dark figure in the corner. Wolf let out a cry. The poor traveler opened his eyes, and recognized the man who had just sent him away.

Wolf was enraged. "What is this?" he screamed. "I told you not to come here. I do not provide shelter to beggars!"

The traveler pleaded not to be sent out into the snow, while Wolf rained down a shower of verbal abuse on his head.

The shouts and the pleading reached the *poritz* in the inner room. He came out to see what all the commotion was about.

"He is a brother of yours, is he not?" the nobleman asked Wolf in surprise. "A fellow Jew. Will you really throw him out into that cold? You people have compassion for one another, do you not?"

"He has no money to pay me," Wolf explained humbly. He had one rule of behavior for nobility, and quite another for a Jewish pauper.

"I am prepared to pay for him," the *poritz* said generously. "What do you say to that, Jew? I take pity on him, where you take none! Let him in. I will pay all his expenses: food and drink, and a bed for as long as he needs it. Whatever he wants goes on my bill."

For a moment, a blush colored Wolf's cheek. "Look how far you have sunk!" screamed his conscience, buried deep inside.

But Wolf ignored it, hurrying to see to the needs of his two guests, placing them in one of his largest rooms and attending to every detail of their comfort.

The pair of travelers stayed in Wolf's inn for two weeks, until the worst of the snowstorm had abated. When the bitter winds finally died down and the snow had begun to thaw, the *poritz* was eager to continue his interrupted journey. Wolf presented him with the bill, which the nobleman scanned with a frown.

"What's this?" he asked sternly. "This bill is grossly inflated."

"Heaven forbid!" exclaimed the innkeeper. "The bill is accurate, down to the last penny."

"You have handed me a bill for two guests," fumed the nobleman. "Do I look like two people to you?"

Wolf was taken aback. The *poritz* was pretending that he had forgotten his promise. Recovering his wits, Wolf said, "Your Honor, if you will recall, on the night you came here you undertook to pay for the Jew who has been staying here at the inn. So I have presented you with a double bill — one for you, and one for the guest who has been sharing your room."

"Do you think I am insane?" the *poritz* snapped. "Am I some kind of fool, to pay the Jew's bill? Where did you get such a stupid idea in your head?"

"B-but — you promised!" Wolf cried.

"I tricked you," the *poritz* returned coolly. "I felt sorry for that frozen fellow. But never for a minute did I really intend to take on his debt."

Anyone with an ounce of sense would have realized then that he was not going to see double payment from the *poritz*. But the love of money had blinded the innkeeper, and he was not prepared to yield. Women, however, have been blessed with extra intuition. Alerted by the shouts, Wolf's wife hastened to the spot and dragged her husband off to another room.

"Wolf, have you lost your mind?" she demanded. "Have you forgotten who rules this land — who are the rulers and who are the subjects? The *poritz* can have you thrown out of your home and straight into prison, to rot for the rest of your life! Give him a corrected bill for his own expenses only, and let him go before he becomes even angrier."

Wolf knew when he was defeated. He sat down and prepared a new bill, for only one guest, and presented it to the *poritz*.

"Now you are talking sense," the *poritz* said, when he saw the bottom line slashed in half. "*This* is an honest bill!"

He paid what he owed, and his carriage was soon disappearing into the distance.

The moment the *poritz* was gone, Wolf ran to the other room, where he treated his Jewish guest to the sharp edge of his tongue. All the anger that had built up, after two weeks of devoted service for which he had expected to be paid in full, went into the tongue-lashing he now vented on the poor Jew. He hurled abuse at the traveler, then pushed him furiously to the door. Wolf's blood did not cool until he lifted his hand and slapped the other man resoundingly across the cheek — before throwing him out.

Less than a quarter of an hour later, a fire broke out simultaneously in every wing of the house. The place turned into a blazing inferno. The entire structure and all its contents quickly turned into a pile of ash. In the confusion, Wolf and his family managed to jump out the windows into the courtyard with only the clothing on their backs.

The fire continued to burn, spreading from the decimated house to the yard, and from the yard to the stables, barns, and coops. It engulfed the huge grain silo and the wine cellars and the produce. Nothing was left of all Wolf's wealth. Even the heavy safe, filled with valuable currency, melted in the awesome heat, and all its contents turned to ash.

Wolf was penniless.

He began to wander, a shattered man, asking for pity where he had shown none. Compassionate Jews did take pity on him. They fed him and gave him to drink; they provided small sums of cash. But Wolf was seeking a great salvation, one that would restore his former glory. He did not know that his fate had been decreed in Heaven. Someone told him about the holy rebbe, R' Meir, who lived in Premishlan, and whose blessing effected wonders.

He came to the rebbe to ask for his blessing, that he might regain what he had lost. But R' Meir had the vision to see all. Knowing that Wolf was coming to see him, he forbade his loyal *gabbai*, Aryeh, to let him into the inner chamber.

"And I ask Your Honor," R' Meir concluded, turning to his guest, R' Hershe'le of Liska. "A man like that, who slapped Eliyahu HaNavi on the cheek — can I let such a man in?"

[This story was told by R' Menashe Rosenfeld, a foremost Karliner chassid in Jerusalem, in the name of the "Bikener Rebbe," who moved to Israel from Hungary, and who heard it passed down, from person to person, directly from R' Tzvi Hirsch of Liska, author of the *Ach Pri Tevuah*.]

The Staff of Life

THERE WAS A LONG LINE OF CUSTOMERS AT THE CHECKOUT counter. Two people began quarreling over their places in line. Someone else asked the person in front of him to hold his place while he ran back to the refrigerated section for some cheese. Yosef, the grocer, was in over his head calculating totals, making change, and marking down what people owed when they bought on credit. But even working at top speed, so that he scarcely had a moment to breathe, he found the time to admonish his customers, "Please, don't crumble the bread. Be careful not to drop the bread on the floor!"

Everyone who shopped at Yosef's grocery was long familiar with his caution regarding the treatment of bread. Those who became irritated with his scoldings and warnings found themselves another neighborhood grocery in which to shop, with a grocer who didn't care what his customers did with the loaves of bread they bought. For all that grocer cared, they could toss the bread in the trash the moment they left his store, as long as they paid for it first.

Yosef was aware that his strictness over the bread drove away some of his customers, but he was unmoved. He continued on as before. Every new customer who entered his grocery received his first lesson in the laws of safeguarding the honor of bread:

"Understand that this bread that Hashem has given us is a gift from Heaven. Think of how many people were involved in producing this bread. Farmers plowed the fields, fertilized it, seeded it, and watered it, praying to Hashem to send rain in its proper time. With anxious hearts, they watched every stage of the growth process, and when the wheat reached its peak ripeness, they harvested it. They took the sheaves they had cut down, and separated the wheat from the chaff."

He went on with his lecture, indifferent as to whether the customer was interested or not. It was his business to educate the Jewish consumer in the proper respect for bread — Heaven's gift.

As evening drew near, the grocery emptied out. That was when Yosef would take his broom and, with sincere reverence, gather the crumbs that had fallen to the ground near the bread shelves. Sometimes he would do this several times a day. Any time he saw a pile of crumbs collecting near the shelves, he would whisk out his broom and a special dustpan, and collect the crumbs into a large, clean plastic bag. He would toss these crumbs to the birds in the grassy area behind the store, so that no stray crumb would come to be tossed disrespectfully into the garbage, Heaven forbid.

To the young yeshivah men who crowded into his store each day, he would offer his decided opinion: "It as clear as the sun at noon that you are poor because you aren't careful about the respect due to bread as it is written, 'Anyone who is disrespectful with bread or bread crumbs will be pursued by poverty' (*Tikkunei Zohar* 15). You buy more bread than you need, and throw half the loaves near the local trash bin … True, you don't actually stick the bread into the trash," he added scornfully. "You put it into a plastic bag near the big bin, so that the municipal garbagemen will be the sinners who place the bread into the garbage truck. But what difference does that make? You are still the ones getting rid of the bread."

The yeshivah men would try to justify themselves to Yosef, explaining that it was impossible to calculate their bread needs with electronic accuracy. They bought a loaf each day; if necessary, they bought two. What to do if, at day's end, half a loaf or less was always left over? Yesterday's bread was stale. The wife and children insisted on fresh bread each morning, which led to all those bread-filled plastic bags beside the neighborhood trash bin. Sometimes there was a quarter-loaf in those bags; at other times a third, a half, or even a nearly-whole loaf tossed beside the receptacle.

"*HaKadosh Baruch Hu* treats you according to the principle of *middah k'neged middah*," Yosef claimed. "You throw bread into the garbage, showing disdain for His gift — and He pays you back in the same coin. Why are you surprised that you never have a *shekel* to spare?"

Yosef himself was true to his beliefs, at home as well as in the shop. Not a crumb of bread was ever thrown away in his house. He conducted a careful investigation into his family's bread needs. If there was ever a bit of bread left over, it was not thrown out, Heaven forbid, but used in a hundred and one different dishes, beginning with fried bread slices and ground bread crumbs for use in beef and fish patties, and ending in sweet bread pancakes and other delicacies whipped up by Yosef's creative wife. Yosef humbly, gratefully, and lovingly accepted the gift Hashem had given him in the form of breads, rolls, challahs, and pitas. What they all had in common was that they were completely eaten, down to the last drop.

And if, in a rare case, a piece of leftover bread was simply inedible for some reason, Yosef would soak it in water and leave it in the garden. The pigeons and sparrows pecked at it, until not even a crumb remained.

With the passage of the years, the grocery's customers grew so accustomed to Yosef's admonishments over the bread that his warnings went, as the saying goes, "in one ear and out the other." Only a small percentage of his customers, however, switched to a different grocery, and this did not have a detrimental effect on his income. By this time, no one gave much thought to the matter anymore.

Until a new family moved into the neighborhood.

Nachum Leibowitz, a *kollel* man, had his first introduction to the strange grocer who took the time out of his hectic routine to carefully sweep up every crumb that accidentally dropped from a loaf of bread and might be trampled on by passing feet.

If Yosef was not your standard grocer, was Nachum not your standard *kollel* man?

Nachum liked to study people. If his sharp eyes caught some unusual behavior, he would not rest until he had asked the reason for it. And Yosef the grocer was certainly unusual. Nachum watched Yosef for several days. He saw the way the grocer raced to fetch his special broom and dustpan to sweep up every stray bread crumb from the floor. He watched Yosef arrange his fresh loaves on their shelves each morning. If one could be said to behave in a loving manner toward something inanimate, that's how Yosef behaved toward those loaves of bread. He lined them up in careful rows, like soldiers on parade, taking care not to let any loaf slip out of place. White bread was lined up separately from the whole-wheat loaves, dietetic bread, and pumpernickel. (The packaged, pre-sliced bread posed no problem in terms of crumbs, because it was in a plastic bag already; but there could be, and sometimes were, whole loaves dropped on the floor!)

Once he had established an acquaintance with the grocer, Nachum decided that the time was ripe for learning what lay behind Yosef's odd behavior. He waited patiently through the heaviest flow of morning customers. When the pace had slowed to a trickle, he approached the checkout counter with a loaf of bread and some milk. Nachum placed the loaf precisely at the very edge of the counter. He lowered his hand, and ... whoops! The bread fell to the floor.

"Careful!" shouted Yosef, his face turning red with excitement and anger. "Look how you threw that loaf onto the floor!"

"So what?" countered Nachum. "It's not a person. It's only bread. You don't have to go crazy over a loaf of bread."

"*What*?" Yosef screamed. "What are you saying? 'It's only bread,'" he mocked. "Do you have any idea what you're talking about?"

Nachum smiled. The grocer had fallen right into his trap. Now Yosef would become agitated enough to tell Nachum exactly what he wanted to know.

"Tell me," he said provokingly. "Don't you think you're exaggerating a little in the way you treat bread?"

Yosef's face turned a deeper shade of crimson. "If you knew what I know," he yelled, "you would not speak with such disdain. You would kiss each loaf of bread and whisper, as I do: 'Thank you, my Creator, for this free gift that You give us.' You would talk very differently."

"So, let's hear what you know that I don't," Nachum invited.

Yosef could not resist the invitation. And that was how Nachum had the privilege of being the first of the grocer's customers to hear the solution to the riddle of Yosef's extraordinary attitude toward bread.

Jerusalem, in the year 5676 (1916), was a hungry city.

World War I, which ended with the Turkish conquerors being chased out of Eretz Yisrael, had wreaked havoc on the poor country's food supplies and left it barren. Many years of drought, an invasion of locusts, and the closing of sea supply-lanes had brought in their wake a terrible famine. In the city of Jerusalem, people scoured the streets for anything edible.

The three Templer sisters managed, somehow, during the first two years of the War. The eldest, Shoshanah, who was 18, worked as a seamstress for the Turkish military machine, which did not yet believe in its own fast-approaching demise. Thanks to her steady job, she and her two sisters — Rivkah, 15, and Shulamis, 10 — did not starve. Each day, the younger sisters waited tensely for Shoshanah's return. She brought her day's wages each evening: one *bishlik* (a small coin). Occasionally, when her military supervisors were especially pleased, she received a bonus of one *lira*.

The Templer sisters had been orphaned when their father, R' Nesanel, perished in an epidemic at the outset of the War. Their mother, Tzipporah (nee Greenfeld), followed a year later. Shoshanah bore the burden of caring for her two younger sisters, and lost sleep making certain that they did not sense any lack.

This was easier said than done.

In the starving city, where whole families nearly died of hunger, the odds that three orphans would remain alive were just about zero to none. But, through Heaven's mercy, Shoshanah's work found favor with the Turkish army officers, who saw to it that she received, from time to time, not only an extra coin but also a small sack of flour. Shoshanah would bring these sacks home and bake little loaves of bread from them — loaves which just barely sustained the three sisters.

The terrible winter of 5677 (1917) arrived. The Turkish Army began to sense its impending defeat at the hands of the British, whose forward movement had begun in Egypt and was slowly approaching Palestine. As the tottering Ottoman Empire fought a losing battle to keep control of Palestine, little attention was paid to the appearance of the soldiers' uniforms. The young seamstress returned from work one day with the bitter news that there would be no going back the next day. The Templer girls' coffers were empty. Now they began to know what hunger really felt like.

The small loaves of bread became a dream of the past — a sweet dream. The house had nothing in it, not even so much as a potato peel. Hunger began to gnaw at their sides. Rivkah was old enough to deal with it reasonably well, but Shulamis, being only 11, began to show alarming signs of the swelling that accompanies malnutrition.

Rivkah and Shoshanah watched anxiously as their younger sister's face began to turn yellow. Despairing, they tried to hide from the young girl the fact that she was about to die of starvation. This was no unusual phenomenon in wartime Jerusalem. Starving people — Jew and Arab alike — dotted the streets, begging passersby for a morsel of bread to keep them alive. But there was no one to offer that life-giving morsel. Everyone was hungry; it was those who managed to obtain the bare minimum who survived.

Shoshanah went out to search the streets for some compassionate Jew who would agree to share his bread to save her little sister's life. She even scrambled through the trash bins, hoping to come across some overlooked piece of food. To her disappointment, she found nothing.

The hours passed. Shulamis groaned weakly, "I'm so hungry. Please give me a piece of bread ..."

She was speaking to the thin air, for Rivkah, too, was away from home. Both sisters had gone out to make one last, desperate search for a bit of food to keep young Shulamis alive.

Shulamis called out to Shoshanah and Rivkah for a long time. When no one answered, she finally heaved herself to her feeble legs and stumbled out into the courtyard. She sat down on the cold ground, drew breath weakly into her lungs, and began crying faintly, "Bread. Bread. Give me bread ..."

No one answered. No one heard her, and no one came to her aid. More hours passed. Night fell, and still the two older sisters stayed away. Shulamis had no idea what had happened to them. Hunger confused her mind. Slowly, she slid to the ground and lay on the frigid earth, at the end of her strength. Her weak cries turned to whimpers, and faded away. Only her big, dark eyes gazed upward at the darker sky, until they closed.

Rivkah was the first to return home. She was in despair. A search of the trash bins had resulted in nothing — not even a crumb. Better to return home and stay with Shulamis, she thought, than to leave her all alone.

To her dismay, she found her little sister sprawled on the ground outside. The girl's breathing was rapid and shallow. She was fighting for her life.

"Shulamis, don't die!" Rivkah sobbed. "Our father and mother have already died. Stay with us!"

Shulamis did not react. Like a madwoman, Rivkah raced into the house. She found a cup of water, drenched a clean rag in it and began to squeeze out the water, drop by drop, into her sister's mouth. Perhaps the water would save her ... Shulamis sucked the rag weakly, and tried to chew it. Hunger was troubling her worse than thirst.

"Shulamis, please hang on," Rivkah begged through her tears. "I'm sure Shoshanah will find something for you."

"Hashem," Rivkah said, turning her face heavenward. "Don't let my sister die. She's just a little girl!"

Shulamis sucked at the damp rag and whispered, "More. Rivkah, give me water, I'm going to die."

"You're not going to die, Shulamis," Rivkah said in a pleading tone. "Shoshanah's going to come home with bread soon. I just know it!"

In her heart of hearts, however, Rivkah had already given up hope. Shoshanah had most likely failed to find food as well. That was why she had not yet returned home. Soon Shulamis would die, and there was nothing Rivkah could do to help her.

Shoshanah darted frantically through the narrow streets of the Old City. Young Shulamis' face swam before her eyes constantly, and her lips murmured a ceaseless prayer on her sister's behalf. She pleaded with her Creator to have mercy on the little girl's life and to reveal to her, Shoshanah, the whereabouts of a piece of life-giving bread.

Suddenly, an idea struck with the force of a lightning bolt. The bakery! How had she not thought of it before?   The small bakery near the *shuk*. She had no way of knowing that the bakery had been abandoned two weeks earlier by its owner, who fled the country after deserting the Turkish Army.

Reaching the bakery, Shoshanah was stunned to find it dark and deserted. She tried the door — and found that it opened easily, unlocked. The place was black as midnight. She walked forward with hands outstretched, groping for the bread trays. These had once held warm, fragrant loaves. Perhaps there were still a few crumbs left behind …

Her fingers touched something hard and round. A cry of joy burst from her lips. It was a dry loaf, baked some two or three weeks before — but it was bread! Old bread that could be softened and eaten.

With supernatural speed, Shoshanah flew through the Old City's streets, loaf in hand. She found Rivkah dipping a rag in water and thrusting it into Shulamis' mouth. Shulamis was only half-conscious.

"Give me the water," Shoshanah ordered.

With trembling hands she broke off a small piece of the loaf and soaked it in the cup of water. She then placed the softened bread into Shulamis' mouth.

The girl's dry lips felt the difference. Her mouth sucked the moisture out of the bread, and then began to chew with a barely perceptible motion of the jaws. The small piece was swallowed. Then came another, and another. Shulamis' eyes opened and the spark of life, nearly extinguished, shone into the night.

At the very last moment, Shulamis had been saved from starving to death.

"Shulamis Templer was my mother, may she rest in peace," explained Yosef to Nachum, who was raptly listening to the tale. "All her life, she treated bread with tremendous respect, for it had saved her life. She never let us throw any away — not even a crumb. Every chunk of bread was consumed in one of a hundred and one ways, but was never thrown into the garbage. You don't throw away a gift from Hashem."

Thoughtfully, Nachum said, "Very nice. But there's one thing I don't understand. We have a tradition that says that anyone who is careful about the honor due to bread will merit wealth. I see you, a man with an average-size grocery. Where are your riches?"

Yosef laughed. "I'm happy with what I have," he said. "That's true wealth. As *Pirkei Avos* says: 'Who is rich? He who is happy with his lot.' I'm satisfied with what I have. I don't need millions."

Indeed, Yosef was satisfied with little. But the story has a surprising twist, which took place about a year later. One day, as the grocer passed a lottery stand, he was seized by an inexplicable urge to purchase a "Lotto" ticket, something he had never done before.

For the first and only time in his life, Yosef bought a lottery ticket. Just that once.

He could not explain why — against all odds and statistics — it was he who, though he invested only a few *shekels* in the venture, correctly guessed all six numbers. In one fell swoop, he collected millions of *shekels* that turned him into a rich man overnight.

A rich man — and a satisfied one.

The Sealed Pipe

THE AXE ROSE AND FELL WITH A METHODICAL RHYTHM. IT made a soaring arc in the air until it was over his shoulder, then fell roundly down onto the hard tree trunk. A small, triangular notch had already been carved out of the trunk, but there was still a long way to go. He would be hacking at it for hours until it finally fell away, broken.

Though the sun did not show itself all day, hiding inside a heavy cloud bank, Kasriel's body was bathed in sweat from his exertions. For years now, Kasriel the woodcutter had stood this way, from morning till evening, plying his axe with the same methodical rhythm. He was known as an expert on all matters pertaining to trees and lumber. Unlike a novice lumberjack, he never struck his ax haphazardly into a tree trunk. Rather, he would walk around it first, checking carefully to find the best place in which to make the breach — the trunk's weakest spot.

So long had Kasriel been working at this trade, that the old question that once used to trouble him rarely crossed his mind any longer. The question was this: Why was it that those who made their living doing backbreaking labor — woodsmen, water carriers, blacksmiths, and harness-makers — earned only pennies, while those who worked at easier jobs made much larger profits? Where was the justice, he would once ask himself. Why do I work until my body feels shattered to pieces, and in the end my family has nothing to eat but a bit of bread and water?

However, as the years passed he stopped embittering his soul with questions of this kind, and humbly accepted his lot as a heavenly decree.

First thing Sunday morning, Kasriel would leave his house and set out for the forest, with plans to return home on Friday afternoon. His wife and children saw him only on Shabbos; he slept in a small shack in the woods to save himself the daily 2-hour walk to the forest and back. On Shabbos he would sit at his table reeling with exhaustion, aching in every bone. By the time the fish course was over, his head was down and his eyes closed.

And only on Shabbos did the family dine on fish and meat. All the rest of the week, they subsisted on just bread and water.

Malkah, the woodsman's wife, paced her house with a heavy heart. When a woman and her seven children are forced to live on dry bread every day, it's no wonder that tears burst out now and then. The children hungered for something to go with their bread — a fruit or a vegetable, perhaps. Malkah habitually returned the same answer: "I know that you'd like a potato or a cucumber, but we have none."

A hundred and more times she said the same words. Her heart ached with pity for her children, who longed for the taste of an egg, or milk. Who dreamed of a fruit in the middle of the week, when even on Shabbos they could afford only a bit of fish and, at rare intervals, a small piece of meat? That day, her youngest daughter begged for a little milk. Her round, innocent eyes looked so pleadingly up at Malkah that she found tears rolling down her own cheeks, bubbling up from the depths of her heart, and joining with her child's until the sobs could be heard outside.

Suddenly, there came a knocking on the door. Malkah hastily dabbed at her face with her apron and went to answer it.

Two gentile men stood in the doorway. The lavishness of their clothing left no doubt as to their being well-to-do.

"We heard someone crying," one of them said, "and we stopped our horses to find out why a woman was weeping so bitterly."

Malkah was speechless. Casting her eyes down in embarrassment, she mumbled some unclear answer.

The men, clearly wishing to be helpful, repeated the question a second time.

She pointed to her thin, pale children and described their poverty, and how she was forced again and again to deny her children the extra food they craved.

The travelers' eyes lit up. "We have a sack of potatoes with us. We can sell them to you, cheap."

"A sack of potatoes?"

"Yes. A full sack."

Despair clouded Malkah's face again. "I don't even have a spare penny to pay for them."

"We'll sell the potatoes to you on credit. You can pay us next week."

One of the men ran back to the wagon and returned with a sack brimming with big potatoes. Without waiting to hear her profuse thanks, they went on their way at once. Malkah wasted no time preparing a tasty potato dish for her hungry little ones.

On Friday, when Kasriel returned from the forest, the children joyfully told him about the treat they had enjoyed during the week. He joined in their happiness, but his overwhelming fatigue stopped him before he got around to asking where the potatoes had come from.

The two prosperous gentlemen appeared again the following week, carrying two sacks — one filled with potatoes and the other with carrots. They presented their wares proudly and were happy to extend Malkah credit this week as well.

The hungry children had treats again that week, and the little house was filled with happiness. There were no more tears.

The third time they came, the men brought onions to add to the potatoes and carrots. They explained to the woman that they were able to handle a few additional weeks of credit. And so, week after week, they came and sold her vegetables, though Malkah had yet to repay so much as a penny of the rapidly accumulating debt. The youngsters enjoyed vegetables and fruit, and occasionally even milk and eggs. Along the way, Kasriel finally heard the story of the two gentiles who came each Tuesday to sell their goods on endless credit.

His forehead creased with worry. "And what will you do when they ask for payment?"

"I don't know," Malkah replied frankly.

As long as they didn't press her for payment, she continued to accept a steady stream of produce, and her children were joyous.

At the beginning of the month of Shevat, the winter suddenly grew fierce. Frigid winds whipped the little house, and heavy snows covered it and the rest of the village. That Tuesday, Malkah was certain, the good-hearted gentiles would not pay her a visit. To her shock, when noon came — in the midst of yet another snowstorm — she heard the familiar sounds outside. Going to the window, she was astounded to see the men lifting full crates of fruit from their wagon.

"What's all this?" she asked. "Why today, of all days?"

Within minutes, the mystery was explained.

"We heard that you Jews will be celebrating a holiday in a few days — 'The Festival of Fruits.' You have a custom of eating many fruits in the middle of the winter. So we've brought the finest fruits you've ever seen!"

"The Festival of Fruits?" Huge question-marks were stamped on Malkah's eyes. "What are you talking about?"

All at once, she realized that they were referring to Tu B'Shevat, the New Year for Trees, on which there is a custom to enjoy all kinds of fruit.

"Well? What do you say?" they asked. "Do you want the fruit?"

"Of course I want it!"

"And what about your enormous bill?" They suddenly brought up the topic that had been put aside until now.

Malkah was at a total loss. What could she say? She hadn't a penny in her pocket.

"We're looking out for your welfare," the taller of the two men told her. "We don't want you to miss out on these really fine fruits. We've brought the best of the best, fruit from far away, unloaded from the ship just a few days ago. Your children will no doubt enjoy them greatly ..."

"You're right," Malkah said, her heart pounding. "But I don't have any money for you. I can't even offer you a collateral worthy of the name — our furniture is broken and we have no gold or silver utensils. My Shabbos candlesticks are made of earthenware."

The shorter of the pair glanced at Shmuel, Malkah's oldest son. "Who says you have to pay with money?"

The oblique message made her heart race even more furiously. "What are you trying to say?" she cried.

"You have a very nice-looking son. A smart boy, too. I have no children of my own. I'd like to adopt him. How old is he?"

"T-twelve and a h-half," she stammered fearfully.

"Excellent. I will leave him with you for another half a year, until he is 13 years old. Then I will take him in payment of your debt."

"What?"

"Yes," the gentile affirmed. "This seems to me a fair exchange. You will still have six children at home, and I will have just one son. What do you think?"

"Never!" Malkah screamed. "Do you think I'm a mother who would give away her own child? Give you my Shmulie when he turns bar mitzvah, so that you may raise him as a gentile?"

"Who said you're giving him away?" the short gentleman asked. "The boy will merely live in my home. You'll be able to visit him from time to time. I will give him in one day what you haven't been able to give him all his life."

"Thanks — for nothing," Malkah was about to reply acidly, but bit back the words at the last minute.

"Too bad about all this fruit," the taller man said. "If you don't want it, then pay another time. But you'd better remember this." A piercing stare accompanied the menace in his voice. "We have a complete list of your debt to us, starting with that first sack of potatoes. If you do not pay us what you owe by the middle of the month, we will take you to court. You'll find yourself sitting in jail."

The cat was out of the bag. They were not interested in her welfare at all, or in her hungry children. They had seen her son and decided to purchase him for a proverbial bowl of lentils. A paralyzing fear rooted her to the spot. She was unable to so much as blink an eye.

After a moment, she recovered sufficiently to think of a plan: She could promise them Shmulie and act as if she agreed to their terms. Then, when her son was approaching his birthday, she'd make sure to get him out of the house.

"I agree," she whispered, inwardly ashamed of what she was doing.

Immediately, the taller of the two gentiles sat down at the table, took a piece of parchment scroll, a quill, and ink from his bag, and asked her to sign a prepared, detailed contract stating that Shmulie would pass into their hands on the day he turned 13, with no objections by his parents.

With trembling hands, Malkah signed the document.

The men beamed. Post-haste, they raced out to the wagon and began removing crates filled with beautiful fruit — fruit such as had never been seen in those frozen lands. All types of fruits, in every size and color. The small house was filled with their fragrance. The children ran from one to the other, picking up samples to taste.

The men left, taking with them the contract that Shmulie's mother had signed.

On Friday, when the woodcutter returned home from the forest, he stood amazed at the sight of all those crates of fruit.

"And it's all on credit?" he asked disbelievingly.

Malkah did not want to lie. She cleared her throat and made vague motions with her fingers, until her husband wondered if her mind had become slightly addled. But she managed to keep her secret — for the time being, at any rate.

Privately, Kasriel was overjoyed at the sight of the fruit. He had the yearly custom of traveling to see the *Saba Kaddisha*, R' Yisrael of Rizhin, each Tu B'Shevat. Every other year, he'd come as a pauper. This year, he would arrive like a rich man!

He didn't press her for answers as to how the gentiles had come to sell her such an enormous quantity of fruit without receiving so much as a kopeck in return. While he realized that his wife was distressed, he had no idea as to the depths of the pit into which she had fallen.

Several days later, with Tu B'Shevat drawing close, Kasriel hired a strong wagon and a pair of sturdy horses, loaded all the fruit onto the wagon, and set off for Rizhin. Unlike other years, the trip through the frozen wastes was colored a rosy, intoxicating hue. How happy the rebbe would be to see such marvelous fruits! Fruits such as these had never before appeared in the Rizhin courtyard.

On his arrival, Kasriel enlisted the aid of the rebbe's helpers in unloading the wagon. The *gabbaim* could not believe their eyes — both because they had never seen such lovely fruits, and also because it was the poverty-stricken Kasriel who had brought them.

They hastened to transfer the fruit into silver bowls. A short time later, the bowls were artistically arranged on the rebbe's table. But the rebbe averted his eyes, avoiding the sight of the fruit entirely.

One of the *gabbaim* decided to act. Cautiously, and with tremendous respect, he inched the fruit-laden bowls closer to the center of the table. Perhaps the rebbe had not yet noticed how beautiful the fruit was.

To everyone's shock, the rebbe reacted severely to the *gabbai's* well-meant act. He ordered Kasriel's fruits removed from his table immediately.

Kasriel felt his heart constrict with anguish and shame. The rebbe didn't want his fruits. He had ordered them removed as though they were polluted. Why?

All the way home, Kasriel thought about it. Finally, he reached the only possible conclusion: "The fruits *were* polluted."

The moment Malkah saw her husband's face, she knew that something had happened. Kasriel did not leave her in suspense for long. He demanded that she reveal the secret behind the fruit.

Bursting into heart-rending tears, Malkah told him everything.

Kasriel's eyes nearly popped out of their sockets. "You signed our Shmulie away to gentiles?"

"I had no choice," Malkah sobbed. "They threatened to bring me to court."

"*Oy!* What have you done?" Kasriel pounded his head with his hands. "What have you done?"

He spent a long time pacing aimlessly around the house, like a caged beast. Broken syllables fell from his lips. Suddenly, he ran outside to the waiting wagon and horses.

"Kasriel, where are you going?" Malkah cried, making a frenzied dash after him.

Wild-eyed, but with a set face, Kasriel turned the horses toward the road. "I'm going back to Rizhin, to try and save Shmulie."

The Rizhiner Rebbe looked visibly shaken by Kasriel's story. "Yes, your son is in a difficult spot. Those men won't easily give him up."

"What do I do?" Kasriel burst out. If the holy rebbe said the situation was difficult, he was fast losing hope.

The rebbe, however, had no intention of abandoning Kasriel in his hour of need. "Bring your son here the week he turns 13, and we will hope that *HaKadosh Baruch Hu* helps us succeed in doing something."

Kasriel's heart eased slightly. The rebbe had undertaken to play an active role in dealing with this sticky situation.

The week before Shmulie turned 13, his father hurried him over to the rebbe's courtyard. The Rizhiner undertook to safeguard him from all harm. On the day he became a bar mitzvah, the Rebbe personally tied on the boy's *tefillin* and participated in the *seudas mitzvah* that took place immediately after *davening*.

That same morning, the two gentiles came to Malkah's house, demanding the boy. In tears, she told them that her son had "disappeared." They bullied and threatened her unmercifully, until she broke down and confessed that he was staying in the home of the Rizhiner Rebbe.

Without a moment's delay, the two men leaped onto their horses and made quick work of the journey to nearby Rizhin.

Contract in hand, they burst into the *beis midrash*, angrily demanding the boy. They had in their possession a signed legal document. By law, the boy was theirs!

The rebbe was unruffled. "A legal contract? Perhaps. I have one question, before we hand over the boy. Will you let me smoke your pipe?"

"Certainly." The man was amused at the paltry request.

"In that case, can you sign a contract saying that you will not take the boy until I've smoked this pipe?"

"Sure, if that's what you want."

The rebbe instructed his *gabbai* to fill the pipe with fresh, fragrant tobacco. He placed the pipe in his mouth, his face pensive. Everyone waited for the smoke to rise from the lit pipe, but the rebbe was in no hurry. He whispered something in the *gabbai's* ear. The *gabbai* appeared confused, then nodded, and ran to do the rebbe's bidding. He returned a moment later with a round container filled with red sealing-wax. Before anyone could unravel the riddle, the Rizhiner

Rebbe had sealed the pipe on both sides. To the stunned gentiles, he said, "Please wait while I smoke this pipe. You'll be waiting forever, though, because I've sealed the pipe with sealing-wax and I don't ever intend to smoke it."

"What is this?" the gentiles screamed. "You tricked us! The boy is ours!" Furious, they waved the contract in the air.

But the rebbe waved a contract of his own. "I have a contract, too," he smiled. "Foolishly, you have given up the boy."

Shame-faced, the two men left the holy courtyard. The rebbe had promised to give up the boy after he had smoked the pipe — but he had not promised that he would ever smoke it!

As a postscript, a brief story: The Satmar Rebbe once asked, "Who is a smart chassid? A man like the chassid who fell ill and was seemingly near death and came to see my father, R' Chananyah Yom Tov Lipa, author of the *Kedushas Yom Tov*. The man's doctor recommended that he travel to Vienna, where there were expert physicians who might be able to help him. But he was afraid that his failing health might not allow him to reach Vienna.

"He went to his rebbe and, in tears, poured out his story. The rebbe said, 'I take responsibility until you reach Vienna.'

"The chassid calmed down. He returned home, and never set out on the intended trip. If the rebbe had undertaken to guarantee that he would remain alive until Vienna, what was the hurry to get there?

"The chassid went on to live another fifteen years!"

[Thanks to R' Avraham Shalom Weinbach, *Shlita*, a friend of my father and of mine, who told me this story.]

"May Hashem Fulfill All Your Wishes"

AFTER THE PASSING OF THE *TZADDIK* R' LEIB SARA'S, PATRON of the thirty-six hidden *tzaddikim* in his generation, the holy task of supporting the generation's righteous men was passed down to the *tzaddik* R' Mordechai, son of the holy Maggid, R' Nachum of Chernobyl.

Like his predecessor, R' Mordechai was constantly traveling. He went from village to village, from town to town, collecting funds for his exalted task. While most people willingly handed over their donations, there were those who did not grasp the matter's importance. These did not respond at once, or else gave only paltry amounts.

Ironically, those who contributed with a lavish hand were overjoyed at the privilege of helping to support the *tzaddikim* of their time — while those who gave ungenerously and with sour faces demanded, in exchange, his blessing for various goals of their own: a good livelihood, successful marriages for their children, health, wealth, and everything good. All in return for a few piddling pennies ...

Very different was the philanthropist, R' Chaim Mendel.

R' Chaim Mendel was known in the vernacular as *"ah sheiner Yid"* — a respectable Jew. He was well-respected, tall and handsome on the outside and pleasant of character within, an individual who found favor in the eyes of Hashem as well as his fellow man. Everyone liked him. Family and neighbors, relatives and friends — and even the gentiles who did business with him — could not praise him enough. He was a special man, inside and out. A learned scholar who could read the "fine print," he was also well-to-do financially. He gave charity generously and readily opened his home to guests. He was a devoted follower of the generation's *tzaddikim*. In short, R' Chaim Mendel had been blessed with all manner of spiritual and physical gifts. A truly lucky man.

Because he was also a smart man, he made sure not to flaunt his success. Moreover, in his desire to help those less fortunate than himself, he employed scores of destitute Jews in his factories and inns, and paid them more than adequately for their services. These men repaid him with love and devoted work. Hence, all his businesses flourished.

In light of all his good qualities, R' Chaim Mendel was universally accepted wherever he went. No wonder, then, that people considered him a leader. He considered himself happy ... until the trouble with his only son, R' Shalom Shachna, began.

Shalom Shachna was a young man blessed with every grace and talent. He possessed a sharp mind and was successful in his learning. He had a fine character and was pious and diligent, devoting all his time to Torah learning and heartfelt prayer. Anyone would have thanked heaven for such a son. His father wished to marry him off to the daughter of a gentleman as prosperous as himself or, alternatively, the daughter of a renowned Torah scholar. When Shalom Shachna reached the appropriate age, matchmakers came swarming round with a host of potential proposals. There was nothing for R' Chaim Mendel to do but investigate and select the best one for his son.

To the complete shock of R' Chaim Mendel and his wife, Shalom Shachna announced that he had no intention of listening to any one of these magnificent marriage suggestions. The dumbfounded parents could not believe their ears. Did their son expect them to pluck him a bride from the moon?

"No, no," laughed Shalom Shachna, a faint flush rising to his still-unbearded cheeks. Then he went on to indicate that, if they suggested matching him with the daughter of Baruch Leib, the forest caretaker, he would not refuse.

"*What*?" shrieked his parents. His mother, Feigel, a good and modest woman, wrung her hands in distress. Baruch Leib was in charge of R' Chaim Mendel's forests. A good Jew, no one had ever raised a voice in complaint against him.But that was the only thing that could be said in his favor. A totally simple man — a forest caretaker!

His daughter Nechama Rickel, on the other hand, was graced with fine *middos*. Modest and kind, she was a fine Jewish daughter with a pleasant manner that won everyone's heart. No one could argue that she would not make some nice young man a good wife. But she was not for Shalom Shachna, the only son of the wealthy R' Chaim Mendel!

It was not Chaim Mendel's way to show disdain for any person, not even Baruch Leib, guardian of his forests. Indeed, Baruch Leib was a good and upright Jew who kept the mitzvos devotedly. He was at shul morning and night and made certain to recite the *Krias Shema* at its proper time each day. But he was unlearned. In every way, he was at the opposite end of the spectrum from R' Chaim Mendel. At one end, the rich and respected philanthropist — and, at the other, a man of low station, simplest of the simple.

It is not surprising that the parents were embittered and angry at their son, who did not know how to appreciate his own standing and aspired to "lower himself" with this alliance.

To the young man, they outlined his elevated stature in the community, and explained that he must not degrade himself by marrying into a lowly family. Their words fell on deaf ears. Shalom Shachna informed them that he would not listen to any other marriage proposal. He had only one burning ambition: to become Baruch Leib's son-in-law!

R' Chaim Mendel and his wife were filled with pain and anguish. They prayed to Hashem to open their son's eyes and give him the wisdom he needed not to embarrass them or himself. They hoped that time would accomplish what logic could not.

Twice a year, R' Chaim was honored with a visit by R' Mordechai of Chernobyl, who came to ask for a contribution for the generation's thirty-six hidden *tzaddikim*. Indeed, had R' Mordechai not found his way to R' Chaim Mendel's home, R' Chaim Mendel would have traveled to see his rebbe. It gave him, however, a special pleasure to host his beloved rebbe on these visits. The Maggid of Chernobyl knew this, and spared no effort on behalf of this tremendous mitzvah — especially since R' Chaim Mendel, overjoyed at his rebbe's presence in his home, doubled and tripled his donation. In addition, he also gave his rebbe a generous sum for other needs.

The day of the rebbe's arrival was one of celebration, as the local people welcomed their exalted guest with song and dance before escorting him with pomp and ceremony to R' Chaim Mendel's house, where a huge feast awaited. R' Chaim Mendel invited all his neighbors to honor his guest, and at the appointed hour there were dozens of men washing their hands and partaking of the meat and fish and other delicious foods. At the festive meal, they heard words of Torah and Chassidus from the Rebbe — most of which was beyond their understanding but which uplifted them nevertheless, banishing the gray sameness of their day-to-day routine.

Bursting with happiness, the men raised their voices in song, in honor of their Creator and His servants. As hearts opened wide, so did purses. Money flowed like water. R' Chaim Mendel led the way with the first donation, and the others hastened to follow his example. The holy Maggid would heap blessing on all their heads for participating in the great mitzvah of supporting the generation's pillars, the hidden thirty-six. Both sides ended the day joyous and satisfied.

That day, after the feast was ended, the rebbe sat conversing with R' Chaim Mendel. In the course of their talk the rebbe offered much sage advice concerning the running of his host's home and businesses.

Suddenly, the chassid turned to his rebbe with a question: "Rebbe, it's been a long time now since I began contributing a large sum for the support of the hidden *tzaddidim*, and I thank Hashem Who has granted me the privilege of doing my share of the mitzvah. But there is something that has been troubling me for some time."

"What is it?" the rebbe asked.

Bashfully, R' Chaim Mendel lowered his eyes. "I have a powerful desire to see the face of one of the hidden *tzaddikim*. I am prepared to give whatever sum the rebbe asks, for the merit of looking — even secretly, and for a brief moment — at one of the hidden ones."

Before the rebbe had completed his consideration of this unusual request, R' Chaim Mendel made a second one.

"rebbe, I ask for a blessing — a proper *shidduch* for my only son, Shalom Shachna."

"Shalom Shachna needs a blessing?" the rebbe asked in surprise. "It seems to me that anyone wishing to connect himself to your family would be the one seeking a blessing. A fine young man like Shalom Shachna must certainly be inundated with proposals."

"True," sighed his host. "Many people have been coming around, asking for a match with Shalom Shachna. But the boy has lost his mind. He wants to marry the daughter of Baruch Leib, who cares for my forests, a simple man who has no understanding of *tzaddikim* and *talmidei chachamim*. When the rebbe honors my home with a visit and I prepare a meal to which I invite one and all, without exception — who is the one person who doesn't trouble himself to show up? Baruch Leib, of course. I'm not complaining about him; apparently his meager understanding does not comprehend what a *tzaddik* is. On the contrary, let him use his energy to care for my trees. But why is my son stubbornly insisting on such nonsense?"

The rebbe looked at him with smiling eyes. "So what is your request?"

"I know my Shalom Shachna well. He is very stubborn. Once he has gotten got this absurd notion into his head, nothing can dislodge it — except the rebbe. If the rebbe, with his *ruach hakodesh*, would reveal my son's true partner in marriage, the one who was designated for him forty days before he was conceived, my obstinate son would let go of this madness."

R' Mordechai had listened attentively. He answered, "What you request is difficult. You wish to see the face of a hidden *tzaddik*, and I do not have permission to reveal their identities. You ask me to reveal your son's true bride? You ask too much! These things are the most secret of all. *HaKadosh Baruch Hu* matches people up — something as difficult to do as the splitting of the Red Sea — and you lightly request to know what is hidden from every mortal person?"

R' Chaim Mendel jumped to his feet, trembling as he realized his error. Kindly, the rebbe invited him to sit, a slight smile playing on his lips. "I am not permitted to reveal the face of a hidden *tzaddik*. However, if you merit it, it is possible that you may see the face of Eliyahu HaNavi, dressed in the guise of one of the hidden *tzaddikim*."

R' Chaim Mendel was stunned. Astonishment paralyzed him and rendered him speechless. He — smallest of the small — to merit seeing the face of Eliyahu HaNavi? Far greater men than he had toiled all their lives long without meriting such a privilege!

"How do I merit this?" His voice was faint. The rebbe's glance was affectionate. "Slow down! You haven't merited it yet. You must work all year in order to do so. When the time comes, I invite you to join me on Seder night. If you merit it, you may see Eliyahu HaNavi at the moment when the door is opened as we recite *Shefoch Chamascha*." The rebbe paused. "As for your second request, regarding a proper match for your son — this, too, will be fulfilled. The matter will become clear from the revelation of Eliyahu HaNavi."

R' Chaim Mendel did not grasp his rebbe's meaning, but he believed that all would become clear in time.

The conversation took place in the fall, in the month of Cheshvan. From that moment, however, R' Chaim Mendel's entire mind was consumed with thoughts of Pesach. In his great eagerness to merit seeing the face of Eliyahu HaNavi, the snowy winter months passed as if they were mere days. He purified himself, praying slowly and fervently to his Creator. His charitable contributions became truly outstanding, especially in the area of *matan b'seiser*, secret gifts. He fasted every Monday and Thursday, studied a great deal of *Zohar* and Kabbalah, immersed in the *mikveh* many times each day, and recited *Tikkun Chatzos* every night amid bitter weeping.

As Pesach approached, R' Chaim Mendel's tension rose accordingly. At the start of the month of Nissan, he gave twice the amount of *tzedakah* that he usually gave each year, and sent a special present to his forest caretaker, Baruch Leib. He felt the need to compensate the man for all the poisoned darts he had thrown with his tongue.

His messenger approached Baruch Leib's home hauling a wagonload of eggs and wine, creams and vegetables, fine matzos and a sackful of nuts.

The offering was rejected out of hand. Baruch Leib told the messenger that he had no need of anything, and the foods would be better off distributed among the truly needy.

R' Chaim Mendel was furious with the man's insolence; a proud beggar who slapped the face of his benefactor! With an effort, he collected his patience, lest his anger rob him of the merit of seeing Eliyahu HaNavi. "I'll deal with him after Pesach," he muttered.

A few days before the holiday, he set out in his lavish coach for Chernobyl. He was no stranger to the rebbe's courtyard, having visited there several times before. Never, however, had he come with such a goal: to meet Eliyahu HaNavi, face to face!

Meeting the rebbe on Erev Pesach, after the burning of the *chametz*, R' Chaim Mendel offered a trembling handshake. Where was the firm grip and famous smile he was accustomed to bringing his rebbe? He was a mass of nerves and tension about this fateful encounter. In every fiber of his being he sensed himself unfit for this great gift; he had not purified himself even to a hundredth of the degree that he should have. He hurried to his inn, where he prepared himself for the meeting like a Kohen Gadol before his yearly visit to the *Kodesh HaKodashim* on Yom Kippur.

After the Yom Tov *Maariv* was said, all the invited guests entered the rebbe's brightly-lit home. Every room was filled with candlesticks topped by glowing flames. The large room in which the Seder was conducted was truly radiant. In the center of the room stood a large table set with silver and gold. The silver matzah plate glistened beneath the *matzos mitzvah* that had been baked that very day. Numerous bottles of wine dotted the table, and silver goblets of every size were set out. Among them, one goblet stood out: the goblet of Eliyahu HaNavi! R' Chaim Mendel's head spun. Another moment, and he'd faint from sheer excitement ...

White-knuckled hands gripped the edge of the table as he attempted to regain a measure of calm. His eyes swept the table, where the Rebbe's holy sons were seated, each in his proper place. R' Mordechai had eight great and holy sons, but only a portion of them — those who lived in the area — were present.

R' Chaim Mendel's lips moved in a silent prayer that rose up from the depths of his heart: "Please, Hashem, give Chaim Mendel *ben* Sarah Raizel the strength to stand firm, and let his eyes see the face of Eliyahu HaNavi. Let his sins not stand in the way. And please, Hashem, send the proper and rightful match to my son, Shalom Shachna *ben* Feigel, in the merit of the *tzedakah* I give to help support the thirty-six hidden *tzaddikim*."

As he concluded his prayer, he felt as though a heavy stone had rolled off his heart. The matter was in Heaven's hands now. He sat down to join in the rebbe's exalted Seder.

R' Mordechai sat on a reclining couch, dressed in a white *kittel* with his *shtreimel* on his head. He read the Haggadah line by line, translating it all into Yiddish with great fervor. His face shone like a burning torch and his eyes sparkled like twin stars. R' Chaim Mendel seemed to see tongues of flame surrounding the rebbe and his holy sons.

After the *Bircas HaMazon* was recited, Eliyahu HaNavi's goblet was filled. The *shamash* went to open the door.

Dozens of pairs of eyes turned toward the open door. R' Chaim Mendel's heart hammered violently in his chest. Flashes of heat traveled through his body. A blurred image appeared, and approached the laden table. A cold sweat popped out on R' Chaim Mendel's brow. Was this ... was this really Eliyahu HaNavi? The face radiated holiness and shone like the noonday sun — but the clothes were those of a coarse farmer. The lines of the figure's face grew sharper. Narrowing his eyes, the more clearly to see, R' Chaim Mendel felt the impact of a resounding blow that seemed to echo through the room. He slid to the floor, unconscious ...

The face he had seen was that of Baruch Leib, caretaker of his forests ...

He woke a short time later and took his seat, trembling uncontrollably. His face was pale as death. Speech was impossible. The Chernobyler Rebbe soothed him, poured him a cup of water, and said gently, "*Nu*, R' Chaim Mendel. Is everything clear to you now?"

As his shaken guest sipped the water, the rebbe continued. "You merited seeing Eliyahu HaNavi, dressed in the guise of one of the thirty-six hidden *tzaddikim*. Now you understand who your *mechutan* is — the hidden *tzaddik*. Now you comprehend, too, why your righteous son has insisted on becoming his son-in-law. Bear no grudge against him. In the merit of the *tzedakah* you give so generously to the *tzaddikim*, you have merited allying yourself, through marriage, with one of them."

The whole city was in an uproar when, not long afterward, the strange match was announced: Shalom Shachna, brilliant son of the wealthy R' Chaim Mendel, was to marry Nechama Rickel, daughter of Baruch Leib, the forest caretaker. No one could understand it.

R' Chaim Mendel attended his son's wedding as though in a dream, beside himself with joy. His *mechutan* appeared dressed in his farmer's clothing, a leather belt circling his waist. On the day following the wedding, however, he disappeared without a trace.

Only R' Chaim Mendel and his son knew his secret. This they guarded zealously, however — as the Maggid of Chernobyl had instructed them.

R' Shimon "Ba'al Shem"

THE AUTHOR OF THE *DOVEV MEISHARIM*, THE RENOWNED *AV Beis Din* of Tchebin, R' Dov Berish Weidenfeld, came to Eretz Yisrael as a post-World War II refugee. He came quietly, residing anonymously for a time in a Jerusalem inn, dressed not in rabbinical clothing but in the clothing of a simple man.

One day, however, his rebbetzin fell ill and required medical attention. He was forced to shatter the walls of anonymity that he had built around himself and become dependent on other people once more. One of those who came to his assistance was an outstanding Torah scholar, who began a Torah discussion with him. The man was astounded at R' Weidenfeld's erudition, and quickly "suspected" the modest individual of being a lion in hiding behind a simple facade.

"Who are you?" he asked.

The Rav of Tchebin tried at first to evade the question. But the other man persisted until the rav mumbled that his name was Dov Berish and that he came from Tchebin.

The man clapped a hand to his head in astonishment. "Your Honor is the famous Rav of Tchebin?"

Immediately, the man went to Jerusalem's rabbis and community leaders, who took the rav out of his seclusion that same day. From his temporary lodging they brought him, for the time being, to a rented, furnished apartment. His reputation began to spread throughout the country.

One day, a meeting of the giants took place; R' Yosef Tzvi Dushinsky came to see the Rav of Tchebin together with a retinue of students. One of these was R' Yisrael Grossman, *Shlita*, Rosh Yeshivah of Pinsk-Karlin (and the source of this story). The two *gedolei hador* embarked on a protracted Torah discussion, after which they conversed amiably about the city of Cracow and its well-known rabbis.

In the course of the conversation, R' Dushinsky asked the Rav of Tchebin, "Does Your Honor know why R' Shimon Sofer, son of the Chasam Sofer and author of the *Michtav Sofer*, served as rav of Cracow? How did the Pressburg *gaon* from Slovakia come to serve as a rav in Poland, and not just anywhere in Poland, but in the very heart of Galicia's Torah dominion?"

Smiling his characteristic modest smile, the Rav of Tchebin replied, "I, too, have wondered about that. I don't know the answer to the riddle. But that's the way it is in the world of *rabbanim*;

sometimes they travel to distant places to take up positions, and don't remain to serve near the place where they were born."

"Indeed," assented R' Dushinsky. "In this case, however, there was a special reason. There is an unusual story behind R' Shimon Sofer's *rabbanus* in Cracow. Have you ever heard it?"

"Never."

"Then I'll tell you about it," said R' Dushinsky.

The Rema's shul was overflowing. Overhead, the brass chandelier had been polished to a high gloss, and its scores of candles cast their brilliance down from the high ceiling. Excited children in their best holiday clothing milled about the nearby street as a large crowd gathered in front of the shul. Those who had managed to wedge their way inside were the lucky ones. But these were few in number, compared to the multitude waiting outside.

There was tension in the air. Clearly, something unique was about to occur in the coming minutes. A candidate for the position of the city's chief rabbi was about to deliver a sermon to the throng.

Cracow was seeking a rav.

For a long time now — ever since the city's last rabbi had passed away — the position had remained unfilled. No one, it seemed, could fill the vacuum. This was not because Poland lacked great *rabbanim*. There were certainly many Torah scholars throughout Poland and Galicia, men well-versed in *Shas* and able to reason and lecture with the best of them.

No, the problem was the first three rows of benches in the Rema's shul.

What, you may well ask, have the first three rows of benches to do with the fact that a large and central city such as Cracow had no rav?

Anyone who has not seen Cracow in its heyday has never seen anything beautiful in his life. The city was filled with shuls and houses of learning, all packed to capacity with outstanding scholars. In the Radomsker *shteibel*, claimed the Levover Rebbe, who had *davened* there in his youth, there were over thirty *bachurim* who knew all of *Shas*. And they were not the only ones of their kind. Dozens of similar *shteiblach* dotted the city's landscape. All of Cracow boasted *talmidei chachamim* who had a firm grasp of *Shas* and its commentaries, men who could move mountains in logic. Not for nothing was Cracow dubbed the "Jerusalem of Galicia." The city exuded the fragrance of Torah. Even its youngsters, the word went, were as full of Torah as a pomegranate is full of seeds.

To be chief rabbi of Cracow meant, simply speaking, to be master of them all. To stand head and shoulders above all those towering Torah scholars!

And in the three first rows of benches in the Rema's shul sat the creme de la creme. These were formidable geniuses whose minds were capable of grasping in a moment what it would take the average person an hour to comprehend. When these men debated among themselves, the sea of Talmud would boil until it seemed that sparks of fire and bolts of lightning flew through the air. Anyone who had not attained a high level of Torah learning could not understand even half of what they were saying.

These brilliant men were the gaunlet that must be run by anyone who wished to be appointed to the position of the city's rav. To date, no one had succeeded.

The position brought more than one outstanding scholar to the Rema's shul in Cracow — only to have him return home, shamefaced.

Cracow's scholars did not give a man much time. No sooner had a candidate begun building up the first foundation of his thesis than he was bombarded with difficult questions that proceeded to demolish it. Weaklings stood no chance. Those who tried for the position had to gird their loins for battle — a battle of Torah. The shul was the battlefield. It became commotion-filled, with shouts flying through the air on every side. Thumbs twirled in the classic scholarly gesture known only to the Jewish people.

The candidates did not yield easily. They stood their ground, arguing energetically and trying to prove that truth was on their side. But candidate after candidate in turn met his downfall in those first three rows, a cauldron of fire from which no one had yet departed unscathed. Every man who entered the Rema's shul for the purpose of vying for the city's rabbinical seat found himself fleeing the place — sometimes in tears. Cracow's scholars would render each candidate into a mere pile of bones.

For both sides, the city's rabbinical seat represented a challenge. Those who came to claim it were eager to prevail over the city's scholars, but all had so far failed. As for the city's scholars themselves, they sought a rav who would succeed in beating them in the war of Torah. They, too, had so far failed in this goal.

In the meantime, the position of chief rabbi remained empty.

HaGaon R' Shimon Sofer, second son of the Chasam Sofer, chanced upon Cracow on the way to visit a spa for health reasons. At that point in his life, he had served as rav and *Av Beis Din* in Hungary's Mattersdorf community for many years, and it had never entered his mind to present himself as a candidate for the position of Cracow's rabbi. During his stay in the city he asked to meet the city's chief rabbi, and was told, to his surprise, that there was none.

"Why?" R' Shimon asked.

"Because of the Torah scholars," his hosts sighed.

R' Shimon's astonishment grew. "What do you mean?"

His hosts related what happened to each candidate for the city's rabbinate — how each one who dared jump into the fray wound up fleeing in shame after the city's scholars had shown him up.

R' Shimon's brow creased. "Is that how it is?" He fell silent. For some time he turned the matter over in his mind, considering it from every angle. By evening, he had decided to apply for the job of chief rabbi of Cracow.

His hosts tried to dissuade him, explaining that he had no idea of the deep mud into which he was about to plunge. "You'll end up running away in disgrace," they warned.

But R' Shimon had made up his mind. The next morning, he went to see the community leaders to inform them that he had decided to present his candidacy for the position of the city's rav. The leaders looked at him pityingly. R' Shimon's reputation had spread far and wide, and he was known as a brilliant scholar as well as a famous speaker. Indeed, they longed for such an illustrious man as their rav, and were confident that he would do a magnificent job.

"But what about our terrible geniuses?" they asked in despair. "They're not people — they're whirlwind angels. Hardly will you have said a word than they'll be bombarding you with the whole *Talmud Bavli* and *Talmud Yerushalmi,* the *Rambam* and the *Shulchan Aruch,* the *Rishonim* and the *Acharonim*, proving that you're wrong and don't know a thing."

R' Shimon glanced at the community leaders with a smile. "Let me worry about that," he said pleasantly. "I'm not at all afraid of Cracow's scholars."

"Please, Your Honor. Consider carefully," they pleaded. "We have your welfare at heart. Many rabbis have spoken the same way before entering the shul, where they encountered something they'll never forget to their last day on earth!"

"Let the people gather in the shul on the appointed day," R' Shimon replied.

The day arrived. There was something in the air, something mysterious and inexplicable. As opposed to the previous occasions, the atmosphere was festive.

Like King David's warriors in their own day, the outstanding scholars seated in the first three rows were poised for battle. There were no *sefarim* open in front of them. There was no need. The entire Torah rested inside their heads, as though inside a box. Impatiently they waited for the *derashah* to begin.

The broad windowsills were packed with people, as was the rest of the shul. No one took the chance of losing his place. The large hall hummed like a beehive.

Then — silence. Absolute quiet fell over the shul. The crowd parted to let the new candidate approach.

Apart from his exceptional height, R' Shimon Sofer was graced with an unforgettable beauty. His eyes glowed and his face possessed an unusual radiance. He looked angelic. He was then 39 years old, physically at his peak. With vigorous steps he went up to the eastern wall and took his place at the *shtender*. There he stood at ease, pausing.

The shul was charged with expectation. All breathlessly awaited the *gaon's* first utterance.

R' Shimon swept the crowd with a leisurely look, unfazed by the many eyes studying him in their turn. He gazed upon the faces of the brilliant men packing the first three rows, not missing the lightning bolts straining to be loosed from their eyes.

"*Morai v'rabbosai* (my teachers and masters)," he began. "Before I begin my *derashah*, I would like to tell you one story. Then I will start."

Expressions of surprise swept along the first three rows. Benches creaked as dozens of men twisted in their seats to meet one another's eyes. Someone called out, "Have we gathered here to hear stories? Speak in Torah!"

Without a moment's hesitation, R' Shimon began his tale.

"You all know that my illustrious father, the great leader of Jewry, Rabbi Moshe Sofer, was rav of the city of Pressburg. I was born there, in the year 5581 (1821). Pressburg's Jews greatly revered and honored my father, and his authority in the city was absolute.

"Now and then, however, an insolent person or two would rise up and do things they ought not to have done. They were dealt with summarily by my father.

"On one occasion, my father was told that a certain butcher, known in Pressburg as a physically powerful man, was selling the people questionable meat. Kosher witnesses came to my father and told him that, despite the fact that the rabbi who served as *shochet* and *bodek* disqualified certain animals, this didn't stop the butcher. Without troubling himself to ask a different rabbi's opinion, he set himself up as the 'rabbi' who rendered the meat permissible, and sold it in his butcher shop as though it were perfectly kosher.

"Several *bnei Torah* approached the butcher to complain. 'Is this possible? For years you've been known as an upright butcher who would not sell unkosher meat for any money. Because of this, housewives rely on you implicitly. How dare you cause them to stumble this way, just for money?'

"The butcher chased them out of his shop with curses and threats. If they set foot in his shop again, he roared at them, he would break their bones!

"The *bnei Torah* came to my father and lodged a complaint against the butcher.

"Father could scarcely believe that the butcher, who was known as a hard man but not a sinner, had changed so drastically — that he was actually prepared, for love of money, to poison his trusting customers with nonkosher meat. After listening to the whole episode in detail, he sent one of his top students to warn the butcher that, should he not desist from his twisted ways, he would meet a bitter end.

"Once again, the butcher cursed out the student. When the student persisted in his rebuke, the butcher slapped him in the face, twice.

"Father was stunned when the student returned to tell him what had happened. He sent two more students, both talented and articulate speakers. Perhaps these would succeed where others had failed.

"The moment the enraged butcher saw the students, he punched them powerfully in the face and then chased them out of his shop the way you would chase away a mad dog.

"Father's patience was at an end. He summoned me, taught me to pronounce a Holy Name, told me what to say, and sent me to the butcher.

"I went to the butcher shop, imbued with my father's strength, and told the butcher as follows: 'You should know that I am armed with a Holy Name that has the power to inflict death. If you promise me that you will stop selling *treife* meat — fine. If not, I will pronounce the Name and you will die on the spot!'

"The butcher was foolish!" thundered R' Shimon Sofer into the packed shul. Every eye was riveted to his face; you could have cut the silence with a knife. "He should have believed me! After all, my father was known as an expert in practical Kabbalah.

"But, again, the butcher opened his insolent mouth to curse me, and raised a wicked hand to strike me. At that moment, I pronounced the Holy Name as Father had taught me, and the butcher collapsed on the spot!

"*Morai v'rabbosai,*" R' Shimon announced forcefully, with burning eyes, "I see Cracow's Torah scholars getting ready to storm me and swallow me alive. Thorny questions are bursting from your mouths, even before I begin to speak. Know this: If your intent is for the sake of Heaven, *l'sheim Shamayim,* then I am prepared to debate with you in a Torah war. This is the way with Torah. But if you wish only to cut me down with words, let me say this: I have not forgotten the Holy Name that my father taught me as a young man. It is ready in my mouth!"

R' Shimon had hardly finished making his remarks when there was a confusion of fleeing figures as the occupants of the first three rows made a break for the door. Awe descended on the shul. The narrow aisles became clogged with running figures, as the brilliant scholars fled in all directions.

In the ensuing silence, the rav delivered an incisive *derashah* without interruption. And that was how R' Shimon began his rabbinate in Cracow, where he served in peace and glory for twenty-three years, from the year 5620 (1860) to the day he left this world on the 17th day of Tammuz, 5643 (1883).

[Special thanks to my friend, R' Shmuel Honig, who heard this story from his grandfather, *HaGaon* R' Yisrael Grossman, *Shlita.*]

Sudden Salvation

R' BINYAMIN BEINUSH, A PILLAR OF THE JEWISH COMMUNITY of Vitebsk, had been blessed. Born into a distinguished family, he was a *talmid chacham* who was also extremely wealthy. The sprawling forests surrounding Vitebsk belonged to him; anyone who wished to cut down trees in those forests had to pay him for the privilege. In addition to the forests, he owned liquor-production facilities that supported scores of Jewish households. He was lavish in his charity and his home was open wide to guests and beggars alike.

His greatest pleasure was to distribute largesse to the poor with a free hand. For the sake of peace, he did not differentiate between Jewish beggar and non-Jewish; the simplest gentile knew that he would not leave that rich Jew's home empty-handed.

No wonder, then, that Binyamin Beinush was loved and respected by Jew and gentile alike. All blessed him in their hearts, and wished him every sort of success. He was the epitome of a good-hearted and generous man.

There is, however, an exception to every rule. Among the gentiles were several envious and mean-hearted men who couldn't bear the Jew's dizzying wealth. They waited for an opportunity to do him harm. If only some "accident" would befall Binyamin Beinush, and end his life! But Heaven itself was watching over him, not allowing him to fall into the hands of the wicked.

Nothing lasts forever. The tables turned when Pavel, the Russian Czar, died, leaving to rule in his stead a new Czar — Alexander I. The new Czar was not known for being overly fond of the Jews. With his rise to power, the country's anti-Semites rose to the fore, certain that the transition would usher in a new era of pogroms against the Jews. The anti-Semitic machinery creaked into action once again, quickly gathering strength. And its primary target was the wealthy Jews, who had always been a thorn in the gentiles' sides. Now, they had found their opportunity to embitter the lives of those Jews.

The Russian priest who entered the tavern did not look any different from the other patrons in the place. To disguise his identity, he was dressed in ordinary clothes. He mingled with the other drinkers and downed a few himself. When he was done, he paid with a large bill. Leaving the tavern, he hurried home, where he inspected his change carefully. His face broke into a broad smile — the smile of a hunter who has successfully trapped his prey. His large bill had been counterfeit!

Several days later, on Shabbos morning, as R' Binyamin Beinush stood in shul together with the rest of the congregation wrapped in his *tallis,* the place was suddenly thrown into turmoil and shock.

In the shul's doorway stood Vitebsk's police inspector, accompanied by several armed police officers. One of these officers asked a worshiper where he could find Binyamin Beinush. The Jew pointed a trembling finger, and the policemen strode vigorously over to the rich Jew.

"In the name of the law, you are under arrest!" the inspector announced sternly.

The color drained out of Binyamin Beinush's cheeks. His skin turned a pasty greenish-white. Before he could utter a word, the police officers tore his *tallis* from his shoulders and handcuffed his hands behind his back. He was dragged roughly outside, tossed into the police wagon, and carried off. A few hours later, word reached the city that the respected philanthropist was in prison for unknown reasons.

Terror descended on the Jews. No one in the community could understand the inexplicable arrest of one of its foremost citizens. That fact alone was enough to throw them into a panic. If this could happen to a pillar of their community, a man close to those in authority and accepted by the gentile population, what mercy could the simple folk expect?

Community activists hurried to the governor's house in an attempt to glean more information about the reason for Binyamin Beinush's sudden arrest. The governor made no attempt to conceal his satisfaction at the upheaval the event had caused among the Jews. Running a hand self-importantly over the medals that decorated his uniform, he said enigmatically, "As far as I know, the order came from on high — directly from St. Petersburg."

"From the Czar's palace?" one of the Jews asked, weak-kneed.

"Yes."

"But what does he stand accused of?" another inquired.

The governor was forced to admit that he had no further information on that score. He had no idea why the wealthy Jew had been arrested.

For a full week, the Jews worked to ascertain the reason for the arrest, and to ease Binyamin Beinush's incarceration. Then their fear doubled as they learned that the prisoner had been removed from his prison in the dead of night, manacled in chains, and taken to St. Petersburg under heavy guard. There he had been thrown into a tiny isolation cell to await trial.

Informed sources claimed that, when the verdict was announced, the prisoner would be sentenced to death by hanging.

The country's Jews had good reason to believe these sources. Rumors such as these almost invariably proved to be true!

In the city of Sokolov, there lived a well-known community activist by the name of R' Nosson Nota. He was close to Minister Potemkin, one of the most important men in Russia at the time. Minister Potemkin respected R' Nosson Nota greatly and affectionately turned the "Nota" into "Netkin," which subsequently became R' Nosson Nota's family name. The Jew's influence with the Russian government had been considerable during the lifetime of the previous Czar, Pavel. Now the real test had come. Would the new Czar, Alexander I, prove equally susceptible to the charms of Netkin of Sokolov?

On the day R' Nosson Nota learned of R' Binyamin Beinush's imprisonment, he leaped into action.

It was the height of a Russian winter. A snowstorm raged, battering the countryside with its arsenal of high winds and frigid temperatures. This was no time for any man to be outdoors. Every sane creature waited snugly at home for the storm to pass.

R' Nosson Nota did not wait — not with a sword dangling over a fellow Jew's head. How could he sit at home in his easy chair, sipping a hot drink by the roaring fireplace, while his flesh and blood — a Jewish brother whose forefathers stood at the foot of Mount Sinai — languished in jail with even kosher food denied him?

R' Nosson Nota stepped out of his house, directly into the path of the furious storm. The shrieking wind whipped him mercilessly as he floundered in the deep snow, but he did not yield an inch. Stumbling and falling, yet rising again and again, he made his arduous way to the city's transportation center, where he hired a carriage and set out on his mission.

True to his heritage, he stopped in Vilna to pray at his ancestors' graves. In the cemetery, almost buried in snow, he flung himself on the Vilna Gaon's resting place and wept long and bitterly over the fate of R' Binyamin Beinush, who was related to the Gaon.

When he had completed his prayers, he proceeded to his lodgings in Vilna. While eating a light supper, he overheard several Jews talking about an important visitor who was residing in their town at the moment. The visitor was none other than R' Chaim of Volozhin, the foremost student of the Vilna Gaon!

"Heaven has brought us both here at the same time," R' Nosson Nota whispered excitedly. He quickly recited the *BirKas HaMazon*, then raced out into the street and hurried with all his strength, in the face of the storm, to R' Chaim's lodgings. The hour was late and he was fatigued from his difficult journey. But if Heaven had offered him a chance to request the *gadol hador's* blessing, how could he possibly pass it up?

The owners of R' Chaim's lodging recognized the activist; R' Nosson Nota was as well-known in Lithuania as he was in Russia. All doors were open to him.

He related to R' Chaim the sad news that had brought him here, and asked for his blessing. R' Chaim did so warmly: "Hashem's salvation is like the blink of an eye. I am confident that you will succeed in your efforts."

R' Nosson Nota lingered some time longer, asking R' Chaim's advice on community affairs and other burning issues. Then, armed with R' Chaim of Volozhin's blessing, he went back out into the freezing cold. The hour was now very late.

R' Nosson Nota had no idea just how quickly R' Chaim's *berachah* would come true.

Instead of returning to his lodgings by the same route, his feet carried him into Vilna's gentile neighborhoods. As he floundered in the deep snow, he was at a loss to explain to himself why he was not making due haste to return to his warm room. He was so tired ...

In the stillness of the night, his ear caught the far-off sound of music. Stopping momentarily to pinpoint from where the music was coming, he began to walk in that direction.

As he neared the source of the music, all doubt fell away. There was no question about it: This was an authentic orchestra. It was comprised of many and varied instruments: horns and flutes, violins and reed instruments, drums and cymbals. Some sort of party was taking place in one of the local palaces. A very noisy party, and growing noisier the closer he came. R' Nosson Nota stood in the street gazing up at the windows of the house, which were concealed by thick drapery. Dazzling light lit the cracks at the sides. He wondered whose home this was, and in whose honor this lavish party was being held.

He was very close to the palace now. The merrymakers' voices and the sound of their dancing feet wafted clearly into the night air, with no concern for the night's tranquility or sleeping neighbors.

A tall, impenetrable wall surrounded the palace, and the gate was securely padlocked against intruders. Beside the gate, in a small booth, sat an elderly porter, shivering violently. It was clear that he was suffering intensely in the frigid air. The old man clapped his hands together in a vain effort to warm them.

Netkin approached. "Good evening to you. It's a cold one, isn't it?"

The old man sighed. "They're in there celebrating, and I have to freeze outside. Do you see how absurd it is? Old Vladimir, 80 years old, stands guard over the young people! If they'd only give me a bottle of whiskey to warm my freezing bones ..."

Netkin placed a few shiny coins into the old man's trembling hand. "Buy yourself a bottle tomorrow, and you can drink it on cold nights. By the way, who owns this palace that you're guarding?"

The old porter quickly hid the coins in his pocket. "Where are you from, the moon? Don't you know that Minister Pollack lives here? They're throwing a big party in honor of the Minister of the Interior, Count Kotzovi."

Netkin's heart began to pound madly.

"Listen," he said, with a pleasant smile. "I can see that you're very poor. Your patched trousers and worn coat tell me that. I am a wealthy Jew, and I'm prepared to give you a hefty reward — if you'll do me one little favor."

The porter stared at him in astonishment. "What can old Vladimir do for you?"

"Find a way to let the Minister of the Interior know that I wish to meet with him urgently. Tell him that 'Netkin,' the Jewish activist, is waiting outside."

The porter shrugged. "Impossible. Look at this gate. There are scores of soldiers and police officers inside, all armed. They won't let anyone in."

His eyes rolled at the sight of the gold coins that sprouted suddenly in R' Nosson Nota's hand.

"You know what?" the porter said with sudden enthusiasm. "I have a brilliant solution! Come into my booth and wait. In an hour or two, the party will end and the guests will start leaving. When Count Kotzovi passes near here, you'll be able to speak to him."

With no better plan in hand, R' Nosson Nota entered the booth. He set himself to wait in the freezing cold, his lips framing words of *Tehillim*.

He stood there for three long hours. The time was approaching 3 a.m. when the party began winding down and the first of the merrymakers emerged from the palace. Ornate carriages appeared on every side, as suddenly as if summoned by a pair of snapping magical fingers, to converge on the palace gates. Ministers and other illustrious personages disappeared into these carriages. R' Nosson Nota spotted Count Kotzovi, walking in his direction. With him was a tall man, a stranger to R' Nosson Nota, wearing resplendent clothing that outshone even the glitter of the snow. The Jew approached the Minister and bowed respectfully. "Count!"

Count Kotzovi turned his head. "Who's that I see?" he boomed. "The Jew — Netkin! What are you doing here, and why do you look so downhearted?" He had sharp eyes.

R' Nosson Nota heaved a mournful sigh. "A tragedy has occurred! An innocent man has been arrested for perpetrating no crime. His life is in danger." He groaned with a deep-seated pain.

The Count pointed up to the dark skies. "It's nearly morning," he said apologetically. "Come to me tomorrow, at 10 a.m. You can give me all the details then."

R' Nosson Nota fell silent. There was no arguing with the Count. He was preparing to leave when the second man, the Count's companion, studied him closely. His eyes glowed with a mysterious fire. He appeared to be young, yet at the same time an individual of strong and independent character. He turned to the Count. "This man says that a tragedy has occurred, and you push him off to tomorrow morning? It would be a better idea to hear him out tonight. Come, let's take him back to our inn with us."

The young man obviously did not suffer from any lack of confidence. He gestured for R' Nosson Nota to climb aboard the carriage. Without hesitation, the Jew did so. He was happy that the conversation had not been broken off.

The horses trotted for several minutes until they reached the inn's courtyard, a place frequented by members of the ruling circle. The three men entered. Count Kotzovi showed Netkin into a room where he could wait until summoned, then went into another room together with his friend.

A half-hour later, Netkin was invited to join them there. This, he perceived, was not just another room at the inn; it more closely resembled a small reception hall. It was spacious and beautifully decorated, the bedknobs overlaid with gold and the easy chairs upholstered with deerskin, their arms worked with pure silver. The room shone with color, highlighting the gold and silver ornaments that graced every corner.

Netkin entered cautiously. Bowing, he remained near the door.

"Come a little closer, Netkin," Count Kotzovi said. "Let's hear what you have to say."

Netkin walked into the room and approached the Count and his guest. With restrained anguish, he related what had happened to Binyamin Beinush of Vitebsk, by orders from on high.

The Count cut him off. "The Jew, Binyamin Beinush, is not innocent as you claim. He counterfeited money, which was found in his factories. It was by my order that he was arrested and his property confiscated."

R' Nosson Nota blanched. A tense silence filled the room. The second man directed a piercing glance at the Jew, who stood with bowed head, his entire body trembling with distress. Suddenly, as though drawing strength from some unseen source, Netkin's head went up.

He spoke forcefully. "I swear by all that is holy and precious to me and to my people that this is a false accusation. The money must have been planted there. Binyamin Beinush is a good and kind man whose entire personality runs contrary to the picture being painted of him in this case. I can bring every resident of Vitebsk — Jew and gentile alike — to corroborate under oath that Binyamin Beinush, a pillar of our community, is incapable of engaging in such a despicable crime."

He spoke with the strength and assurance of a man who is sure of his ground. Count Kotzovi turned to his guest and said, "I've known this Jew from Sokolov for years. He can be relied on. He never lies, and his word is undoubtedly good. If Netkin says that Beinush of Vitebsk is no criminal, it is clear that the case of the counterfeit money is nothing but a fabrication."

The other man was silent. Addressing R' Nosson Nota now, the Count continued, "Netkin, were the matter up to me, I would free Binyamin Beinush on the spot. But you know that pardon for prisoners lies in the hands of the Czar alone."

Hot tears trickled down Netkin's face. "In that case," he pleaded, "will Your Honor give me a letter for his majesty, the Czar? In just a little while, when morning comes, I will set out for St. Petersburg and ride directly to the royal palace. I will throw myself at the Czar's feet and beg for mercy for this precious soul, who is innocent of any crime."

The stranger and the Count exchanged a glance. The tall man whispered a few words into the Count's ear, then turned his burning glance back on the Jew. Gently, he said, "There is no need for a letter, I think. You can go home. We will try to have the Jew freed soon."

"'We will try'...?"

Suddenly, Netkin grabbed his head with both hands. He blushed like a child. Emotionally, he turned to the "stranger" and choked out, "If Your Majesty will permit me to fulfill an edict of our Sages, I would like to recite a special blessing for his honor and glory."

"Permission granted," the man said with a smile.

R' Nosson Nota replaced his hat, which he had taken off earlier out of respect for the Count. With concentrated fervor, and with a joyous countenance, he blessed Hashem and the mortal royalty: *"Baruch she'nasan mikevodo l'basar v'dam!* Blessed is He Who shares His glory with mortal man!"

Czar Alexander I of Russia took pleasure in the Jew's shrewdness, which had allowed him to identify his monarch without ever having laid eyes on him. The Czar kept his promise. When Netkin arrived in Vitebsk to relay the good news, he was told that R' Binyamin Beinush had already been freed from prison and all his property restored to him.

"Now I know," declared R' Nosson Nota, "how mighty is R' Chaim of Volozhin's blessing. He promised me that Hashem's salvation is like the blink of an eye."

R' Nosson Nota's relations with the Czar Alexander I continued to be excellent from that day on. Thanks to his special friendship with the royal house, the activist was able to labor successfully, on numerous occasions, on behalf of his Jewish brothers' welfare.

The Amulet

THE PATIENT'S FACE WAS SHRIVELED. HIS LONG STRUGGLE with the Angel of Death was about to end, with a decisive victory for the Angel. The house in the Batei-Ungarin section of Jerusalem was filled with people waiting sorrowfully for the soul to depart the body.

With difficulty, the dying man opened his eyes. He searched for his beloved son. Finding him, he whispered with labored breaths, "Remember me to our rebbe, R' Dovid'l, may he live."

The spark of life was suddenly extinguished. His head fell forward. Cries of "*Shema Yisrael!*" tore the silence. In the presence of his family and several close friends and neighbors, thus departed the soul of one of Jerusalem's finest chassidim: R' Yehudah Leib Deutch.

His son, R' Matisyahu Deutch, did not waste a moment. He knew what he must do, and time was very short. This was Friday afternoon, and the custom in Jerusalem is not to leave a dead body unburied overnight. Late as it was, the funeral must be conducted before Shabbos. Immediately, R' Matisyahu sent a messenger to the Old City, to his rebbe, R' Dovid'l Biderman of Lelov. The messenger relayed the deceased man's last request: that he be remembered to his rebbe.

R' Dovid'l grasped the chassid's intent. R' Yehudah Leib had been a clever man. Knowing that he was at death's door, R' Yehudah Leib's intention had not been to ask that the rebbe pray for his recovery. His request must have been for the rebbe to do him a favor elsewhere — in the World of Souls!

R' Yehudah Leib Deutch had come to Eretz Yisrael from the city of Stropkov. As soon as he had met R' Dovid'l, he became one of his closest chassidim and clung to him with such a powerful bond that he was often able to run from his home in Batei-Ungarin to the rebbe's *beis midrash* in the Old City without growing tired, even when he was no longer a young man.

The entourage returned from the funeral, comforted by the fact that they had been able to bury the deceased before the onset of Shabbos. In great haste they immersed in the *mikveh*, dressed for Shabbos, and raced to shul.

Shabbos passed. That night, the chassidim sat in R' Dovid'l's shul for the *melaveh malkah seudah*, where they ate the remains of the Shabbos food — a bit of challah and some smoked herring — sang the *zemiros* designated for *Motza'ei Shabbos*, and waited for the rebbe to signal for *mayim acharonim* to be brought to the table.

But R' Dovid'l was in no hurry. Lost in thoughts of his own, he was far away from that place and time.

All at once, he began to tell a story.

There were two chassidim who wished to travel to Lublin for Rosh Hashanah. With all their heart they longed to be near the Rebbe — known far and wide as the Chozeh of Lublin — when the shofar would be blown on the Day of Judgment.

But it looked as though their desire, strong as it was, was not to be fulfilled.

Both chassidim were destitute. They had left home nearly empty-handed, with only a few pennies and several crusts of bread between them. The pennies were sufficient for only a short journey. They were then forced to explain to the wagon driver that they had no more money. He, refusing to transport them for free, promptly set them down on the high road.

They stood at the side of the road, downcast and worried. They were far from home, yet not far enough along to reach Lublin on foot. What to do? Should they celebrate the holiday among the trees? Blow the shofar among gentiles?

Their stomachs growled. Hungry and thirsty, they began to search for someone who would give them a little food. But food would only sustain them physically; they thirsted for spiritual sustenance as well.

The two stood and considered their situation. As is known, most Jews at that time were just as poverty-stricken as they were. Apart from a few men of means, the majority tilted the economic scale downward. The two friends knew that asking their fellow Jews for aid in reaching Lublin would not help them achieve their goal. A different solution must be sought.

One of the two was impressive-looking, with a long flowing beard and deep-set, kind eyes. He was also a learned man. The other's appearance was simpler. The pair decided to pretend that they were a rebbe and his *shamash*, assistant. The more distinguished-looking of the two would henceforward be the "rebbe," while his friend would be the helper in his holy work. They would wander from village to village, the "rebbe" bestowing his blessings and the "*shamash*" serving his needs and collecting the donations they hoped to garner from good-hearted Jews.

As they continued on the road to Lublin, the "*shamash*" prepared to start spouting wonders about his rebbe's greatness. So far, however, they had not yet reached even the suggestion of an inhabited settlement.

For a long time they trudged down the road that ran between the trees, without sight or sound of a village or town. They had nearly given up hope when, at the end of their strength, they came to a small Jewish village just off the high road. Every Jewish village had its inn — a "*kretchmer*" as it was known — and the innkeepers were generally men of means!

A man in his late 30's stood in the inn's courtyard, shining his shoes till they gleamed in the sun. A brown horse paced to and fro in a bored way, stopping occasionally beside its master, who ran an affectionate hand over its smooth flank.

"*Reb Yid!*" the "*shamash*" addressed the man. "I have some news today. A *tzaddik* has come to town. A great rebbe is on the way!"

The Jewish innkeeper reacted in a decidedly negative manner. "Don't tell me any stories of 'rebbes' and their miracles. You can take your rebbe and go somewhere else. Just don't bring him here."

The "*shamash*" stood open-mouthed for a moment. But the long road to Lublin and a swiftly-approaching Rosh Hashanah did not allow him the luxury of taking umbrage. Besides, the innkeeper had not been mocking; he sounded bitter. Clearly, something had goaded him to speak in such a disdainful way about "rebbes."

"What's the matter, *Reb Yid*?" he asked sympathetically. "Why do you speak that way about great men?"

"Great men," scoffed the innkeeper. "Permit me to laugh. I've been to every rebbe in the country, and none of them has managed to bring about the salvation I need. Why should I believe in them?"

The *shamash* entered the yard. Drawing closer, he extended a friendly hand to the innkeeper. "I see that you're speaking from distress. Well, you know what they say: If you've got trouble on your mind, share it with someone. Why suffer alone? Let me bear it together with you. Maybe I can help."

He spoke sincerely, and his words fell on receptive ears. The innkeeper studied him closely in silence for a while, then said, "To my great sorrow, I am childless. It's been fifteen years since I married, and there have not been any children. What haven't I done, and who haven't I seen! All the *tzaddikim* and rebbes have blessed me and prayed for me. I know that their blessings were sincere — but they haven't helped. So I've stopped believing in rebbes. Don't bring a rebbe near me."

It occurred to the *shamash* that he could solve the problem in a flash, simply by revealing to the innkeeper that his "rebbe" was really not a rebbe. Instead, he assumed a caring expression and smiled radiantly, "The rebbe who's on his way here is not like all the others. He is something altogether different."

He wasn't lying. The "rebbe" who stood a short distance away, awaiting his signal, was indeed different from other rebbes. In fact, he wasn't a rebbe at all!

The innkeeper waved an impatient hand. "I already told you not to talk to me about it. Big rebbe, small rebbe, they're all the same to me. I've given up on every one of them."

He fell suddenly silent. The chassid was certain that he was about to be sent away, together with his "rebbe." But the innkeeper's face softened.

"Tell me," he said. "Does your rebbe know how to write a *kemei'a* (amulet)?"

"Certainly. What a question!"

"In that case, you are both welcome to come inside, with all due respect," the innkeeper said, abruptly reversing direction.

The chassid ran to summon the "rebbe," who emerged from his place of concealment and walked over to the inn's yard with measured step and honorable bearing. They entered the inn, where the *shamash* explained to the rebbe that the innkeeper was childless and wished to receive a *kemei'a*, to summon the blessing of children.

The "rebbe's" face had been serious till then; now it turned downright solemn. He asked the innkeeper to fetch a bottle of ink and some parchment.

The items were quickly brought. The "rebbe" asked the other two men to leave the room while he wrote the *kemei'a* on a piece of parchment. When the ink had dried, he rolled up the parchment, slipped it into a cloth holder, and summoned the innkeeper back. Soberly, he handed over the amulet.

"Give this to your wife. I warn you in the strictest terms not to show it to any living being in the world, or you will lose its benefit."

"No one will know she has a *kemei'a*," the innkeeper promised.

"A year from now, your wife will be holding a son!" Warmly, the "rebbe" pressed the inkeeper's hand.

The man's face lit up with joy. Though he had stopped believing in rebbes, he still clung to his faith in amulets. He handed this one happily to his wife, then served his guests a meal fit for a king. Meat and fish and all sorts of delicacies found their way to the table. He poured them glass after glass of wine and liquor. For a long time he stood over his guests, treating them with enormous honor.

His enthusiasm did not wane until he had given them a large sum of money — which covered all their expenses to Lublin and back home again after the holiday.

A year later, the two friends returned to Lublin for Rosh Hashanah. This time, there was no need to pretend they were rebbe and *shamash*, as they had managed to save enough money over the course of the year to pay for the trip. Their journey took them once again past the same village in which they had stopped the year before. With an exchange of meaningful glances, they requested that the wagon driver make a detour around the village. The "*kretchmer*" in which they had stayed, it will be remembered, was located on the high road. Passing through would mean encountering the innkeeper's fury at the deceit they had perpetrated.

Taking the long way around, they reached Lublin on Erev Rosh Hashanah, just as the large congregation was completing its recitation of the *Selichos* known as "*Zechor Bris.*"

The *beis midrash* was filled to capacity. An atmosphere of awe permeated the place. The two chassidim were absorbed into the crowd and began to make their way toward the eastern wall. Their first order of business was to receive the rebbe's welcoming blessing.

They slowly moved closer to the Chozeh, and closer ... and then halted in shock.

Seated beside the rebbe was the same innkeeper whom they had fooled the year before, and whom they had sought to avoid that day. He was wearing a *tallis* and conversing with the rebbe. He must be denouncing the pair of them this very minute!

At a total loss, they stood rooted to the spot. What to do? Should they try to escape? But they had not come all this long way only to run away on the eve of the holiday. Ignore the innkeeper and walk over to greet the rebbe? That would lead to their leaving in shame.

They stood transfixed, bereft of ideas. They had no choice but to listen to the innkeeper's conversation with the rebbe.

Their breaths froze and their hearts skipped a beat. It seemed that the man was the father of a baby having a *bris*! A son had been born to him the week before, and he had come to honor the rebbe with the role of *sandek*. Listening further, they heard the innkeeper describe, in meticulous detail, the scene that had taken place the year before.

"I tell Your Honor, I've never seen such a miracle-worker in my life. He promised me a son the following year — and here I am, a year later, with the son I've brought with me!"

"Do you have any idea who that rebbe was?" questioned the Chozeh of Lublin.

"No, Rebbe," the innkeeper answered emotionally. "I'd never heard of him before, and I had never seen him before or since. But this much I can tell Your Honor: If I saw him, I would recognize him immediately. He had a very distinguished appearance."

The happy father's eyes swept the crowded shul. Suddenly, he gasped. "Whom do I see? It's that rebbe — the very one who brought about the miracle last year. And his *shamash*, too!"

Caught in a trap! There was no escaping now. With a crook of his finger, the Chozeh invited them to join him. Slowly they approached, knees quaking. They were certain to be soundly rebuked by the *tzaddik* any minute now — a scolding they would never forget.

To their relief, the rebbe did not rebuke them at all. Instead, he ordered them to remain until after the *bris*. Afterwards, the happy father of the newborn heaped the spurious "rebbe" with compliments.

The Chozeh said, "There was an iron curtain standing between this childless man and his Father in Heaven. All the prayers said by various *tzaddikim*, and the blessings they bestowed, were useless. No prayer or blessing was able to pierce that curtain. Then the two of you came, and the 'rebbe' here gave him the *kemei'a,* in which he had written just five letters: S - K - T - D - M."

The "rebbe" blushed furiously. The Chozeh of Lublin knew things that had taken place in the utmost secrecy!

The Chozeh continued: "S - K - T - D - M are the intitials of five Polish words: '*Stare krowy takze daja mleko.*' Translated, that means, 'Old cows also give milk.'

"When that *kemei'a* reached heaven, those on high burst into such hearty laughter that the iron partition was cracked, and all the prayers and blessings of the *tzaddidim* were able to do their job. That was how this Jew merited a son, at whose *bris* the two of you were present today."

R' Dovid'l finished telling his story, thought a moment, and then added, "Last night, our friend R' Yehudah Leib arrived in the Heavenly Court. Among other things, they asked him, 'And who is your rebbe?' R' Yehudah Leib replied, 'R' Dovid'l of Yerushalayim.' A great laughter burst out in heaven. 'What? Is Dovid'l also a rebbe?' While they were laughing, R' Yehudah Leib 'slipped' into the World that is all good."

Seeing the impression his tale had made on his listeners, and their inclination to discuss it at length, he quickly changed the subject. "*Nu*, bring the *mayim acharonim*, it's time to *bentch*."

But even long years after that *Motza'ei Shabbos*, the impact of the story remained in the hearts of those who had been privileged to hear it that night.

[R' Shmuel Aharon Shazuri-Weber, who was present at that *melaveh malkah* described above nearly ninety years ago, retained it in his phenomenal memory, and relayed it to R' Chaim Weinstock, *Shlita*, of Jerusalem.]

The Case of the Traveling Epidemic

THE SHULS IN THE CITY OF ALEK WERE CROWDED WITH worshipers. It was not Yom Kippur, yet the heart-rending wails that emanated from the shuls would have had any passing stranger believing that he had read his calendar wrong. Though it was not Yom Kippur, everyone was fasting, praying, and weeping bitterly with much pounding on their hearts, just as they did on Yom Kippur.

What was going on?

A brief tour of the small city's cemetery could tell the full story. Scores of fresh graves had been dug there in recent weeks, in the wake of a terrible epidemic that had swept through Alek suddenly, and with devastating consequences. The epidemic had focused strangely on the Jewish side of town, as though the gentile population possessed some secret protection against the Angel of Death. Of late, it seemed as if all the Angel's fury was directed at the hapless Jews — and particularly at Jewish children and babies. Passing through the rows of new graves, a visitor would have seen, to his horror, that most of them were small. The city was filled with tears; there was no family that had not lost a relative. And, after the high toll of children taken by the plague, it seemed to become the turn of the parents. But the youngsters bore the brunt of the epidemic's fury.

As always in times of trouble, the Jews had gathered in the shuls to pour out their hearts in prayer. They were pleading with their Creator to halt the Angel of Death in its tracks.

Their efforts appeared to be futile. Not only did the epidemic not slow down — it seemed to strengthen, exacting its intolerable price in lives. Alek's Jews were afraid there would soon be none of them left at all.

But there was a single hope left. A great *tzaddik* resided among them: R' Tzvi Aryeh, widely known as "R' Hirsch Leib Aleker," an outstanding student of R' Yechiel Michel, the Maggid of Zlotchov.

R' Hirsch Leib was known for his tremendous power of *tefillah*, which had helped save his fellow Jews from all manner of evil decrees. Squarely facing off with his opponent — the prosecuting angels who wished to harm the Jewish people — he would fearlessly counter by expounding on the merits of his fellow Jews. In this way, he had succeeded in rescuing quite a number of his brethren from an evil fate.

The Jews of Alek began streaming to the *tzaddik's* home day and night. The cries of mothers whose young ones had been torn from them because of the epidemic pierced his holy heart. Women who had lost two or three children stood wailing in his room, pleading, "Let the rest survive!" A young widower who had lost his bride of just half a year broke down in agonized tears. Old folks who had lost their children in the prime of their lives wrung their hands and gazed at him with eyes full of questions.

R' Hirsch Leib stood in his room, begging Heaven's mercy for his brothers and sisters, and praying that the remnant survive. To his terror, he sensed that his plea was not being accepted. Heaven was rejecting his prayers. He pounded with all his might on the Gates of Mercy, and was shaken to the core when the Gates remained locked. It was as if the decree had been sealed in blood: to destroy the Jews of Alek, young and old, in one fell swoop.

In that difficult hour, R' Hirsch Leib decided to take a step of last resort: He would choose an atonement to suffer in the people's stead. He relied on the verse, "*V'eten adam tachtecha,* And I will put a person in your stead (*Yeshayahu* 43:4)," about which our Sages have commented, "Do not say '*adam*,' but '*Edom*' (*Berachos* 62)." There were many descendants of Edom living nearby who never failed to take every opportunity to hurt the Jews in any way possible. Up to that point, these wicked men had been untouched by the virulent epidemic. The time had come to transfer it to their courtyard. After all, why shouldn't they bear their share of the burden?

That very day, the heads of Alek's Jewish community were summoned to the *tzaddik's* home. R' Hirsch Leib made an unusual request.

"I need 160 crowns (valuable coins also known as *kronen*) — the numerical equivalent of the word *tzelem* (cross) — in order to conduct a *pidyon nefesh* (redemption rite) for our community."

The leaders needed no explanation as to why the *tzaddik* could not donate the money from his own pocket. A single glance at his shabby home, rickety furniture, and threadbare clothes was enough. R' Hirsch Leib was destitute. It was open to question whether his home contained even a single crown in case of emergencies.

They set out to accomplish the task. Before the day was out, they had combed Alek to collect the requisite 160 crowns, which they brought reverently to the *tzaddik's* home. With all their hearts, they believed that R' Hirsch Leib had the knowledge to conduct a *pidyon nefesh*. All of the Jews in Alek had been involved in the secret reason behind the collection; there was not a single family that did not contribute at least one crown.

They gathered around the *tzaddik's* house, where many dozens of Jews waited impatiently to hear the result of the ritual. Brought to the edge of despair by the events of previous weeks, they hoped to hear that the Angel of Death had at last turned its blade on their own greatest enemies. Hot tears fell on open books of *Tehillim*, as they sought to strengthen their defender in his holy mission.

R' Hirsch Leib remained closeted in his room for a long time, with the piles of coins before him. His lips whispered various words known only to those versed in the secrets of Kabbalah. His *gabbaim*, peeking through the keyhole, saw him pass the coins from hand to hand as he whispered, eyes closed and face radiant.

When he was done, he called back in his *gabbaim*. Pointing to the glistening pile of coins on the table, he said, "Take the crowns and scatter them near the homes of those known to be the biggest Jew-haters, those who have persecuted the Jews the most."

The *gabbaim* hurried away to do as they had been bidden. Carrying bags of gold coins, they began strolling through the streets of the gentile neighborhood, tossing the coins toward the houses as they went. The gentiles, who had been following with great satisfaction the epidemic's sweeping progress through the Jewish quarter, stared in astonishment as the bearded Jews walked through their streets tossing coins out of sacks. Their neighbors, the gentiles decided, must have gone mad with grief. Some suggested that since the Jews were all destined to die, they must have decided they had no further use for money. On one point, all the gentiles were agreed: a great deal of cash, in the form of valuable coins, was rolling through their streets, free for the taking ...

In a flash, they were sniffing around on the ground, eagerly gathering up the coins. Quarrels and fistfights broke out over the disputed ownership of one coin or another, as the slower among them tried to wrest the coins away from their quicker friends. A hail of curses and abuse by the disappointed was showered on the heads of the lucky ones who had the muscle necessary to protect their loot.

By the time the *gabbaim* returned to R' Hirsch Leib's home, not a single crown remained on the ground. They had all been snatched up. It is interesting to note that the lion's share of the coins found their way into the homes of Alek's most vociferous anti-Semites.

✿

The *pidyon nefesh* began having an effect within 24 hours.

Suddenly, for the first time since it began, the epidemic did not exact its toll of victims from the Jewish quarter of town. It was as though it had halted in its tracks. In the gentile neighborhoods, however, cries of anguish began to waft from the windows of homes where family members had suddenly fallen deathly ill.

The observant took note that that the epidemic hit hardest in those homes that had garnered the most coins the day before. Those who had felt themselves unlucky the day before — because they had not been quick enough to reach the coins — now realized that they had been fortunate. They were enjoying continued good health, while those who had snatched the coins lay in their beds, writhing in pain.

By the next day, the first deaths were recorded in the gentile population. These were clustered primarily around the homes of the most virulent anti-Semites. The rising death toll stood in contrast to the total cessation of fatalities in the city's Jewish quarter. The tossing of those valuable coins began to seem far less "foolish" a move than the gentiles had originally believed it to be; apparently, the coins had transferred the illness from one place to the other. The Jews had imbued the coins with magical properties and sent the Angel of Death to haunt Alek's gentiles. The city was in an uproar.

There was, however, one rabid anti-Semite who had not participated in the great coin hunt: the city's priest. This was a man who never lost an opportunity to denounce the Jews from his pulpit. He accused the Jews of being the root cause of every gentile trouble, of sowing disease, of crucifying their annointed one ... Two days ago, he had watched enviously as the lay townsmen crawled on the ground collecting gold coins and growing unexpectedly rich. He himself did not crawl; it was beneath his dignity to do so. Should he, a respected man of the cloth, pluck money from the gutters like a beggar? But his eyes had started out of their sockets at the sight of the coins glistening at his feet and snatched up by hot, eager hands. It had taken all his self-control to restrain himself from joining them. He assumed an expression of lofty scorn for those who were squabbling like hens over every stray coin, at times pummeling each other to the point of bloodshed.

"Fools," he spat. "Money-hungry fools!"

Head high, he entered his house — privately wondering why he didn't have a clever servant to do the dirty work of collecting the booty for him.

Two days later, the priest was celebrating his spurious "moral triumph." People were whispering that the enchanted crowns scattered by the Jews had sowed death and destruction, transferring the plague from the Jewish section of town to the gentile one.

The priest's hatred leaped to a new high. He did not wait for the following Sunday to preach his sermon. Right then and there, he went out into the street and addressed the gathering crowd.

"Do you know what has brought this dread disease upon you?" he thundered. "The coins that the Jews spread. And do you know which Jews those were? They were sent by the *tzaddik* — the well-known Jewish '*rabbin*.' "

The time had come to announce the news he had worked so hard to uncover. Standing at his full height, he cleared his throat and shouted, "I have learned from witnesses that the *rabbin* was locked in a room with those coins, and immediately afterwards sent his assistants to scatter them in our neighborhoods. Since then, as you know, the epidemic has begun its rampage in our midst!"

The incitement worked. Inflamed, the crowd began to shout angry curses about the Jews in general, and the *tzaddik* in particular. Like a herd of obedient sheep, they trotted after the priest as he led the way to the mayor's house, to demand that the Jewish rabbi stand trial for the crime of causing an epidemic in the heart of the gentile population.

The mayor of Alek was no Jew-hater, and he was not at all convinced that the rabbi had been involved in the matter. Under intense pressure from the mob, however, he was forced to concede. He sent a summons to R' Hirsch Leib's home; the rabbi was to appear before him to answer to the charge of spreading a fatal disease.

Alek's Jewish community was terrified to learn that their holy rebbe was to pay the price for his devotion to them. Their fear leaped to a new high when they learned that the gentiles, whose hatred was being constantly fanned by the wicked priest, were preparing to launch bloody pogroms the moment the *tzaddik* was convicted. Not only would the rabbi pay for the crime, but the entire Jewish population of the city would pay as well.

"We've jumped from the frying pan into the fire! Saved from the epidemic, only to be massacred by those murderers," whispered the Jews, their faces ashen. Those of little faith started packing, ready to flee the city in the dead of night, until the danger passed.

The rebbe himself was not concerned. He sent word to every shul in Alek reassuring the people that there was nothing to fear. "Even if they convict me, the haters of Israel will not have dominion over us. Not so much as a child's fingernail will be harmed," the rebbe promised with full confidence. The words were like a balm to his people's fearful hearts.

As the epidemic continued to rage unchecked in the gentile neighborhoods, the gentiles' fury grew with each passing day. In that charged atmosphere, even a tiny spark could set off a huge conflagration. Everyone — Jew and gentile alike — waited tensely for the trial, which was scheduled, with astonishing speed, for later that same week. It was clear to all that the rebbe's conviction in the case of the traveling epidemic would be the cue for a horrific massacre. The haters of Israel armed themselves with knives and axes, while the Jews poured their hearts out in prayer, night and day.

On the appointed day, the rebbe, accompanied by his two faithful *gabbaim* and surrounded by police officers, walked into the courthouse. The city's Jews watched and prayed as his tall, erect figure was swallowed up into the building. From that same portal, a few hours later, would emerge the verdict.

The mayor of Alek also served as its chief judge. He sat in the center of the dais, with two additional judges on either side of him. On R' Hirsch Leib's entrance, the mayor honored him by rising to his feet and remaining that way until the rebbe was seated. No one who saw this was surprised: the mayor was known to harbor a longstanding admiration for the rebbe, having more than once expressed the opinion that the rebbe was a genuine man of G-d. For the rebbe's supporters, the identity of the chief judge came as a relief; but the sight of the prosecutor — the rabidly anti-Semitic priest — froze the blood in their veins. His hardened expression swept away any doubt that he would rest content with anything less than the severest punishment — and that he would not hesitate to give the signal to start a bout of brutal Jewish bloodletting.

"You may begin the proceedings," the judge instructed the prosecutor.

The priest stood up and launched into his accusation: The accused was guilty of disseminating disease in the heart of Alek's gentile population. He had accomplished this through the tossing of gold "crowns" into the gentile neighborhoods, after which the Jews had stopped dying and gentiles began to take their place.

"How was the epidemic transferred?" the chief judge wanted to know. "And don't give me some old wives' tale about magical coins. We're not chatting in the market square and I'm not about to accept such nonsense."

The priest paled. With those few words, the mayor had taken the wind out of his sails. The use of a magical enchantment was the central point of his case.

Without giving him time to recover, the mayor went on. "In your opinion, had the coins been handled by patients who had been ill? Was that how they transferred the epidemic?"

The priest gazed wildly around, as though seeking some source of support from the mob roiling outside the courthouse doors. Anticipating events, the mayor had made the trial a closed affair, with only a few chosen spectators permitted inside the courthouse.

"I can't explain exactly how the plague was transferred," the priest said after some consideration. He knew that the mayor had laid a trap for him, and did not wish to fall into it. "I know only one thing. That rabbi"

— he pointed at R' Hirsch Leib, whose face was tranquil, as though the proceedings had nothing to do with him — "closeted himself in his room with those coins, 160 of them, and then sent his men to spread them in our streets. From that day, the situation turned completely around. The Jews began to recover, while our people began dropping like flies. These are the exact facts, and not wild guesses or exaggerations."

"Well spoken!" the mayor said approvingly. "What, then, do you think of the following idea, based on the facts you've just presented? Because the disseminators of the plague were the coins the rebbe ordered thrown in your neighborhood, he must be punished accordingly. You, my good priest, shall go from house to house collecting all those crowns — 160 of them, I believe you said? — and return them from whence they came; that is, scatter them in the Jewish streets. That's where they came from, and that's where they belong."

The priest gaped disbelievingly at the mayor. Without pause, the judge slammed his gavel down and announced the verdict:

"The priest must gather all the coins and scatter them, in person, among the Jewish homes in Alek. Sentence to be carried out immediately!"

Forced to be a Rebbe

O N THE EVE OF ROSH HASHANAH ONE YEAR, A JEW BROUGHT A gift to the Vizhnitzer Rebbe, R' Chaim Meir Hager. The gift was the head of a sheep, one of the auspicious symbols for celebrating the new year. The rebbe was pleased with the gift, and tasted the meat on Rosh Hashanah night, reciting the words, "*Yehi ratzon sheni-heyeh l'rosh v'lo l'zanav,* May it be Your will that we be a head and not a tail."

Unfortunately, the meat was spoiled. It made the Rebbe violently ill with food poisoning, forcing him to remain bedridden for an extended period of time.

Many weeks later, the Rebbe had recovered sufficiently to get out of bed and stand on his feet. At his doctors' suggestion, he went outside, toward evening, for a stroll in the fresh air. Flanked by his helpers, he walked down the main street of Vizhnitz. He smiled his sweet, wise smile at one of the men accompanying him, his relative, R' Dovid Koshitzky.

"You are a descendant of R' Naftali of Ropshitz," the Rebbe said. "Let me tell you a story about your ancestor — a story you have certainly never heard."

The men perked up their ears as the rebbe began his story. All through the story, the smiles never left his listeners' faces.

Among those who clustered around R' Naftali of Ropshitz were not only ordinary chassidim, but also *talmidei chachamim* whose entire essence was bound up in Torah and in the service of Hashem. These men had all but renounced the material world them. A little bread and water was sent to them from the rebbe's house, a meager meal,but one which satisfied them completely.

Among these "regulars," one stood out. R' Yitzchak was a man in his prime. There was nothing in his life apart from his devotion to Torah and Chassidus, and a burning belief in *tzaddikim* which expressed itself through a powerful connection to his rebbe.

Hashem had blessed R' Yitzchak with numerous daughters. The first of them, Shaindel, had already turned 15 1/2 and was ready, according to the custom of the time, to go to the *chupah*. R' Yitzchak's good wife generally tried, as far as possible, not to burden her husband with household matters. Now, however, with a grown-up daughter and not a penny in the house for a dowry, she asked her husband to do something. Without a dowry, they would have to settle for a mediocre young man for their Shaindel, which was less than that excellent girl deserved.

"And what shall I do?" countered R' Yitzchak. "Shall I leave the holy Torah and go into business, or take up some craft?"

"Heaven forbid. That never entered my mind! But when you next travel to Ropshitz to see the holy rebbe, don't forget to mention our daughter and get his blessing and advice."

"What are you thinking?" R' Yitzchak was astounded. "Shall I interrupt the rebbe's holy thoughts with such trivialities? Shall I steal his precious time with the emptiness of this world? People come to the rebbe in order to purify and elevate themselves, to acquire wisdom and to uproot their bad traits. Mundane matters — for the rebbe? What are you thinking?"

Vehemently, she answered, "If you're not prepared to speak to the rebbe, then I'm coming along with you. I'll walk right in and bring our situation to the rebbe's attention. You'll be embarrassed!"

Taken aback by the threat, R' Yitzchak promised to do as she had requested. His wife packed his *tallis* and *tefillin*, his Shabbos clothes, a loaf of bread and some water, and they parted in peace.

But when R' Yitzchak arrived in Ropshitz, his first order of business, after receiving the rebbe's greeting, was to sit down in his usual place in the *beis midrash* and immediately lose himself in higher matters. His companions were engaged in similar pursuits: one praying long hours, a second poring over his *Gemara*, a third purifying his thoughts over a *sefer Tehillim*, fervent tears pouring down his cheeks. Several weeks passed as though in a dream. When it was time for R' Yitzchak to leave, the rebbe's famous *gabbai*, Yehoshua, brought him to the rebbe's room, his *kvittel* and his meager contribution in hand.

The rebbe read the names on the note and asked at once, "How old is your daughter, Shaindel?"

"She's 15 1/2."

"*Nu*, it's time to find her a *shidduch*. Have you set aside an appropriate dowry?"

R' Yitzchak spread his hands. "From where would I have it? I toil in Torah. Must I abandon my beloved *Gemara* and find a job?"

"No, no," replied the rebbe. "A person must only make a small effort, the *Ribbono Shel Olam* will take care of the rest. Next week, on Thursday, leave your home and travel to the resort town of Durna. Stay there over Shabbos and then return home. Salvation is near."

On R' Yitzchak's return from Ropshitz, his wife and daughters welcomed him eagerly. "Did you speak to the rebbe?"

Beaming, R' Yitzchak replied, "There was no need to say a word! The rebbe himself asked me Shaindel's age, and advised me to spend next Shabbos in Durna. He said that everything would fall into place."

They could not see how a trip to Durna would solve their problem, but they possessed a deep and implicit faith in the advice of *tzaddikim*.

It was a wintry week after Chanukah. After *davening Shacharis* and having a bite to eat, R' Yitzchak left his house on Thursday morning without the slightest idea of how to get to Durna. Wishing to save himself the trouble of carrying a heavy bundle, and because Shabbos was approaching, he wore his Shabbos *kapote* and his *shtreimel* on his head.

To his good fortune, coaches with passengers who took pity on him passed and took him along. Each one took him a little further along his way. And so he traveled on, until it was mid-afternoon and he was standing on Durna's main street.

Now what? He had his bundle containing his *tallis* and *tefillin*, a few *sefarim*, and a bit of dry bread that, when soaked in water, might be edible. He began to walk.

As the rebbe had mentioned, Durna was a resort town. During the summer months the place bustled with life, its streets swarming with vacationers. The air was clear and invigorating. Great Torah figures would stroll its streets deep in conversation, their *meshamshim* following behind. Rich men enjoyed the comforts the city offered, and lazy men found ample scope for their idleness. When summer ended, however, the place emptied. Winter's snow and icy rains precluded coming and going. Durna was in hibernation. From every chimney, smoke spiraled upward as the townspeople hunkered down in their homes.

At one window stood a housewife, a simple villager, with time on her hands. During the summers she and her husband earned their living hosting some of the many vacationers who passed through their town, but the winters held no such livlihood. She stood gazing through her window, in the vain hope that a miracle would occur and bring some sort of guest — or anything at all to add a little color to the drab winter's day.

She was all too familiar with the small daily happenings in the street outside: the clip-clop of the passing horse, the blacksmith's pounding, the rumble of the lumber wagon, and the water-carrier's sneeze. Suddenly, she rubbed her eyes disbelievingly. What was this? A tall, venerable-looking man with a flowing beard was walking down the street carrying a small cloth bag. It was a holy man, coming to stay in town at the height of winter. Perhaps she would have the privilege of hosting this *tzaddik*!

With a happy cry, she ran into another room and said breathlessly to her husband, a simple villager like herself, "Did you see who's passing in the street? It is a holy man, a great rebbe! Quick, go out and invite him to our house. Maybe our home will be blessed!"

The man raced outside to see if his wife had exaggerated in her description. When he saw R' Yitzchak, he admitted that she had been absolutely correct. This was indeed a holy man, a *tzaddik* with an exalted countenance and the purified image of a veritable angel, descended from heaven straight to their modest street, where he walked with a measured, tired gait.

Quick as a flash, the man ran inside again to instruct his wife to prepare a hot stew, some cake, and whiskey with which to welcome this important guest. He put on his Shabbos clothes and went outside to greet the illustrious *tzaddik*. In awe and humility he approached R' Yitzchak. "*Shalom aleichem*, Rebbe."

R' Yitzchak halted. He heard only the greeting and missed the title. He shook the villager's hand with his own travel-stained one.

"I am the first to greet Your Honor, holy Rebbe," the villager announced joyfully. "Please give us the privilege of providing you with lodgings. Refresh yourself with something warm in my house, taste some whiskey and sweet cakes made by my wife herself, and bestow your blessing on our simple home."

R' Yitzchak stared at him, thunderstruck. He glanced over his shoulder to see if the man was, perhaps, addressing someone else, but no one stood behind him. This naive man was indeed addressing him as "Rebbe"!

"I am not a rebbe, and not even a *talmid chacham*," R' Yitzchak said. "I am just a simple Jew. But I will accept your invitation with happiness. Since leaving home early this morning, I haven't eaten a thing. I am hungry and thirsty, and the cold is piercing my bones. I will eat and drink in your house, and perhaps I will also rest a little under your roof."

The villager refused to accept R' Yitzchak's disclaimer. On the contrary, it only elevated his guest in his eyes: Not only was this man a great rebbe, he was also a tremendously humble one!

"Rebbe, please stop," he cried with a victorious smile. "All great rebbes modestly say, 'I'm no rebbe.' You're just like the others."

"But I really am no rebbe!" protested R' Yitzchak. "I'm not a hidden *tzaddik*, and I am certainly no rebbe or leader. I am a simple chassid, a student of the holy Rebbe, R' Naftali of Ropshitz, and nothing more."

His host wasn't listening. Respectfully, he took R' Yitzchak's bundle and ushered him into the house.

The table was set with cakes and delicacies, and there was whiskey to warm the traveler's frozen bones. He drank a sip or two, tasted a cake, and ate a bowl of stew to restore his strength, then thanked his hosts for their goodness and hospitality. They, for on their part, could not understand what sort of thanks were coming to them. Was it not their obligation to honor the great *tzaddik*?

As R' Yitzchak warmed himself by the stove and chatted with his host, the man's wife hurried over to her neighbors to pour out the story of the illustrious guest who had honored them with his presence. "A holy man! And so modest!" were just two of the epithets she used in describing him. The other women, surprised to hear that someone had come to their town on such a dreary winter's day, hastened to the house to take a peek.

One look was enough to make up their minds. "You foolish thing," they scolded her. "You don't understand what *tzaddikim* are like. This man is much more than you've said. He's a tremendous rebbe — the greatest of the great!"

The naive women ran to fetch their husbands. Before R' Yitzchak knew what was happening, the simple, good-hearted Jews had formed a long line, all desirous of pressing the "rebbe's" hand and greeting him with a fervent, "*Shalom aleichem,* Rebbe!"

"I'm not a rebbe," R' Yitzchak was quick to correct them. "What's gotten into all of you? I'm just a simple Jew, an ordinary chassid. Please, leave me alone."

But they saw his protestations as the clearest sign that he was indeed a rebbe — one of the great ones — a towering rebbe whose humility and modesty led him to conceal himself in this way. Despite all R' Yitzchak's protests, the line only grew longer.

"It's time for *Minchah*," someone called out.

At once they all left, with R' Yitzchak at the center of the excited group, bewildered as to how he had come to be there and how to react to the strange drama in which he found himself unexpectedly playing the starring role.

By the time the procession reached the shul, the news had spread as if on wings. A great and noble *tzaddik* had come to stay in their town! Durna was beside itself with joy. In shul, every man came over to greet the "rebbe."

Desperately, he pleaded, "Have pity, leave me be, I am nothing," but they continued on exactly as before. The line continued to grow until the *chazzan* stepped up to begin *Minchah*.

Between *Minchah* and *Maariv* a regular daily *shiur* was scheduled, dating back dozens of years. On this festive day, however, a spontaneous gathering took place the moment *Minchah* was over. Included in the crowd were Durna's leading citizens. They were radiant.

"How fortunate we are to have the privilege of hosting the *tzaddik* in our town!" they told one another happily. "In his humility, he keeps repeating like the refrain of a song, 'I am nothing.' He will wish to conduct a modest Shabbos here, as if he were a simple person. Will we let him? Will such a Shabbos be allowed to pass without a '*tisch*' (table) for everyone to attend?"

The main speaker was the *rosh kehillah*, the wealthy community leader, whose opinion was voiced more loudly than the rest. "First of all, it is highly unfitting to let the *tzaddik* stay in lodgings so far from the shul. It's a disgrace to make this exalted man walk such a distance to shul several times a day."

"And another thing," someone else took up the thread, "can we allow such an illustrious rebbe to remain in the home of such simple folk?"

The decision was unanimous: The holy rebbe must stay in the *rosh kehillah's* home, located just steps away from the *beis midrash*.

"*Rabbosai*," he cried, "the time is short, and we've got plenty to do. We must prepare lavish Shabbos meals in honor of the exalted Shabbos we are anticipating, with Hashem's help. Everyone in town will participate in preparing the food for the meals the rebbe will conduct in the *beis midrash* on Friday night and at the *seudah shelishis*."

Meanwhile, as the commotion raged behind him, R' Yitzchak was immersed in a *sefer*. He had no inkling that the commotion was all about him. Without his knowledge, several decisions had been made for him; a wagon was sent post-haste to his hosts' simple home to fetch his belongings and bring them to the *rosh kehillah's* ornate mansion near the shul. Receiving word of her illustrious guest, the rich man's wife began urgent preparations in his honor.

After *davening*, the seven most important community leaders approached the "rebbe" and explained that it was not fitting for a man of his stature to lodge in the home of such simple folk. Moreoever, the streets were difficult to traverse because of rain and snow, and his chosen lodgings were far from the shul. In short, the honored rebbe was presented with a *fait accompli*: His belongings had already been tranferred to the *rosh kehillah's* home. To R' Yitzchak's distress, the crowd surrounded him on every side when he emerged into the street, as if he were a *chasan* walking to his *chupah*. His new host walked beside him, glowing with satisfaction. Someone stepped forward to serve as the "rebbe's" *shamash* and *gabbai*, and the large entourage arrived at the mansion amid much joyous clamor.

After a royal dinner in the rich man's lavish dining room, he pleaded with his exalted guest, in the name of the entire community, not to disappoint them in their expectation of seeing him conduct a holy "*tisch*," sprinkled with words of Torah as the *Shechinah* itself spoke from his throat, and with Shabbos *tefillos* to uplift every soul.

R' Yitzchak sighed brokenly. "I've already told you that I'm not a rebbe. Honor removes a man from this world ..."

"Yes, yes," his host smiled calmly. "That's exactly what all great rebbes say. But it seems to me that our Sages have instructed: 'Do everything that your host asks.' The townspeople are working hard to prepare wonderful Shabbos meals. The rebbe will surely not wish to distress this holy *kehillah* who want just one thing: to bask in the radiance of the *Shechinah*."

Meanwhile, people had begun to collect outside, each desiring a private interview with the "rebbe." The self-appointed *gabbai* wrote *kvitlach* and organized the crowd into an orderly line, as if he had been doing it all his life.

To R' Yitzchak's dismay, he found himself greeting visitors, offering advice, reading *kvitlach* and bestowing blessings like an expert rebbe. At first, he tried to object, "I'm not a rebbe, nor the son of a rebbe," but the people would not desist. When he protested that he did not know how to read a *kvittel* and knew nothing of the soul, and was certainly not on a level to offer blessings to his fellow Jews, he was told, "Are we not taught, 'Do not let the blessing of the common man be light in your eyes'?"

R' Yitzchak continued to protest, explaining to everyone that a mistake had been made. He wasn't a rebbe, but only a simple chassid. His words fell on deaf ears. After a great deal of fruitless argument, he accepted the decree with resignation and blessed the people warmly — upon which the notes and gifts began to flow in earnest. A not insignificant pile of money began to accumulate on the table before him.

Suddenly, sounds of a dispute were heard outside. Someone cried, "Let me in at once — it's a matter of life and death! Help!" Other voices, calmer ones, attempted to soothe the speaker.

The Jew wept bitter tears as he told his story. His small daughter had been confined to bed for five weeks with a raging fever. Expert doctors had examined her and prescribed medicines that had done no good at all. The illness had continued to rage within her with increasing intensity, until she now lay hovering between life and death. Then the girl's father heard the welcome news: A *tzaddik* had come to town! The distraught father had come post-haste to receive the rebbe's blessing for his daughter's recovery.

Those waiting in the long line explained to the brokenhearted father that he must not place any great hope in this rebbe, for he was a stubborn *tzaddik* who insisted that he was no rebbe at all. But the man was in despair and would not give up. His daughter's life was in danger! He begged and pleaded until several people gave up their places in line and let him in ahead of them to see the rebbe.

The anguished father entered the "rebbe's" room and burst into a fresh bout of tears. "Please, let the rebbe bless my sick daughter!," he cried.

R' Yitzchak trembled. Up until now, with the burden of playing the role of "rebbe" thrust upon him, he had been dispensing blessings of a general nature. Here, however, was a situation in which a girl's life hung in the balance! Sorrowfully, he told the father, "They have lied in saying that I am a rebbe. It's somebody's idea of a joke. I am a simple Jew, like yourself. I can't help myself, let alone others."

Hearing this, the father's knees buckled. He fell on his face and lay prostrate before the "rebbe," shaking with heartrending sobs. "Has the rebbe seen in Heaven that I am to be consoled for the loss of my poor daughter? Has her decree been sealed? Oh, woe is me! Woe is me!" His wails could easily be heard outside in the waiting room.

R' Yitzchak was deeply shaken. The innocent man had taken his words in exactly the opposite way than what he had intended. "*Reb*

Yid," he explained, "I am not a rebbe and have not seen what transpires in Heaven. I only wished to say that I am a simple man."

In fear and despair, the father of the sick girl banged his head on the floor. "Aaaah! My daughter's fate is sealed. The rebbe cannot help her!"

R' Yitzchak's heart melted. Tears flowed from his eyes. Now he understood what a real rebbe went through. The people's agony lay heavy on his shoulders. To encourage the weeping man and to keep him from dissolving in pain, he blessed him wholeheartedly, saying that Hashem should send his daughter a full and speedy recovery. Hearing the *berachah*, the man got up from the ground, wiped his tears, and returned home with a heart considerably lighter.

The moment he left, R' Yitzchak bent his head and wept for the situation in which Hashem had placed him. A simple village woman had erred, and all the rest had been drawn in after her error.

The next morning, in the midst of *Shacharis*, the father of the sick girl burst into the shul. His face glowed with joy as he held up a bottle of schnapps and a big cake.

"The rebbe is an angel of Hashem!" he cried. "I returned home yesterday to find my daughter feeling better already. Her fever dropped from the moment the rebbe gave his blessing, and this morning she's completely herself again, as though she had never been ill. And he says he's no rebbe ..."

The *beis midrash* exploded with excitement. When R' Yitzchak heard the reason for the turmoil, his pain doubled. That night, on Shabbos, his protests were fruitless. Against his will he stepped up to the *bimah* and davened *Kabbalas Shabbos* and *Maariv* for the enthusiastic congregation. Afterwards he conducted a public "*tisch*," complete with *divrei Torah*, the distribution of "*sherayim*" — food from the rebbe's plate — the pouring of fine, aged wine from his host's wine cellar with a "*l'chaim!*" for the crowd, heartfelt Shabbos *zemiros,* and energetic dancing. When he returned to the mansion late that night, the entire crowd accompanied him with song and dance.

The same scenario replayed itself in the morning, and again at the third Shabbos meal, as the people responded with an outpouring of fervor to the presence of the *tzaddik* in their midst.

After a sumptuous *melaveh malkah* repast, R' Yitzchak sat in his host's lavish home trying to concoct a strategy for escaping the honor that had been thrust upon him. His unseeing eyes gazed at the rich drapes and rugs around him. His host, meanwhile, stood in the front hall with his wife, who declared, "Shall we host such a great *tzaddik* without receiving a *berachah*? Without an explicit blessing, he's not leaving that room!"

Her husband said, "I've pleaded with many *tzaddikim* already. I don't want to be a bother."

"Let me do the job. *I'll* be the bother!"

Together they entered the room and stood humbly before the "rebbe."

"This time, we are not here as hosts, but rather as people in need of salvation," the *rosh kehillah* began. "It's been seventeen years since we were married, and we have not yet been blessed with children."

R' Yitzchak felt as though he were caught in a steel trap. What had begun as a trickle had turned into a flood, and now he was being asked for a tremendous salvation. "I've already told you that I'm no rebbe, and I haven't changed my mind about that."

As she had promised, the wife — twice as stubborn as her husband — took over. Copious tears flowed until she succeeded in dragging from R' Yitzchak an explicit blessing stating that, with Hashem's help, the following year she would bear a son.

The couple left the room overflowing with happiness — but not before they deposited a giant "gift" of money on the table. R' Yitzchak nearly fainted with the power of his distress. What had become of him these past three days? He had become a counterfeit rebbe — a rebbe against his will!

He crammed the money into his bag and stuffed all the *kvitlach* — each filled with its own brand of misery and longing — into his pockets, slung his bag over his shoulder, opened the door, and slipped secretly out into the night. He left without parting from his host or expressing his gratitude. He could not bear another moment of this charade.

R' Yitzchak walked the streets alone. There was no living soul outside to see him at that late hour. He walked until he had left the town limits behind, stopping when he reached a crossroads. Where to now?

He was still standing there, at a total loss, when a wagon came down the road. Even in the dark he recognized its passenger: the holy Rebbe of Ropshitz!

"Rebbe!" R' Yitzchak ran toward the wagon. "See my misfortune. They turned me into a 'rebbe'!" And he proceeded to relate everything that had transpired from his arrival in Durna. He told R' Naftali of all the honor he had been forced to bear. When he was finished, he placed the *kvitlach* and the money in the rebbe's hands.

The rebbe listened attentively to the story and accepted the *kvitlach* — but returned every last cent of the money to R' Yitzchak. "I will worry about the *kvitlach*. That is my work, and my burden. But the money is yours. I am no highwayman, to rob my fellow travelers in the middle of the night ... I will not take money that precious brothers gave to you and not to me. Go choose a fine *chasan* for your daughter, and may you see *nachas* from all your offspring!"

Not long afterward, Shaindel became engaged.

Some time later, their second daughter reached marriageable age. R' Yitzchak's wife asked him when he was planning to visit the rebbe ...

R' Yitzchak declared firmly, "This time, I will not mention our daughter to the rebbe. I suffered enough in Durna."

Once again, she threatened to see the rebbe herself. He was undeterred. "I am not afraid. Do as you please."

The argument continued for several days, until a messenger unexpectedly came to R' Yitzchak: The rebbe had summoned him to his presence at once.

With pounding heart he made the trip to Ropshitz, knowing what he could expect there.

The moment he arrived, he was taken to see the rebbe.

"How old is your second daughter?" R' Naftali asked.

R' Yitzchak stammered a reply, and the rebbe once again instructed him to travel to Durna. "You were very successful there last time," he said with a smile.

R' Yitzchak burst into tears. "I am repulsed by the honor. If I at least deserved it ... But I know my own worth. I feel like a liar and a cheat. I suffered very much in Durna."

"The Torah says, 'And he set his shoulder to suffer.' In this world we are obligated to suffer. For our children's sake, we are obligated to suffer," the rebbe answered firmly. "Next Thursday, return to Durna wearing your Shabbos clothes, and wait for salvation."

So R' Yitzchak went back to Durna, as his rebbe had ordered. He stepped down into the street, and all was exactly as it had been the year before. There was the village woman peering out her window, just as before. Catching sight of R' Yitzchak outside, she emitted a cry of surprise, her voice resounding through the town. "It's the *Navi* in our midst! The rebbe lives ten hours away from Durna, and the *rosh kehillah's* wife gave birth only an hour ago — yet here he is!"

Before he could gather his wits, people began to flock in his direction. The Jews of Durna surrounded him with joyful cries of "*Shalom aleichem*, Rebbe!" — and the old argument commenced once more; he claiming "I'm not a rebbe," and they just as staunchly clinging to their own opinion.

They were still arguing the point when the *rosh kehillah's* ornate carriage pulled up beside them. The man himself jumped out, ebullient, and kissed R' Yitzchak's hand.

"An angel of G-d was sent to us, to help us celebrate the *shalom zachar*!" Taking R' Yitzchak by the arm, he said, "Please, I beg Your Honor, don't disappear in the dead of night again like Yaakov fleeing Eisav. I will gladly provide your lodging and everything else Your Honor might need, if you'll only give me the privilege of hosting you until after my son's *bris* next Thursday, so that I may honor the rebbe with being *sandak*, of course."

R' Yitzchak climbed aboard the carriage, which proceeded at a snail's pace in the dense crowd. His insides were churning. He had not anticipated this. The honor he had garnered the previous year was nothing compared to what lay in store for him now.

As the carriage neared the rich man's mansion, cries of "Make way! Make way for the rebbe!" resounded. R' Yitzchak entertained a strange notion. "Maybe — just maybe — this really *was* my doing. I've never wasted a moment away from Torah and *tefillah*. Maybe the child really was born through my blessing?"

He rejected the idea at once, and banished it from his heart. "I gave the *kvittel* to the rebbe. It was certainly his doing." Yet the notion would not leave. "Maybe it *was* me?"

"No! I am positive that it came about through the rebbe's powers."

"Still ... I, too, have amassed a few merits in my time ..."

And so on, and so forth.

Hundreds of guests streamed into Durna for the following Shabbos, having heard about the holy rebbe. R' Yitzchak understood that his denials were useless. His rebbe had urged him to accept his suffering with love. R' Yitzchak saw hundreds of Jews, led fervent prayers in shul, and conducted exalted "*tisch*" after "*tisch*," all without the same degree of pain and heartbreak that he had felt the year before. For four days he welcomed visitors like a rebbe, and not one person heard him object, "But I'm not a rebbe!"

When the time came for the *bris*, he was honored with the role of *sandak* before thousands of onlookers, and heard himself addressed by the title "*Adoneinu Moreinu V' Rabbeinu*, our master, guide, and teacher," without a single word of protest.

After the ceremony, his host asked him not to leave just yet, but to remain until the third day after the *bris milah*. R' Yitzchak obliged. This second Shabbos, too, was an uplifting experience. Many in the future would speak of those two wonderful Shabbasos in Durna. Between the two, R' Yitzchak met with numerous individuals who had come to him for advice and a blessing. The donations kept pouring in.

Before his departure on Sunday, his host and the host's wife — holding her newborn son — entered his room and, as a token of their deepfelt gratitude, presented him with a check worth half their enormous fortune.

It was as a rich man that R' Yitzchak traveled to Ropshitz, in a beautiful coach harnessed to four sturdy horses.

On his arrival at the rebbe's house, in an uplifted frame of mind, Yehoshua the *gabbai* stopped him cold in his tracks.

"*Shalom aleichem*, R' Yitzchak. It's unbelievable! Just 10 minutes ago, the rebbe came out of his room and instructed me to let everyone in to see him today — except R' Yitzchak. You don't have permission to enter."

"What have I done wrong?" cried R' Yitzchak. "The rebbe himself ordered me to go to Durna. Because I've spent two Shabbasos there, do I deserve such a punishment?"

Curtly, the *gabbai* answered, "That's what I was instructed by the rebbe. I can't change his orders."

Heartbroken, R' Yitzchak went into a quiet corner of the *beis midrash*, where he sat and learned, recited *Tehillim*, and waited for the rebbe to "make up" with him. Four days passed. And still, the *gabbai* stood firm as a rock: He could not go in.

On the fifth day, the *tzaddik's* door opened. The rebbe was on his way to a *bris*, scheduled to take place in a nearby town. R' Yitzchak threw himself at R' Naftali's feet, weeping and wailing. "Why has Your Honor pushed me away? Why am I forbidden to enter? I am ready to repair whatever I must fix in my character! Please, just open the door a crack, so that I may know where I have erred."

R' Naftali of Ropshitz's gaze was piercing. "It seems to me that you were entertaining the thought that you were already a rebbe — a great rebbe. Maybe you're a great *tzaddik*, too! Well, I know of several barren women. Perhaps you can bring them salvation? I have some people who desperately need healing. Can you offer them a speedy recovery? And what about all those who need to make a living? Here, I'll give you my *kvitlach* so you can *daven* for them."

R' Yitzchak's bones turned to water as he heard the rebbe's final words: "I have time for simple Jews. For great 'rebbes' like you, I have no time."

R' Yitzchak was an intelligent man. He understood at once that all the "miracles" he had seemingly brought about had not come through any power of his own. They were all from Hashem, and came because of the rebbe's *davening*. Who had waited for him at the Durna crossroads in the middle of the night, if not the rebbe? To whom had he given all the *kvitlach*? How could he have entertained such a nonsensical notion, when the rebbe had only suggested the plan in order to help him financially? In his own foolishness, he had fallen into the trap of conceit.

Banishing every shred of arrrogance, he declared to his rebbe on the spot that he repented of his conceited thoughts, and longed for the rebbe to open his door and his heart to him again. The rebbe, who of course had been acting for R' Yitzchak's own benefit, acquiesced at once.

R' Yitzchak returned home, with his bundle of money and the check for half the rich man's worth. He married off all his daughters honorably and without financial strain, each one to an outstanding Torah scholar, and was privileged to see further generations of righteous offspring from these unions. Now he could continue traveling to Ropshitz from time to time, without apprehension. The "danger" of his trips to Durna and the burden of being a "rebbe" were removed forever, because the blessings he had gleaned from that town remained with him for the rest of his life.

[Special thanks to R' Yitzchak Brichta of Jerusalem for this unusual story originally related by the Vizhnitzer Rebbe, *ztk"l*, author of the *Imrei Chaim*. The tale was written down by the Rebbe's *shamash*, R' Shimshon Lerner, *Shlita*.]

All in the Hands of Heaven

THERE WAS A SOUND OF MANY FOOTSTEPS OUTSIDE — THE footsteps of dignified men imbued with a sense of the hour and the responsibility it had placed upon their shoulders. Then came the knock at the door.

The woman of the house hurried to open it. She was surprised at the sight that met her eyes. Standing on her doorstep was a group of highly respectable, impressive-looking men.

"Is R' Meir Yehoshua at home?" they asked.

She gestured toward an inner room. "He's in there, learning. Please come in."

The delegation entered R' Meir Yehoshua's room, greeted him politely, and immediately placed a rabbinical contract on the table. The contract was signed by all the heads of the Jewish community of Rivitz, a small city in Poland.

"We have come to ask you to return with us, to serve as rav of our *kehillah*," they said simply. "We've heard of your greatness in Torah. Unanimously, we've agreed to accept Your Honor as the new rav of Rivitz."

R' Meir Yehoshua was indeed great in Torah, and his reputation had spread far and wide. He and his family were suffering from severe financial constraints. Nevertheless, he did not accept the proposed contract at once. As the delegation waited, he read the contract carefully. Then, humbly, he said, "If the matter were up to me, I would be prepared to accept. I would gladly undertake the rabbinate of Rivitz. But — I am a chassid. I must travel to see my Rebbe, R' Yissachar Ber of Radoshitz, to hear his opinion."

They were disappointed, having expected to return home with the new rabbi in tow. However, they had no option but to agree that a chassid who refrained from asking his rebbe's advice about such an important step was no chassid at all.

A timetable was set: R' Meir Yehoshua had a month in which to give them his answer.

R' Meir Yehoshua had not spoken the exact truth when he said he would ask his rebbe. He did not intend to ask at all.

There are two kinds of chassidim. The first kind does not take a step without consulting his rebbe. His faith in *tzaddikim* is the guiding principle of his life; anything his rebbe tells him to do — whether the chassid likes it or not — will be done.

The second kind of chassid does not ask his rebbe. He knows that there is nothing in the world that runs itself. Everything is overseen by Divine Providence. One is not appointed to a respectable community's rabbinical seat because he learned more pages of *Gemara* or sections of the *Shulchan Aruch,* nor because he managed to charm this community leader or that one. It happens because it has been decreed Above. This kind of chassid knows that his rebbe needs to hear no question from him. It's enough simply that the question exists. The chassid will receive his answer without even phrasing the question.

R' Meir Yehoshua was this second type of chassid. He traveled to Radoshitz for Shabbos with no intention of asking his rebbe about the position he had been offered. Shabbos would be filled with time spent in his rebbe's presence, listening to his *davening* and his *divrei Torah.* Certainly, among all the things the rebbe would say, there would be some hint for him, R' Meir Yehoshua, about which way to proceed — a hint that would answer the unasked question. It would resolve his doubts and set him on the correct path. And if no hint was forthcoming — that, itself, would be his answer. If his rebbe saw no need to address the question of the rabbinical position at all, then there was nothing to talk about!

One must be on a high level to think in this way.

R' Meir Yehoshua spent the entire Shabbos in Radoshitz, steeped in Torah and *tefillah.* The rebbe neither discussed the topic of the rabbinical contract openly, nor hinted at it. The chassid had his answer: On his return home, he would return a negative response to the Rivitz proposal. Nothing happened of its own accord; all was in Heaven's hands. And if the rebbe had not said a word about it, this was a sign that Heaven did not want to see R' Meir Yehoshua serve as rav of Rivitz!

On Sunday morning, he went in to take his leave of the rebbe. The rebbe discussed matters of Torah and Chassidus with him at length, as always. R' Meir Yehoshua extended a hand in parting and was ready to leave the room, when the rebbe looked at him with a broad smile and said, "I hear they've offered you the position of rav in the city of Rivitz. Is this true, that you — and here, for the first time since they had met, the rebbe used the indirect form, '*ir,*' of the word 'you,' in place of the direct form, '*du*' — have been chosen as the city's rav?"

R' Meir Yehoshua speedily extracted two points from this: (1) His rebbe had "heard" of the proposal from an unearthly source, and (2) the rebbe agreed with the proposal, as seen by his use of the honorific word, "*ir*." The rebbe was already according him the respect due the designated rav of a city.

He could have left the room then, his answer in hand. However, in the normal course of human dialogue, the rebbe had not yet actually answered the question. Humbly, R' Meir Yehoshua said, "Indeed. They came to propose that I serve as rav of Rivitz. That's why I came here this Shabbos, to hear the rebbe's opinion."

R' Yissachar's face expressed surprise and self-deprecation. "To hear my opinion? What I have to say? What have *I* to say? The answer is not dependent on what I say, but on what He says." The rebbe pointed upward. "There, in *Shamayim*, you (again, the use of the honorific term) have already been named rav of Rivitz. It has been decreed that you take up the burden of the city's rabbinate."

R' Meir Yehoshua stood before his rebbe, eyes closed as he swayed gently in awe and humility. If this were Heaven's decree, then he must accept it with love!

He wished to leave, but the rebbe stopped him. With a warm "Mazal tov!" the Rebbe drank a "*l'chaim*" together with the designated rabbi, and then asked him to sit.

"When you arrive in Rivitz to serve as rav," the rebbe said, "you will naturally deliver a sermon. I would like to honor you with the gift of a special *derashah* (sermon). I will tell you how I was appointed rebbe over a group of chassidim, so that you may learn from the tale that there are no coincidences in this world. Everything happens only through Divine Providence. All is decreed Above; nothing happens by itself. A man's entire life cycle, and everything that occurs in his life — from the trivial things to the biggest ones of all — are all decreed in Heaven. A person has hardly any say in the matter. No one asks him. It's all decided for him — up Above!"

The city of Pshedworz, in Poland, was well-known in chassidic circles. Its houses of learning hummed with Torah, as pious young men sat over their *Gemaras* in fervor and purity.

In one *beis midrash* sat a young man whom everyone called "Berel the *Batlan*," Berel the Idle One. He was always reciting *Tehillim*.

No one had ever seen Berel open a *Gemara*. All he seemed to be able to do was recite *Tehillim*. He barely knew how to review the weekly Torah portion as prescribed by our Sages, *shenayim mikra v'echad targum*. People doubted whether he was even able to understand a Rashi.

"Berel the *Batlan*" succeeded in fooling everyone. In reality, he was R' Yissachar Ber, later to become the renowned "Alter of Radoshitz," whose Torah was repeated everywhere. In his youth, however, he disguised himself so well that people took him for a complete ignoramus. Secretly he would visit his rebbes, the holy Maggid of Kozhnitz, the Chozeh of Lubin, and the Rebbe of Peshis'cha. Apart from his rebbes, no one knew his true nature.

The epithet of "*Batlan*," attached to his name, was something he had deliberately cultivated. He appeared to be the kind of unprepossessing young man who would never amount to much.

The nights, however, belonged to Berel. After everyone left the shul, he would set aside his *Tehillim* and rush over to the bookcase like a starving man. He would learn *Gemara* and its commentaries until morning's light, when the early risers would begin coming to shul. They would find him sound asleep on his bench, and shake their heads at the idle young fellow who wasted his days doing nothing and his nights in sweet slumber.

The month of Tishrei found him in the city of Kozhnitz, near his rebbe; after Succos he started out on the return trip to his home in Pshedworz. Was he planning to return to his little *Tehillim*? Berel was planning nothing. He knew that he had a wife and children whom he was obligated to support. He also knew that everything was decreed from Heaven. No one does anything on his own. Therefore, Berel would not interfere with what Heaven had in mind for him. *Kol haneshamah tehallel Kah*, with every breath one must extol Hashem. Each breath he took was the only breath in the world. The one that would come afterwards would be a new life-force sent by Hashem. Why worry about his next breath?

On the road home, he encountered an unfamiliar Jew, a man well on in years. After they had talked awhile, the man invited Berel to come to his house and serve as a *melamed*, a tutor, for his young sons.

This was the first time anyone had offered him the position of teacher. In fact, it was the first time anyone had offered him any sort of job. Back in Pshedworz, a negative image of idle uselessness clung to him. Berel knew that the suggestion came not from here, but from Above.

"So how can I refuse?" he thought to himself. To the man, he said aloud, "I agree!"

If Heaven had sent him a job, was Berel permitted to ask for a salary? Without a word about payment, he followed the man home to his isolated little village.

The man had three sons. They were a happy, lively bunch, red-cheeked and light-footed, but the boys had never yet opened a book and knew nothing but their games among the ducks and calves. Berel labored with each of them individually, each according to his age and level of understanding. Gradually, the boys became enchanted by the young man with the keen glance, and found themselves falling under the influence of his fervent piety. No longer did they leap and run among the farm animals, or race to the river to bathe in the heat of midday. Now their companions were the *Mishnah* and *Chumash*. The large letters shone for them, as though illuminated by their tutor's magnetic explanations and by his eyes that seemed always to glow with a wonderful light.

After Berel had studied with the boys a set number of hours each day, he was free to do as he wished. With no one watching what he did, he gave free rein to his true desires. There was no longer any need to hide behind a cloak of idleness. He was free to serve his Creator with all his heart.

The children's father was not generous with him. Once a month he paid Berel a miniscule salary — a mere few rubles. Berel never asked for a penny, having privately determined to accept whatever was offered him as the salary decreed for him by Heaven. If Heaven wanted him to have more, he would receive it without having to ask.

He had almost no expenses, and was able to save virtually every penny he was paid. He then sent the money by messenger to his hungry family.

At the winter's end, the father gave Berel a gift of some 30 rubles, thanked him for what he had taught his children, and sent him home without a word about returning after Pesach for the summer semester. Berel did not take the initiative, not even to ask, "Weren't you happy with the work I did?" He accepted his payment happily and traveled home to celebrate Pesach with his family.

The hot days of summer were upon them. Berel understood that Heaven was hinting for him to stay home, so he stayed. He returned to his former occupation: idleness. When the others saw him, he had his *Tehillim* in hand or was asleep on his bench. When they could not see him, he studied Torah and served his Creator with all his heart and soul.

His last penny was gone. The 30 rubles he had been given in parting were spent. At first, he borrowed a bit of money, providing as collateral the few meager possessions he owned: the Shabbos candlesticks, one or two ornaments, a pillow, a blanket. Within a matter of weeks his home was bare of anything of value. Nothing was left but the pile of rusted bars and springs that served his family as beds, and which the moneylender had refused to accept as collateral.

A terrible hunger gripped Berel's family. There was no food at all in the house. Everything had been eaten, down to the last bread crumb. Where were they to turn now?

Every day was like Yom Kippur: one long fast. There was nothing to eat or drink, and no one to interest himself in their fate. Who cared about a "*batlan*," a strange creature who knew how to do nothing but mumble chapters of *Tehillim* from morning to night?

Several days of fasting passed in this way. Berel and his wife felt their strengh ebbing away. Berel sat at the table, *Sefer Tehillim* in his enfeebled, trembling hands, and whispered to himself, "If someone would bring me just 3 pennies now, enough to buy a loaf of bread, he would purchase his World To Come in a moment!"

Suddenly, inspiration struck. How could he have forgotten? He had the new *gartel* (silk sash) that he had bought for Pesach. It was worth exactly 3 pennies! With the last of his strength he ran over to the moneylender's house and secretly "hocked" the *gartel* for the pennies, which he used to buy a large loaf. He and his family happily ate bread that night.

And then, again, there was nothing in the house. After two more days of fasting, the family was once again starving. All through the ordeal, Berel had acted in secrecy, believing that everything that happened to him and his family was between him and his Creator. No one must know, lest they disturb the special private bond that existed between Berel and his Creator.

His faith was now being put to the test. No one knew of the horrible conditions in his home. No one in Pshedworz had a clue that a sterling young man was about to perish from hunger.

But faith triumphed!

Several days earlier, one of their neighbor's children had fallen ill. The child's fever rose, his body convulsed, and the doctors prescribed medicines but to no avail. The little boy was hovering at death's door. His mother cried to her husband, "Hurry, run over to 'Berel the *batlan*.' It seems he knows how to say *Tehillim*. Give him a few pennies to say some for our son's recovery!"

"Berel?" the husband repeated in astonishment.

"It can't hurt. Our son is dying!"

The neighbor raced to Berel's house, handed him *chai* (18) coins, equal to about 6 pennies, and asked him, in tears, to recite *Tehillim* on behalf of his little boy. "He's literally on his deathbed," the father said brokenly. Before the dumbfounded Berel could say a word, the father turned and hurried back to his son's side. If he could do nothing else, he would at least be present to say the "*Shema*" at the final moment.

Berel wanted to say *Tehillim* immediately — but one look at his wife's pinched, pale face told him that in a very short while she, too, would be at the point of departing this world.

"It seems to me that saving her life is no less a mitzvah than saying *Tehillim*. Let the reward of that mitzvah stand in place of the *Tehillim*."

Drawing on superhuman reserves of strength, he ran to the bakery and bought a loaf of bread. He brought it home, where the two of them washed their hands and broke their long fast.

After the first *k'zayis*, Berel began to wonder if the little boy had died in the meantime, his blood on their hands. Trembling, he and his wife left their house and took advantage of the night's darkness to stand beneath their neighbor's window and peek fearfully inside.

To their joy, they did not hear the *"Shema Yisrael"* being recited. There was none of the grief or bustle that accompanies a tragedy. What they did hear was the little boy crying — his first cry in several days. He'd been too weak to utter a sound until then.

They returned home and, with peaceful hearts, resumed their meal. With every bite they took, another small improvement took place in the sick child.

The little boy recovered. From that day on, people began to come to Berel to ask him to pray for them as well. They brought *kvitlach* and small donations, which served to save the family from starvation. Suddenly, the people saw that the *"batlan"* was no idle fellow at all. He had pulled the wool over all of their eyes. In reality, he was a pure and holy soul — a veritable angel from Heaven.

"And why am I telling you all this?" R' Yissachar Ber of Radoshitz asked his student, R' Meir Yehoshua. "Now that you've been appointed to the ranks of Jewish leaders, take these words to heart. Your rabbinical seat has come to you from Heaven, not through men of flesh and blood. Do not flatter anyone, and do not be afraid of anyone. No one is capable of harming you or benefiting you without Heaven's permission. Conduct yourself on an exalted plane, caring only for Heaven's glory and not for any man's!"

Three Gabbaim and Two Decrees

I T WAS HARD TO LIVE AND IT WAS HARD TO DIE, FELT THE JEWS
of Rimanov. As if it were not enough for a family to tragically lose
a loved one, they also had to contend in this difficult hour with the
local *Chevrah Kaddisha*, who took advantage of the bereaved family's
vulnerability and grief to drastically overcharge them for burial plots.
There were a few cases in which extremely poor families were unable
to meet the inflated prices — and others who had the courage to refuse
to pay the high costs.

These few were severely punished. Or rather, their dear departed
ones were punished. The *Chevrah Kaddisha* of Rimanov refused to
bury them, leaving the bodies above ground overnight, or even for two
or three days. Cowed by this desecration, the family members broke
down and submitted to the outrageous prices, just to see their loved
ones buried at last.

This dismal state of affairs formed a shameful noose around the
community's neck. The Jews' distress at the extortion reached astro-
nomical heights, but no one dared say a word. Meanwhile, the burial
society grew even more brazen.

Rimanov was the home of the holy rebbe, R' Menachem Mendel,
who could not bear to witness the terrible extortion. On one occasion,
after a corpse was left unburied for *four* days, the rebbe summoned
the three *gabbaim* of the *Chevrah Kaddisha* — Langeh (tall) Pinny,
Shloimy Wasserstrum, and Mottel's Arik (Aharon, son of Mordechai;
known also as Arik the Red) — and told them bluntly:

"I was going to ask you not to put the financial squeeze on
bereaved families, but I know that you will not heed my request. And
just as it is a mitzvah to say something that will be listened to, it is a
mitzvah not to say something that will not be heard. But this much

I decree: Never, except for extraordinary circumstances, is a body to be left unburied for even one night. It must be buried that same day — on the day of death!"

He spoke with finality. The *gabbaim* ground their teeth, knowing full well that they had just lost the best weapon in their extortion game. They were helpless to counter the rebbe's unequivocal authority. While they were able to remain indifferent to the sight of a penniless and brokenhearted widow, and could coldly raise the price of a burial plot for a young orphan who didn't know which side of a coin was up, in the face of the towering rebbe's implacability they melted. He had taken all the wind out of their sails.

"We promise," they said feebly.

The situation in Rimanov changed — for the short term. There were no more opportunistic demands on mourning families, no more extortion of money with threats of non-burial. The city's dead merited prompt and respectful burial. With their fangs extracted, the *Chevrah Kaddisha* had lost its bite. The price of graves sank, and tranquility was restored.

But a few months of peace came to an abrupt end.

In one of the villages outside of Rimanov, a Jew died. He had rented from the local *poritz* a tavern for the area's gentiles, which he managed, along with a restaurant and small inn for passing Jewish travelers.

His family loaded his coffin into a wagon and brought him to the larger city of Rimanov for burial in its cemetery. When they heard the price the *Chevrah Kaddisha* was demanding, their collective hairs stood on end. Five hundred gold coins — and not a penny less!

This constituted a fortune, a sum well beyond the grasp of anyone in the area. It was a sum to be found only in a rich man's purse.

The *Chevrah Kaddisha* was well aware of this. They also knew that the dead man had been a successful proprietor and doubtless wealthy beyond belief. Like most human beings, they tended to exaggerate.

While the tavern-keeper had not been a pauper, neither had he been a wealthy man.

His widow suspected that an error had been made. The burial society must certainly have meant 50 gold coins. How was it possible for Torah-observant Jews to demand such a grossly inflated price? She was not trying to purchase a whole city for her husband — just a cemetery plot. How could they ask a widow of modest means for a king's ransom? Her husband had been tragically cut down while still a relatively young man, leaving behind young orphans whom she must now feed.

She attempted to set the *Chevrah Kaddisha* straight about their "error." "You meant 50 gold coins, didn't you?"

"No, no," they declared. "We assure you, we meant not a penny under 500 gold coins. Hand over the money, and we will immediately conduct a beautiful funeral for your husband. He will be buried in a respectable plot looking out over Rimanov."

The widow tried desperately to think. "I may be able to get 100, somehow ..."

"Sorry. The price is 500."

She went on thinking out loud. She could ask her rich brother-in-law, Zelig, for a loan on easy terms. "Maybe 200 coins ..."

"Do we look like horse traders to you?" the burial men flared. "There is no bargaining. The price of the grave is 500 gold coins."

In despair, the brokenhearted widow tried for a long time to soften their hearts. It was like talking to stones.

"Mother, let's leave these wicked men," her oldest son — a lad of 15 — said, wiping his reddened eyes with his handkerchief. "We'll bury Father somewhere else."

She agreed. Angrily, she got up and left, with harsh words for the stone-hearted men who had not been prepared to budge an inch for a widow.

The *Chevrah Kaddisha* was taken aback. Taking the body to another city meant leaving it unburied overnight.

They recalled all too clearly the promise R' Menachem Mendel had extracted from their three managing *gabbaim*. Now that promise was about to be blatantly broken. One of the members rushed into the inner room where the *gabbaim* sat, and directed their attention to the stormy argument taking place between the widow and their colleagues in the next room.

"It seems to me," said the man, "that the widow's decision to take the body elsewhere changes the picture entirely. That would mean the burial does not take place until tomorrow — and then we'll be in trouble with the rebbe. We'd better lower the price to make immediate burial possible."

But the *gabbaim*, believing the dead man to have been very wealthy, countered brilliantly: Their promise not to delay burial was relevant only for people who lived in Rimanov proper. As the tavern-keeper came from a nearby village, there was no problem with delaying his burial for a day, or even two.

The *gabbaim* were certain that no one in Rimanov would enter into battle for a family of strangers from an outlying village.

They were mistaken. The incident grew wings and spread through Rimanov. Everywhere the story was heard, a storm erupted. It was all the people talked about. Three things bothered them: First, the breaking of the promise to the Rimanover rebbe; second, the blatant disrespect for the dead; and third, the terrible treatment toward the departed man's family, doubling the tragedy they had already suffered.

So widespread was the talk that the story finally reached the rebbe's ears. He sent his *gabbai*, R' Hershele, to summon the three *gabbaim* to him at once. But the three, anticipating the rebbe's forceful reaction, had prudently left town before the summons came.

Night fell. The dead man lay unburied.

The next morning, the rebbe stated his decree regarding the three errant *gabbaim*:

"They will not merit burial in Rimanov, their native city, but will be buried elsewhere. And none of the three will be buried until three days after their deaths."

Many years passed. People's memories grew hazy, and they forgot the rebbe's words. But Heaven remembered.

Langeh Pinny's sons married women from Hungary and moved to that country. An elderly man now, Pinny traveled to Hungary to visit his offspring. While still on foreign soil, he suddenly fell mortally ill. On his deathbed, he adjured his sons solemnly, "Carry me back to Rimanov and bury me near my fathers."

Several days later, the *gabbai* died.

His sons loaded the coffin onto a wagon, hitched up their horses, and set off at a rapid clip on the road to Rimanov. Day and night they rode, until on the second night they glimpsed Rimanov from the high road. At that moment, the horses inexplicably halted.

The wagoneer stroked their necks and urged them to move, but the horses didn't budge.

Angry now, he struck them with his whip, lightly at first and then in a rage. But the horses stood as though riveted to the spot.

"Don't worry," the driver reassured the anxious family. "I'll switch these horses for a more manageable team." He went at once to find more tractable horses, and returned a short time later leading a powerful-looking pair. The switch was made.

But — wonder of wonders — no sooner were the new horses (which had trotted to the spot willingly enough) harnessed to the coffin-bearing wagon, than they, too, became paralyzed!

Not even the most sluggish intellect could remain unmoved at this turn of events. The *gabbai's* sons suddenly remembered the rebbe's words: "They will not merit burial in Rimanov, their native city, but will be buried elsewhere. And none of the three will be buried until three days after their deaths."

The rebbe's decree was coming to pass before their very eyes. It was futile to try to press on for Rimanov; it was as though an impenetrable partition stood between Pinny and the city of his birth. The sons conferred, and reached a decision: If their father was to be buried in a strange place, better that he be buried near his own children.

The wagoneer harnessed his own horses to the wagon once more, and turned them around so that they faced the direction from which they had come. Suddenly, the horses' legs were working again. Fleet as deer they flew down the road until, less than 24 hours later, they reached the Hungarian city from which they had started. There, Pinny was buried — a full three days after his death.

When Shloimy Wasserstrum heard what had befallen his old friend Pinny, his heart sank like a stone. All these years, he had been waiting, hoping that their long-ago sins would be forgiven and forgotten. Now he stood witness to the harshness of the judgment.

Shloimy thought about it for several days, and concluded that he would not merit being buried in Rimanov. What the rebbe had promised would come true — somehow. Even if Shloimy were to nail himself to his home, a wind would come and bear him off like a feather to another city.

"Why suffer," he asked himself, "when I can do things in a civilized manner? Instead of torturing myself with worry and doubt, and waiting with folded hands for the decree to come true, I can plan ahead."

He bought a ticket and set sail for Eretz Yisrael. "Let's do this right," he explained to his wife. "I won't be able to be buried here in Rimanov under any circumstances. Let us go up to the Holy Land. Then, perhaps, the other part of the decree will be forgiven, and I will merit being buried without delay."

The trip was wonderful. The sea was smooth as glass beneath a smiling sun. Every morning, Shloimy sat comfortably on the upper deck, enjoying the pleasant salt air.

When the captain announced to all the passengers that they would be weighing anchor in the port of Yaffo in just three days, Shloimy's heart gave a sudden leap. A cold sweat popped out on his brow. Feeling ill, he clawed at his aching chest. The sailors hastened over and poured cold water on his face, to no avail. Within minutes, Shloimy had passed on to a better world.

The captain wished to follow seagoing custom from time immemorial and to toss the body over the ship's side. This was to prevent any of the other passengers from catching a possibly contagious disease. But Shloimy's sons set up a loud protest, explaining to the captain the concept of a Jewish burial. They talked and pleaded and poured out their hearts. "How can you do something like this to us, a bereaved family that has just lost a loved one?"

The same words that had been uttered repeatedly by distraught mourners back in Rimanov were heard again now, from the mouths of the sons of the man who had caused those mourners so much suffering ...

In the end, after many tears had been shed and hearts gnawed with bitterness — and after a good deal of money in bribes had changed hands — the captain agreed to allow the body to be stored in the cargo area down below, among the mice and other rodents, until they made port.

Shloimy Wasserstrum was buried in the soil of Eretz Yisrael three days after his death — exactly as the rebbe had decreed.

The third *gabbai*, Mottel's Arik — also known as Arik the Red because of the color of his hair — had been endowed with a great deal of brazenness and chutzpah, which had greatly influenced his colleagues in their heartless behavior. He had been the agitator, ever inciting them to new heights of sin.

Arik heard what had happened to his two friends, but his stony heart did not budge. "That won't happen to me," he said confidently. "I'm going to plant myself right here in Rimanov. Not even a herd of elephants will be able to drag me out."

He was as good as his word. When several of his grandchildren married in other cities, he refused to leave Rimanov to attend the weddings. He feared that he had only to step out of his native city for the situation to become completely out of control ...

Arik lived long years, until his changing beard and hair earned him the nickname Arik the White. The holy rebbe had passed on many years before, his words all but forgotten. As Arik grew more feeble, the hope remained burning inside him that he would be buried in Rimanov, near his fathers. This hope rested on the fact that he was approaching the end of his life and the city had not yet cast him out.

Arik fell into his final illness. He left this world in the manner of *tzaddikim*, on a wintry Erev Shabbos, very near candlelighting time. "Had he died just half an hour earlier, there would have been time to bury him before Shabbos," his colleagues in the new *Chevrah Kaddisha* of Rimanov said in distress. "But it's too late now."

The third *gabbai's* funeral was postponed until Sunday morning.

The sky was deeply overcast, and the wailing wind ushered in a powerful blizzard. Despite the bad weather, a large crowd gathered near Arik's home on Sunday morning to accompany him to the cemetery. On reaching it, they discovered to their dismay that the grave had not yet been dug.

"What's going on?" the burial society members fumed at the gravediggers. "Why haven't you dug the grave by now?"

"What can we do?" they shrugged. They pointed to the plot. "The frozen ground is hard as a rock."

"We've never heard of such a thing! Is this the first grave that's ever been dug in Rimanov?"

Taking up sharp, metal spades, all the members of the *Chevrah Kaddisha* threw their weight into the task. But the ground seemed obstinately unyielding. Even straining with all their might, they managed to move only a few grains of earth.

For seven long hours they toiled, while the body lay on the ground in humiliation. Most of those who had accompanied the body to the cemetery soon fled the icy winds and heavy snows for their own warm homes. Only a handful of family members and the members of the Burial Society remained in place, digging and digging until they managed to carve out a narrow hole in the ground.

The grave was small, but there was no other option. They took up the body and approached the hole.

To their shock, the discarded earth began to roll in from the sides, back into the hole. Within moments the grave was closed up as if it had never been dug!

Once again, the dead body was placed aside. The digging recommenced. The work was easier now, because the soil had already been dug up once. However, for each spadeful they lifted up, two more rolled back in. They would lift the earth up the sides of the grave — only to see it fall back inside. Again and again this occurred, until the diggers finally understood that Heaven itself was battling their progress. It was nearing nightfall, and still the dead man remained unburied.

At that moment, an elderly member of the *Chevrah Kaddisha* slapped his forehead with a heavy sigh. "*Oy*, how great are the rebbe's words. See how they come true!" And he proceeded to tell his younger colleagues and the dead man's family members, who had forgotten the incident, about R' Menachem Mendel of Rimanov's awful decree on the three *gabbaim*.

Arik's sons ran to R' Menachem Mendel's successor, the holy R' Tzvi Hirsch of Rimanov, and told him what had occurred. They pleaded with him to lift the longstanding decree.

R' Tzvi Hirsch, aged and compassionate, heeded the sons' words. He sent his helper to the cemetery, to stand at the former rebbe's grave and to say the following:

"I come here in the name of your student and successor, R' Tzvi Hirsch, may he live and be well, who is too feeble to come in person. The rebbe asks Your Honor to take pity on the dignity and honor of the departed *gabbai's* family, and on the health of the *Chevrah Kaddisha*, who have been toiling unsuccessfully since morning to bury the dead. Your Honor's decree was '*middah k'neged middah* — measure for measure.' Just as they postponed the burial of others, so they, too, would have their own burials postponed. But please, have mercy on the men of the *Chevrah Kaddisha*, who are at the end of their strength. To take the body for burial in another city is impossible now, as the roads are impassable due to snow and mud. Please, remove the decree so that this man may be buried in Rimanov."

No sooner had the rebbe's representative left R' Menachem Mendel's graveside than he heard a surprised shout from the diggers: "The earth is soft!"

The rebellious soil stopped rolling inward to the grave. The frozen ground responded suddenly to the spades. The earth opened its mouth to receive the aged *gabbai's* mortal remains — just minutes before sunset.

It was exactly three full days from the moment of the *gabbai's* death.

On a Deserted Island

THE *TZADDIK,* R' PINCHAS OF KORITZ, KEPT TEN MEN (DUBBED the "ten *batlanim*" by some of the townsfolk) learning day and night in his *beis midrash.* With no other source of livelihood, their support fell on the rebbe's shoulders. Each Friday, he would give the head of the *chaburah,* R' Yaakov, the sum of 10 rubles, which R' Yaakov divided among the group. R' Yaakov Danan was an outstanding *talmid chacham* and renowned for his piety. R' Pinchas relied on him implicitly, and entrusted him with important missions, as we shall see in the following story.

One week, as R' Yaakov counted the money, he found to his surprise that there were only 9 rubles instead of the usual 10. He wished to return to the rebbe's room to point out the error, but R' Pinchas' door was closed. His awe toward his rebbe did not permit him to knock.

The rebbe had given him only 9 rubles, and they belonged to his companions. Not to him! Naturally, he would not deprive one of them and take the money for himself. Faithful treasurer, he distributed the 9 rubles, leaving himself without a penny in hand with which to purchase the Shabbos necessities. So great was his distress and that of his family, that the holy day seemed almost like an ordinary one.

He wanted to share his pain with his rebbe, but R' Pinchas' door was open to him only once each week.

On the following Friday, the rebbe handed R' Yaakov the money hastily, and just as quickly dismissed him. It seemed to R' Yaakov, as he handled the slightly diminished purse, that things were once again not as they should be. He had already left the rebbe's room when he counted the coins. To his anguish, he found again only 9 rubles. The door was closed firmly behind him.

Now he knew with certainty that this was no oversight. The rebbe had deliberately given him 1 ruble less, both this week and last. With no other option open to him, R' Yaakov went to his humble home, fetched his *shtreimel*, and pawned it for 1 ruble, which he used to buy food for Shabbos. When the rebbe caught sight of him without his *shtreimel* on Shabbos, he would doubtless ask what had happened, and R' Yaakov would explain.

The rebbe saw, but did not ask.

On the third Friday, as well, the packet contained only 9 rubles. Even as he handed over the money, R' Pinchas was already ushering R' Yaakov out the door, which he hastened to close behind him.

R' Yaakov had no choice now but to pawn his Shabbos *kapote*. This time, he was sure, when the rebbe saw him wearing his weekday clothes, he would certainly ask for an explanation. To his distress, the rebbe avoided him completely, and his unusual garb raised no questions.

"Next Friday," R' Yaakov resolved, "I won't leave until the rebbe has heard what I have to say. Perhaps he will explain the whole matter to me then."

The following Friday, however, the rebbe once again gave him 9 rubles and immediately dismissed him. There was no chance for R' Yaakov to utter a word. His protests fell on a closed door.

He was now in truly dire straits. He had nothing with which to feed his hungry family. Moreover, he was deeply distressed by his rebbe's coolness toward him.

The matter soon became widely known. News of a seeming rift between the rebbe and R' Yaakov spread through the city. The proof: R' Yaakov was not even being paid his salary.

On Sunday, Zelig the flour merchant approached him. He owned a giant flour mill which produced regular flour as well as semolina, bran, and rye.

"R' Yaakov," Zelig said, "in town, you're known as R' Yaakov 'the *batlan*' (useless fellow), but I believe you're no *batlan* at all. I have a proposal you won't be able to refuse. As you know, Thursday here in Koritz is market day. On Wednesday, you will receive a sack of flour from me, on credit. On Thursday you sell it, bit by bit. I guarantee you'll make a bigger profit than the ruble you once received from the rebbe each week."

R' Yaakov was bereft of alternatives. Though enormously distressed at the prospect, he was forced to accept Zelig's proposal. He sold the sack of flour and made a profit of 2 rubles. On the following Wednesday, he took five sacks of flour from Zelig, and made 10 rubles. In this way his business grew, week by week, until one day Zelig came to him and declared, "I was right: You're no *batlan*. Why should you stand in the marketplace like a beggar? I'll open a shop on the main street, and you'll conduct an honorable business there."

The plan was put into action. R' Yaakov was extraordinarily successful at the business endeavor. His profits grew daily. Eventually he abandoned the flour business and opened a large general store. In the swirl of his activities, he stopped his long-established practice of coming to R' Pinchas every Friday, to accept the 9 rubles to be apportioned among his fellow "*batlanim.*"

In a nearby village lived the local nobleman and landowner, Duke Vasili Mazovitzki. One morning, the Duke was seized with a powerful desire to drink a jug of orange juice. As his own storehouses were completely bereft of oranges at the moment, he sent his steward to nearby Koritz to buy a crate of them.

The moment the oranges arrived, the Duke's servants were quick to squeeze them. Humbly, they presented the jug to their impatient master. He took one sip, then spat the juice out with a grimace. "Bitter as death!"

He raised his voice. "Paul!" His steward came running. "Why did you buy bitter oranges?"

Paul turned crimson. "T-t-the o-o-o-r-r-ranges w-w-w-were b-b-b-bitter?" he stammered.

This inflamed the Duke further. "Would you like me to force you to drink this entire jugful? Go back to the city and bring me some sweet, ripe oranges!"

"But there's no other store in town that sells oranges, sir."

"Are you sure? I'll send someone to check. If it turns out you're lying, the birds will be pecking at your hanging corpse!"

Paul shook like a leaf. "Th-th-there is one other store, sir. B-b-b-but it belongs to a Jew."

"What difference does that make? You can buy the oranges from a demon for all I care. Just bring me some sweet oranges!"

Paul returned to the city and entered R' Yaakov's general store, where he purchased a crate of oranges.

By the Duke's order, the crate was carried immediately to his room. He marveled at their beauty and took even greater pleasure in drinking their juice. So taken was he by their delicious taste that, on one of his next visits to town, he paid a visit to R' Yaakov's store. There, he was struck by the way business was conducted, as well as by the store's neat, well-organized look. "From now on, all the needs of my estate will be supplied from this store alone!" he declared to his steward.

If R' Yaakov had been considered a prosperous man before, now that the Duke had begun to patronize his store he became one of the city's wealthiest citizens. The Duke's patronage trebled and quadrupled the profits of his general store.

Before long, R' Yaakov was summoned to the Duke's mansion. The Duke had a startling proposal for the Jew. He offered R' Yaakov the job of managing his estate, overseeing all the Duke's considerable property: eight medium-sized villages in the area apart from the city of Koritz, and dozens of forests. "I haven't met a single person as clever as you, Yaakov," Duke Vasili said warmly. "I'd like you in charge of all my businesses."

"What about my store?" R' Yaakov asked.

"Your family can run the general store."

R' Yaakov wanted to refuse the offer. It would mean leaving his family for long periods of time, and staying on the Duke's estate. But, giving it a second thought, he changed his mind. This position was likely to hugely increase his worth. Besides, it was rather dangerous to refuse one of the Duke's proposals. R' Yaakov accepted the job.

Before long, R' Yaakov was transformed into one of the country's elite. His management of the Duke's vast estate brought other side businesses in its wake, all of which added considerably to R' Yaakov's personal financial worth.

One day, they were going over the estate's weekly accounts when the Duke abruptly changed the topic.

"I want to tell you something," the Duke confided. "When I plucked you out of your general store and brought you here, it was not for lack of qualified men. No, I had a different purpose in mind for you. What I saw in you that others lack is an outstanding loyalty and faithfulness. In the short time that you've been with me, you've passed through many a test and emerged with flying colors. I see now that none of my other men is your equal. I cannot trust anyone but you."

"Trust anyone — with what?" a startled R' Yaakov inquired.

The Duke smiled. "I am going to answer your question," he said.

✦

"I am growing old, and I have no sons. As my death draws closer, it has been my fear — my terror — that I shall leave no memory of myself behind in the world. I will be buried in a grave and forgotten! Then, after some thought, I came up with a brilliant idea. I shall have a statue erected in the center of town — a statue bearing my face! Talented sculptors will duplicate my image in gold and diamonds, and my memory will thus be preserved for hundreds of years.

"For several years now, I have had well-known artists here on my estate, all of them laboring on this one great task — to sculpt a perfect replica of me. But all their efforts have been in vain. The statue is lifeless. It lacks a soul. I discussed this with the artists, who explained that the job requires an extremely delicate hand, and that only the greatest experts can accomplish it. I launched a thorough investigation to find the man who might be able to complete my sculpture, and discovered that there is a deaf artist in India whose entire collection of work is a reflection of this type of delicate hand. This artist does not wish to travel here for all the money in the world. I must send the statue to him, in India.

"I've been searching for a reliable person who will agree to bring the sculpture to India — and I think I've found him. Say 'yes,' and I'll shower you with gold. All the wealth I have is worth nothing, as long as the statue remains incomplete."

R' Yaakov trembled. Such a long trip was not at all to his liking. He had no desire to board a ship and ride the waves on an endless journey. He had a fine life here, and no wish to leave it.

But how could he refuse the Duke, especially after all the Duke had done for him?

"Give me three days' time to think it over and consult with my family," he requested after some consideration.

"Very well." The Duke's thoughtful gaze scanned R' Yaakov's face, as though asking himself if he had truly found the faithful retainer he had been seeking.

⌒⌒

After much deliberation, R' Yaakov's family agreed that the one man who could provide the answer to R' Yaakov's question was his rebbe, R' Pinchas of Koritz.

R' Yaakov promptly set off for the rebbe's house.

The veteran *gabbaim* greeted him warmly, as an old friend. To his dismay, however, they informed him that the rebbe was closeted in his room, with instructions not to let anyone in to see him.

R' Yaakov was disappointed. This was strange behavior for a rebbe whose door had never been closed to anyone. He returned home, and came back to the rebbe's house on the following day, at a different time. Again, he found the door closed to him. For three days he returned, but he never succeeded in seeing the rebbe. Apparently, his helpers were deliberately denying him entry.

His time was nearly up. Soon he must present himself to the Duke with his answer. Finally, he went to the rebbetzin and gave her a note in which he wrote down his pressing question, along with 200 rubles in cash. "Please," he pleaded urgently, "when the rebbe's door opens, give him this note and the gift."

The rebbetzin was happy. Her home was poverty-stricken; 200 rubles could accomplish quite a lot. But when the rebbe opened his door a short time after R' Yaakov left, she was taken aback by his reaction to the money. The rebbe took the purse and hid it somewhere, refusing to enjoy a single ruble.

R' Yaakov packed his things, went to the Duke's mansion, and gave him his positive answer. He would go.

A wide smile adorned the Duke's face. His eyes sparkled with joy as he called, "Paul, Antony! Come here!"

His two top servants were before him in a twinkling.

"Yaakov has agreed to make the trip," the Duke announced, making no attempt to conceal his happiness. "Bring him the boxes."

The servants disappeared. When they returned, they bore two boxes, one of which was well bound with dozens of ropes.

"Listen carefully," the Duke said in a low voice. "The sculpture is in the bound box. The other box contains enough money, and more, for your trip and all your expenses until your safe return. You must exert extreme vigilance to see that no one steals the money — and certainly not my precious sculpture. Your life is worthless if anything happens to it."

A few days later, R' Yaakov boarded a ship bound for India.

His constant vigilance over his boxes aroused the greedy captain's suspicion. With his vast experience, he had learned to discern between ordinary passengers and those who were traveling with great wealth. This Jew fell into the second category — and in a big way, judging by the anxious glances he kept casting at the two boxes he had brought with him.

"Look out, Jew," he chuckled to himself. "I'll be finding a way to transfer your money soon enough."

They sailed peacefully for several days, plowing through uniformly blue seas. On the fourth day, the ship docked at a small island.

"We'll be stopping here briefly," the sailors announced. "Passengers may disembark and walk onto the island to stretch their legs."

Before the passengers left, they were given the signal: Three blasts of the ship's whistle would tell them that it was time to board ship again. R' Yaakov alone was given a different message: "When you hear four blasts, hurry back"

R' Yaakov strolled on the island, feasting his eyes on the stunning scenery as he waited for the sound of the ship's blasts. Two hours after he had gone ashore, he heard three blasts of the ship's horn. "They said four," he told himself. "This signal must be for the sailors' use. We're not sailing yet."

He continued his stroll. The sun began to sink in the west. "What's this?" he wondered in alarm. "Why haven't the four blasts sounded?"

He returned to the pier — to find the ship gone! Too late, he understood how he had been tricked. The captain had fixed his sights on R' Yaakov's precious boxes. He was lost! Bitter tears coursed down his cheeks. He was abandoned, a prey for any wild animals that might prowl this island ...

In time, he pulled himself together. Everything that Hashem does is for the good. His eye fell on a small case lying on the sand. Approaching it, his heart lightened. His *tallis* and *tefillin* were inside. The captain had been greedy for his money — but he had left behind R' Yaakov's precious heritage when he threw the case over the side.

⌒∞⌒

R' Yaakov lived on that deserted island for six months, alone with his Creator. During that time, he experienced a tremendous spiritual awakening. He found trees bearing sweet pears, and a cold, clear brook running alongside them. Each time he assuaged his hunger with the pears and slaked his thirst with the clean, good-tasting water, he recited the blessings with enormous fervor, sensing Hashem's closeness, and His guiding Hand even in this forsaken place.

By the end of half a year, he was wild-looking and thin as a whip. His hair had grown long and his clothes were ripped and stained. But his spirit did not desert him. And then, one day, he heard the blast of a ship's horn! He raced to the shore.

The ship's passengers were taken aback at his unkempt appearance. However, once they listened to his explanation and realized that he was a man of culture, they were happy to take him on board with them. Before many days had passed, he was standing once again on his native soil. Joining a band of beggars, he approached the city of Koritz.

He was terrified. What would the Duke do when he heard that the statue had been lost?

Discreetly, he asked about the Duke — and was told, to his relief, that the Duke had died several weeks earlier. A heavy stone rolled off R' Yaakov's heart.

Almost at once, the stone was back in place. There was more news: It seemed that R' Yaakov's own home, and all his wealth, had gone up in flames when a fire had burned the house down to its foundations.

Thankfully, his family was unhurt. But they were destitute now, living on other people's charity.

Now R' Yaakov understood the saying of *Chazal*: "One must bless Hashem for the [seemingly] bad things that happen to him, the same way that he blesses Hashem for the [obviously] good things that happen to him." He had just heard two pieces of news, one of them good, and the other bad indeed ...

He passed through the city gates. He did not make for his scorched home, nor for the humble shack in which his wife and children now dwelled. First of all, he made his way to the home of his rebbe, R' Pinchas of Koritz.

He found the table in the rebbe's house set with all manner of delicacies. The members of the household told R' Yaakov that the rebbe had issued instructions, a short time earlier, for a feast to be prepared for an important guest who was on his way.

When R' Yaakov saw his rebbe, he burst into tears. He wept a long time. "Look what has happened to me since the day the rebbe stopped paying me my regular salary!"

The rebbe greeted him with powerful and open affection. He comforted R' Yaakov and soothed him. When the tears had dried up, R' Pinchas said, "Tell me, how many *berachos* did you recite on that deserted island?"

"Very many *berachos*," replied R' Yaakov.

"Did you say them with concentration and fear of Heaven? Did you have the holy Names in mind?" the rebbe pressed.

Shaken, R' Yaakov answered, "Yes. With very great concentration and intent."

R' Pinchas smiled. "Now I can reveal what lies behind all this. A long time ago, Heaven revealed to me that a forlorn soul has lived on that deserted island for hundreds of years, awaiting its *tikkun*, correction. That soul experienced enormous pain as it waited for a Jew to come along and redeem it from its prison. There was no other way to do this than to have a Jew come and recite the *Birchos HaNehenin* (blessings before and after eating) with the right intentions.

"I conducted many fasts and other ordeals for the sake of that soul, but succeeded only to this degree: A person's messenger is like the person himself, so there was no need for me to travel there myself. I could send a representative in my place. And because you are a fine and upright man, R' Yaakov, I chose you to travel to that island and help that suffering soul. No one but you could have done it.

"But, had I revealed my purpose to you, would you have agreed to go through everything you did — poverty and riches, the voyage and the long stay on that island? Most certainly not! Therefore, I had no choice but to act as I did."

R' Pinchas stood up, went over to a corner, and picked up a dusty purse. "Now, here is the 200 rubles that you gave my wife. I knew you would need every bit of it, so I never touched the money. Take it, and use it to marry off your daughter, who has come of age. Tomorrow, return to my *beis midrash* and join the nine other '*batlanim*' waiting there for you. Return to your learning as before, and I will care for all your needs."

Judging With Favor

I N HIS TIME, THE HOLY MAGGID, R' AVRAHAM OF TRISK, WAS considered the rebbe's rebbe in Poland. He was one of eight famous brothers, sons of the holy R' Mordechai of Chernobyl. R' Avraham of Trisk was a wondrous man, utterly detached from this world. It was said that he served as a living example of the fact that a person can survive in this world without eating. He would fast from Shabbos to Shabbos, and on Friday night, after a week-long fast, would crumble up a piece of challah and place just a few crumbs in his mouth. When the fish was served, he would eat just the eye, after which he would drink a small cup of milk. This was the way he ate all three Shabbos meals — an eating that was no eating, but which armed him with the strength to fast through the following week.

Even in later years, when he no longer had the strength to fast from Shabbos to Shabbos, he would fast for most of each day, and only in the evening drink a bit of hot water mixed with milk.

This behavior earned him a reputation as a holy man. Taken together with his awesome wisdom, he was a magnet for swarms of Jews from every corner of Poland and Russia. Among the thousands who came to see him were also many of the generation's rebbes.

When the *gaon* R' Aryeh Mordechai Rabinowitz, great-grandson of the Yid HaKadosh and grandson of R' Yehoshua Asher of Parisov, went to live in Eretz Yisrael together with his son, R' Yehoshua Asher Rabinowitz, they traveled to many rebbes, taking their leave. In due course they arrived in Trisk, eager to receive the holy Maggid's blessing for their journey.

The moment they entered the town, they sensed something strange in the atmosphere. Though it was an ordinary weekday, men, women, and children were streaming toward the *beis midrash* from every direction. When stopped and questioned, several people hurriedly told the newcomers that something very unusual was about to happen in the *beis midrash* — something inexplicable. Their faces filled with curiosity, the townspeople made no attempt to conceal their eagerness to be present at this rare occurrence. Though the travelers, father and son, had no idea what was happening, they decided to hasten to the *beis midrash* as well.

Hundreds of Jews crowded into the big shul, whose every part, including the women's section, was filled to absolute capacity. And yet, no one — not even the children — uttered a word of complaint. Everyone waited in silence.

Two men entered the shul and walked up to the *bimah* in its center. They were dressed in the clothes of well-to-do gentlemen and bore the air of those who are accustomed to being served. Their faces, however, were troubled, and their eyes, normally so tranquil, expressed terrible pain.

The two stood at the *bimah*. One of them gazed out fearfully over the huge throng. For a prolonged moment he stood frozen in place, as though struck with paralysis. Finally, he managed to overcome the stage fright that had gripped him at the sight of the enormous crowd waiting tensely for him to speak.

⚜

Yehoshua Lubliner and Pesach Moshe had been the best of friends from their childhood. When they grew up and married, they became business partners as well. Fortune smiled on them and they grew rich, and then richer.

On their most recent trip to the big market at Leipzig, they planned, as usual, to buy quality goods at cheap prices, and to sell those goods in other cities at a handsome profit. But even "cheap goods" cost a great deal of money when the quantities in question are very large. Taking with them a large sackful of cash, the two set out for Leipzig.

As they rode along in their coach, nibbling on tasty snacks and enjoying the pleasant scenery, they were suddenly shocked by an agonizing spectacle. A Jew was dragging himself painfully along the side of the road. Sweat poured down from his face as he lugged a heavy sack that hung from one shoulder. Stopping their coach, the businessmen called out, "*Reb Yid*, why are you walking on foot?"

The man set down his sack. Breathing heavily, he replied, "It's nice of you rich folk, riding in a comfortable coach, to stop for a poor man like me."

The travelers exchanged a glance. Pesach Moshe, generally the spokesman of the pair, said with a smile, "So, will you tell us why?"

"I'm on my way home, after a good few years working as a *melamed* (private tutor) in the home of a local wealthy family. I'm trying to save money by traveling on foot."

"What is your destination?"

"Leipzig."

"Climb on up," Pesach Moshe invited cordially. "We're going there ourselves."

"Bless you!" Taking a firm grip on his sack, the man clambered aboard the coach.

The trip lasted several days. On Friday afternoon, they stopped at a town just off the highway, and began to prepare themselves for Shabbos.

The rich men did not forget their companion. This Shabbos, they informed him, his expenses were on them. The *melamed* thanked them emotionally, and hastened to make his own Shabbos preparations.

Not for a moment did the two entrepreneurs regret having invited the poor Jew to join them. All through the trip he had been learning quietly, and throughout Shabbos he proved a veritable treasure-house of Torah thought. Whether he was speaking of the weekly Torah portion, *Midrash*, halachah, or *pilpul*, the *melamed's* words sparkled like gems.

As soon as Shabbos was over, the travelers were in a hurry to resume their journey. But before they went, being businessmen who knew the value of money, they stopped to count theirs. To their shock and dismay, they found a bundle of 200 coins missing!

Again and again they re-counted the coins, but the missing bundle did not appear. It was as though it had sprouted legs and simply walked off. They wrinkled their brows, trying to solve the mystery. Suddenly, it occurred to Yehoshua Lubliner that the bundle's "legs" might well be none other than the *melamed's* hands. He voiced his suspicion to Pesach Moshe.

"The *melamed* — a thief?" Pesach Moshe said incredulously. "Impossible! We saw this Shabbos what a big *talmid chacham* he is."

"It says '*kabdeihu v'chashdeihu* — honor him and suspect him.' Up till now, we've honored him. Now we must suspect him as well. Come on, let's go have a talk with the fellow."

In a flash, Yehoshua Lubliner was on his way to the *melamed's* room. He found the *melamed* reciting the prayer of "*V'yitein lecha*" from a *siddur*.

"My friend, I see that you're saying '*V'yitein lecha* — and it shall be given to you.' Perhaps you've already given to yourself? Did you by any chance covet a certain bundle among our many bundles?" Yehoshua Lubliner spoke sternly. "Perhaps you thought of fulfilling the saying, 'One benefits, while the other doesn't lose'? In that case, I'm here to tell you that you must fulfill the positive commandment of returning that which was stolen!"

The *melamed* turned pale with shock. "I did not touch anything that is not mine."

He was denying it, Yehoshua thought. That was to be expected. Had they really thought he would confess so easily? On the other hand, maybe he was telling the truth. They might have cast their suspicions on an innocent man. Apologizing for his accusations, he resolved to continue the search for the bundle. They would seek it in every possible place.

The two friends looked in every suitcase. They upended every sack. They ran their hands along the coach's sides, and came up empty-handed. The bundle of 200 gold coins had disappeared as though swallowed up by the earth itself.

Unless ... unless it had been the *melamed* who had "swallowed" it.

Seeing that the missing money was not to be found anywhere, the heavy cloud of their suspicion fell once again on the head of their fellow traveler. If a lie has no feet to stand on, neither has a bundle of cash. If the money was gone, it was doubtless to be found among the *melamed's* belongings. Pesach Moshe approached him and said quietly, "If you didn't touch anything and are a perfect *tzaddik*, you certainly will not mind if the two of us conduct a search of your clothing and pockets."

"You can search wherever you like," replied the *melamed*. "I guarantee, you will find nothing. I have never touched a penny that is not mine."

"Take off your coat," Yehoshua Lubliner ordered.

Without a word, the *melamed* obeyed.

Yehoshua ran his hands carefully up and down the coat. At first, he felt nothing but cloth. When he reached the hem, however, his fingers came upon something fat and bumpy.

"I've found something!" he cried. He continued to finger the coat, with his friend Pesach Moshe helping him. They found a thick bundle hidden among the folds. It had been sewn into the hem with red thread, and was well-wrapped in the extra cloth that tailors tended to leave at the bottom of a garment in case it required lengthening in the future. The *melamed*, apparently, needed the big hem not in order to make the coat last longer, but in order to conceal his ill-gotten gains. Pesach Moshe and Yehoshua Lubliner counted the money: 200 gold coins!

It was the exact number of coins in their missing bundle. In their fury, they began to beat the *melamed* mercilessly. The poor man kept crying, "I didn't steal your money! I never took a thing! The money is mine!"

In their anger, it never occurred to the pair to judge the *melamed l'chaf zechus* — in a favorable light. They did not stop to think that perhaps they were mistaken and were accusing an innocent man. They continued to beat him, shouting, "Thief! Why did you take our money?"

The noise brought the innkeeper's wife running. "Was the thread used to sew the bundle red?" she inquired.

"Yes!"

"Then he is certainly the thief," she stated. "Now I understand. Yesterday, on Erev Shabbos, he came to me and asked for some red thread with which to sew his clothes. He must have wanted the thread to sew the stolen bundle into the hem of his coat!"

This information kindled the rich men's rage to a fever pitch. They redoubled their blows, striking the *melamed* cruelly and repeatedly as they screamed, "Wicked one! Ungrateful wretch! Is this the thanks you give for the favor we did you? Taking money that is not yours — and then compounding the sin by denying your guilt?"

At last, they calmed down. Taking their bags and bundles, they left the inn. The poor, beaten *melamed* was left behind in the inn, his heart filled with grief at the suspicion that had been cast on him. He had nothing now; the earnings of several years' work were lost. And, on top of everything else, his entire body was one enormous bruise from the painful blows he had sustained.

The next day, the partners were on their way when the sound of hoofbeats reached their ears. A voice called out to them to halt. Turning, they found the postal wagon pursuing them.

They pulled up at once. Perhaps something had happened at home, and their families had sent the news to them. Would it be happy news or, heaven forbid, the opposite? And, if the latter were the case, would the problem be a financial one or — heaven forbid — sickness in the family?

If the postal wagon had taken the trouble to find them on the high road, they certainly would stop and wait to hear what it was all about.

The driver approached them. "Is there anyone here by the name of Yehoshua Lubliner?"

"It is I," Yehoshua replied.

The postal driver handed him a telegram from his wife:

"Yehoshua, a few hours before you set out, I needed a large sum of money. I took a bundle of 200 coins from you. When you count your money, don't be upset when you find one bundle missing."

The hands holding the telegram began to shake. "*Oy! Oy!*" Yehoshua screamed pitifully. "We suspected an innocent man!"

"What happened?" Pesach Moshe demanded.

Without a word, his friend showed him the telegram.

Pesach Moshe's face turned white.

They had beaten an innocent man. He had spoken the truth when he had claimed that the money was his — money that he had worked long years to earn. In their blindness, they had not believed him. They had broken his bones and taken his money. Who knew what state he was in now?

Covered in shame, they made all possible haste back to the inn where they had left the poor *melamed*. They were determined not only to restore his money, but to add on any amount of additional compensation — all for the sake of his forgiveness for the beating, and the disgrace they had heaped on his head.

On their arrival, they were told that the *melamed* had been grievously injured. Of a fragile constitution even before the beating, the heavy blows had brought him to death's door. The rich men summoned a doctor at once, promising him a fortune in gold if only he would restore the *melamed* to health.

The doctor shook his head sorrowfully. "He's too badly hurt. It's only a matter of hours now."

Indeed, within only a few hours, the *melamed* gave up his suffering soul.

When they saw what they had done, the friends' hearts almost stopped beating with the overwhelming force of their pain. How many terrible things they had done! They had suspected an innocent man, beat him mercilessly, scorned and shamed him — and caused his death! They had turned the *melamed's* wife into a widow and his children into orphans. And all because they had not judged him favorably.

Beside themselves with grief and remorse, they decided to go to their rebbe, the Maggid of Trisk, to ask for a way to atone for their terrible crimes.

The penitents wept copiously before the rebbe, begging for an atonement equal to their sins.

"The tremendous pain you are feeling, and the deep remorse you are experiencing in your hearts, are themselves a huge atonement for you. But that's not enough."

He ordered the rich men to support the *melamed's* family in exactly the same measure that they supported their own. And when the time came for the *melamed's* children to marry, the rich men must take care of them as they would take care of their own children.

"The second atonement," the rebbe continued, "is this: You must go into exile for a full year. Exile, our Sages have taught, atones for sin."

The Maggid of Trisk then added, "There is a third atonement, as well. Gather together everyone in Trisk, young and old, in the big shul, and confess what you've done before them all. Everyone will then learn a lesson about how important it is to judge our fellow man favorably. Even when the suspicion seems almost certain, as in your case, there is always room to judge favorably. The humiliation you will undergo in telling the story in front of the huge crowd will serve as a correction for your soul and an atonement for your sin."

When the tale was finished, there was an aura of trembling and awe in the crowded shul. Everyone present was able to witness the dire consequences of judging others in an unfavorable light. Innocent blood had been shed, and an entire family left bereft and orphaned. One and all, they learned the crucial lesson: the absolute imperative of always judging one's fellow man favorably.

[Source: HaGaon R' Fischel Rabinowitz, *Shlita*, Rosh Yeshivah of Yeshivas Tiferes Yisrael of Rizhin, and a member of the *Moetzes Gedolei HaTorah*.]

DECEPTION

A N EPIDEMIC HAD ERUPTED IN LODZ, A LARGE INDUSTRIAL city in Poland. Hundreds of people were felled as the sickness raged through the city. There was no visible source of the plague, and no one to tell them its source. The city council summoned prestigious doctors and consulted with them about how to curtail the epidemic's deadly sweep.

The doctors pointed out the lack of hygienic conditions in the city. The sickness was spreading, they claimed, because the city was far too crowded. With houses crammed tightly together, roof touching roof and balcony touching balcony, each building was bursting with residents. Many of these homes belonged to the poorer strata of the population — people who knew nothing of hygiene. Their children scrambled in dirt and filth, spreading germs and disease. In short, explained the learned physicians, conditions in the city were abysmal, and were providing an easy breeding ground for the epidemic.

"So what do we do?" asked the city leaders. "Send away our poorer citizens? That would stand counter to every precept of law and ethics!"

"There's no need to send them away. The sickness will finish them off in any case." This was said by the mayor, a shrewd man. "The question is, what to do about the overcrowding in our city."

Experts sat in conference for long hours, debating the question: How to thin out the population of their city without causing too great an outcry. Finally, one of the expert advisors declared, "We can't change the past. It's the future that concerns us now. We must enact a law prohibiting new people from settling in Lodz from now on."

After further prolonged discussion, the Lodz authorities made the following special announcement in the city:

"From this day forward, no complete family may move to Lodz. This is strictly prohibited by law. Only a family of which some members already live in the city may join their relatives in Lodz. For example, a woman may join her children or her husband, and the opposite. Any head of a household who breaks the law and moves to Lodz with his whole family will be prosecuted to the full extent of the law — including the death penalty — as he will thereby be endangering the tens of thousands of residents already in Lodz."

Along with the decree, the city elders added a list of additional orders. To minimize the danger of contagion, any victim of the epidemic must be buried immediately and without benefit of a funeral ceremony. Every corpse must be covered over with a thick layer of lime, calculated to eat quickly away at the diseased flesh. Also, no buried body could be exhumed, thereby allowing the germs of disease to be returned to the open air.

The epidemic did not end on the day the law was put into effect, but life did become extremely difficult for those who wished to settle in Lodz. Border police scrutinized every person who came to the city gates, and bombarded them with piercing questions: Who are you? ... Where are you headed? ... Whose children are those with you? ... and so on. Anyone who looked like the head of a household trying to slip in and mingle with the citizens of Lodz was immediately sent away in disgrace, as though to say, "Our city is suffering with those who are already here — and now you've come to add to their number?"

⌒∽⌒

In a city near Lodz lived a Jew named Yonah Kinstelicher. He was a prosperous entrepreneur whose business concerns all centered in Lodz. For a number of years he had been traveling regularly to and from Lodz. At last, he grew tired of making these frequent trips, and made up his mind to move to Lodz permanently. Unfortunately, the epidemic had just broken out at that time, and a strict ban was placed on new residents.

But Jewish nature does not accept edicts of this sort passively. If a decree has been made to the effect that no new Jews could move to Lodz, that just made it necessary to devise strategies by which to outmaneuver the edict.

Yonah's sharp mind found no rest until he had latched onto a clever plan. First he sent his wife and children to live in Lodz. His wife told the border guards that she had come to join her husband, already living in the city. She named the man in whose home her husband had stayed on his business trips to Lodz, and who had been adequately compensated for his part in the subterfuge. He came forward to greet his "family," playing his part like a veteran actor. Two weeks later, Yonah arrived, presenting himself as the brother of the woman who had arrived two weeks before.

The ruse worked. The members of the Kinstelicher family were reunited — but not in tranquility. Suspicion was everywhere. The plan which had succeeded in pulling the wool over the eyes of the border patrol at the city gates was not sufficient to close the mouths of gossipers and talebearers. Were anyone to get wind of the fact that Yonah and his wife and children constituted a nuclear family, it was highly possible that someone would bring the accusation to the authorities, who encouraged such tale-telling. Moreover, the city's residents themselves — Jew and non-Jew alike — supported the new law. They viewed every new arrival as a minor angel of death who had come to add to their pain and strengthen the epidemic.

Therefore, Yonah and his wife spread their own version of their story throughout the city: She was a women who had come with her children, to join her husband, but he had passed away suddenly. They were now living with her divorced brother. To maintain the ruse, the children were trained to call their father "Uncle," even at home.

A full month passed in their new home. It seemed that life had returned to normal. And then — disaster struck.

The raging epidemic did not differentiate between new citizens and old. Even-handedly, it lashed out at them all.

One day, Yonah's wife fell ill. With each passing hour, her limbs felt heavier and her hands more feeble. By the end of two days' suffering, she gave up her soul and became yet another victim in the plague's terrible toll.

Her family's mourning was heart-rending. The orphaned children wailed until it seemed as if the very walls were crying along with them. Their father wept bitterly; he looked like a person whose world had collapsed around him. He knew he must collect himself to handle the situation — but before he had recovered sufficiently to act, or even to think how to act, there came a pounding on the door. The *Chevrah Kaddisha* (Burial Society) had arrived with lightning speed, to remove the dead body from the house. They were conforming to the law which stated that victims of the plague must be buried with all possible haste, to lessen the chances of spreading contagion to the city's living residents.

As Yonah and his children stood beside the still-warm body of their beloved wife and mother, weeping over their bitter loss, the men came to take her away.

The wails intensified. The children did not want to part from their mother so soon. They begged to be allowed to remain with her for a few minutes longer, but the *Chevrah Kaddisha* set briskly about their task of speedy removal. In anguish, the youngsters flung themselves on Yonah, screaming, "Father, Father!"

Father?!?

The members of the burial society knew the Kinstelicher family. Like everyone else, they had been told that Yonah was the children's uncle. Indeed, until that moment the youngsters had called him "Uncle." They had all played their parts so well that no one suspected a thing. Now, the men were stunned to hear the young orphans screaming, "Father!"

As for Yonah, he was carressing his poor children with the kind of love not usually seen in uncles. He was crying with them, but not as an uncle.

It had been Yonah's wish to deceive the authorities and citizens of Lodz — and he had succeeded. The *Chevrah Kaddisha* firmly believed him to be the children's uncle. Of this, they were certain. But — was he also their father? How could an uncle also be a father?

In very short order, they jumped to the wrong conclusion.

Glaring at the weeping widower, they took away the corpse without a word. Two of them went directly to the home of the local *dayan*. "A terrible thing has happened in our city. A man has married his sister!" they fumed. "They have broken a strict Torah prohibition, and their children are *mamzerim* beyond all doubt. Where should we bury the dead mother?"

The *dayan* considered aloud. "Bury her in the regular cemetery? Out of the question! Not after she transgressed such a severe prohibition. Bury her on the other side of the fence, together with all the apostates and sinners and suicides?" He paused, then came to his decision. "Yes. Bury her on the other side of the fence! That's the proper procedure for one who has flaunted the Torah's laws and deliberately trampled them!"

The *Chevrah Kaddisha* hastened to carry out the *dayan's* instructions. A short time later, the body was deposited in a deep pit behind the fence, in the despicable part of the cemetery where the most heinous sinners lay buried. The corpse was covered with a thick layer of lime, to destroy the germs of sickness and keep the living citizens safe.

The widower and his children did not accompany their wife and mother to her final resting place. The *Chevrah Kaddisha* explained to them that this was the custom in Lodz when dealing with epidemic victims: Bodies were disposed of with all possible speed, without benefit of funeral or eulogies, and immediately covered with a thick layer of lime.

Exhausted and broken, Yonah collapsed onto his bed that night. His sleep was disturbed by nightmares. His dead wife came toward him, face streaming with tears. Never in his life had he seen such weeping. "Oh, oh, how can it be that they've done such a terrible thing to me?"

"What has been done to you?" Yonah asked in the dream.

"They buried me with the worst sinners of Israel," she said amid the endless tears. "I can find no peace with such wicked neighbors. I will never be at rest, as long as I lie near apostates and sinners like these. How did you let it happen, Yonah?"

In a cold sweat, Yonah awoke.

No one had told him where his wife was buried. Certainly, he thought, the *Chevrah Kaddisha* would have placed her in a respectable location, as befit an upright woman. Confused and bewildered, he finally concluded that the dream was nonsense. It was only a nightmare. Not only had he lost his young wife and was left a widower with little children dependent on him, but he was also beset by bad dreams to shatter his equilibrium.

All the following day, he tried to shake off the lingering effects of the nightmare. But the dream returned that night, its power redoubled. His wife pleaded and screamed, "Why won't you take pity on me? You have no idea what torture it is for my *neshamah*, to be in this place that is no resting place at all. The worst suffering you can imagine is only a pale shadow beside my present suffering! My body can find no rest in the grave, because of the pollution, the disgusting contamination, spread by those near me. Please, do what you can to move me to another place, where there are kosher people!"

Thoroughly shaken, Yonah woke from the second dream, once again bathed in a cold sweat. If it happened once, a dream could be labeled nonsense. Twice, it called for an investigation! Bright and early the next morning, he set out for the cemetery.

He walked alongside the fence, peeking among the thorns and tall grass that had been allowed to sprout between the graves. To his horror, he found a small placard stuck in the soil of a fresh grave, on the other side of the fence. Reading it, his heard lurched with pain. It bore his dear wife's name.

The dreams had been true after all. Now he knew the reason for her weeping and wailing. Surrounding his wife were the city's most terrible sinners!

On the spot, he resolved to summon the *Chevrah Kaddisha* to a *din Torah* in the presence of the city's chief rabbi, the holy *gaon* R' Eliyahu Chaim Meisel. Let them explain why they had perpetrated such an outrage on his good wife. And then, let them be forced to move her body to the proximity of good Jews.

"Why have you done this terrible thing to my wife?" the widower demanded in a trembling voice. "What is her sin, that you have punished her so severely?"

The members of the *Chevrah Kaddisha* looked at him the way one would gaze at a foul trickster. What a nerve he had, to speak this way!

"Let the rebbe hear the whole story," they addressed R' Eliyahu Chaim. They related the way they had caught the children calling their mother's brother "Father," and concluded that a grievous sin had been perpetrated. A man had married his own sister! Therefore, the *dayan* had ordered the burial she deserved. All had been done according to Torah law.

"And what have you to say?" the rabbi asked the widower gently.

Yonah told the great rabbi who his wife had been. He described her goodness and righteousness, her kind and charitable nature, the prayers that had emanated from the depths of her heart, and the acts of purity and faith. Gulping back sobs, he managed to relay the information that, due to Lodz's strict immigration laws, he had been left with no option but to present his wife as his sister, just as our forefathers, Avraham and Yitzchak, had done in their time.

The rabbi listened to the story, deeply shaken. He recognized in Yonah an honest man, good-hearted and truthful. Forced by circumstances to claim his wife as a sister, Yonah had stumbled unwittingly into a difficult complication, which had resulted in his wife's being given an unfitting burial.

"And what do you have to say now?" he asked the members of the *Chevrah Kaddisha*.

"We apologize with all our hearts for the terrible error we inadvertently made," they exclaimed. They, too, were shaken to the core by what they had just heard. "But we had no choice. We were forced by law to bury the woman quickly. There was no time to investigate, or to learn the truth that the man and his wife were legitimate in the Torah's eyes."

"Can the mistake be rectified now?" the rabbi pressed. "You've heard how much the poor woman is suffering."

"Impossible," they stated. "The temporary law, enacted because of the epidemic, absolutely prohibits removing a corpse from the grave, no matter what! A dire punishment awaits anyone who breaks this law. It is a matter of public safety. The corpse can spread the terrible sickness that is still upon it, even after it has been in the grave."

R' Eliyahu Chaim gave the matter thought. Two sides stood before him, and both were right. Yonah was correct in asserting that a terrible wrong had been done his good wife — but the *Chevrah Kaddisha* was correct in claiming that they had acted in error, and that removing the body now would constitute a danger to life. Which side to favor in his judgment?

He sat considering for a long time. And he prayed for heavenly guidance in rendering his decision.

"Here is what I think," the rabbi said at last. "It is true that a pious Jewish woman is suffering from the proximity of all kinds of wicked and depraved souls. It is also true that it is impossible to remove her from the grave. Therefore, I undertake to learn *Mishnayos* and say *Kaddish* for the elevation of her soul."

Yonah was not pleased with the judgment, and continued to reiterate his poor wife's suffering. The rabbi assured him that there was nothing more he could do.

Several weeks later, the chassid R' Nachman Yosef Wilhelm, assistant to R' Eliyahu Chaim Meisel, encountered the widower walking down the street. Yonah approached him and, with a radiant face, exclaimed, "You have no idea what the holy rabbi has accomplished! Two weeks after the *din Torah*, my wife came to me once again in a dream. This time, her face was lit with a great light, and a sense of satisfaction and peace radiated from her.

"'Yonah, my husband, you don't know how much my situation has been eased,' she told me. 'From the moment the rav began saying *Kaddish* and learning *Mishnayos* for the elevation of my *neshamah*, it is as if a steel wall separates me from all the graves around me. It is as if I have been moved to a different grave! You have no idea how much they esteem R' Eliyahu Chaim Meisel in heaven. Now I am at rest, in peace and tranquility, and all the suffering of my grave has been removed.

"'And because I am at rest, I must leave you, my dear husband. From now on, I do not have permission to reveal to you what is transpiring Above.'"

At that moment, her image disappeared and Yonah woke up. This time, he was free of the cold sweat. He, too, was at peace.

[Source: A *gadol* who heard this story from the R' Nachman Yosef Wilhelm *zt"l*, who was present during all stages of the story, from its beginning to its end.]

A Subtle Hint

EVERYONE IN KARLIN WAS PLUNGED INTO MOURNING. THE chassidim walked about bent and downcast, and heartbroken cries resounded from every mouth. The news had just arrived from the city of Drohovich that their young rebbe, R' Asher of Stolin, had suddenly passed away on Friday, the 15th day of Av, 5633 (1873).

How brief his reign had been! His father, R' Aharon of Karlin, author of the *Beis Aharon*, had departed this world on the 17th day of Sivan, 5632 (1872). A little over a year had passed since then. The chassidim had hardly recovered from the previous tragedy when the second one landed on their heads.

The young rebbe had recently traveled to the health resort of Truskavetz, near the city of Drohovich in Eastern Galicia, then under Austrian rule. The city was universally known as "Himacz" (rendered into English, the initials stood for "His Majesty the Czar"). Some of the chassidim were privy to the fact that R' Asher had once turned to his father, R' Aharon, and told him, "Father, Himacz is mine." No one had grasped his meaning — except for his father, who spoke with his holy son in the language of hints.

When R' Asher had arrived in the environs of Drohovich, he was told that a cholera epidemic was raging in the city. Members of the rebbe's entourage tried to dissuade him from entering the disease-ridden place, but he refused to heed their pleas. Instead, he went to the home of the city's spiritual leader, the holy *gaon* R' Eliyahu Horoshovsky, a foremost student of the Belzer Rebbe. The two were closeted together for a short time.

"I know you are concerned for my welfare," the rebbe told his chassidim when he left. "But I had to enter the city at any price."

The price was steep indeed. As he left the city, his face wore a mysterious expression, and he asked his companions to recite, using the well-known melody, the section from the Yom Kippur liturgy: "You have arranged all of this in honor of Aharon; you have made him the instrument of atonement for Israel." A short time later, he began to feel ill. He had caught the deadly disease.

His distraught chassidim tried to bring him back into the city. They were still on their way, with the rebbe supported in the arms of one of his companions, when his life expired and his soul flew away in holiness.

That was when it came to light that the rebbe had known he was fated to be stricken with the sickness. Perhaps his intention had been to give up his life as an atonement for his people. Apparently, this is what he had spoken about with the city's rabbi. Indeed, in his *sefer Eizor Eliyahu,* R' Eliyahu Horoshovsky wrote, "And so it happened that the renowned *tzaddik,* R' Asher'l of Karlin, came here and was caught in our city, and died with only half his life span over, in order to atone for the sins of the city."

Indeed, immediately afterwards, the epidemic came to a complete end.

⌒♪☾

When the rebbe took sick in Drohovich, his only son, R' Yisrael, was a young child just 4 1/2 years old. He was playing in the yard, holding a sceptre in his hand. Suddenly, the sceptre's tip fell off and rolled on the ground.

The little boy sighed from the depths of his heart. "*Oy,* the head fell off ..."

Then he turned to the men who were in the yard with him, and spoke the same words that had been said a short time earlier by his own father: "'You have arranged all this in honor of Aharon'. Those words are about my grandfather. 'You have made him an instrument of atonment for Israel.' That was my father. 'In place of Aharon, from his root, he will stand.' That is me." This episode was all very strange — veiled, mysterious, and troubling. Some time later, the telegram from Drohovich arrived with its tragic news. The chassidim were plunged into mourning.

During the seven days of mourning, the chassidim came to comfort the young widow, Rebbetzin Sarah Devorah, daughter of the rebbe, R' Elimelech of Grodzisk.

The rebbetzin sat on the ground, her face a mirror of grief over her loss. Her arms embraced her little boy, the heir to Karliner Chassidus, R' Yisrael Perlow, who would be known as the *yenuka,* or "child-rebbe."

The chassidim sat silent, heads bowed. What was there to say? They had sustained loss after loss, and were bereft as a flock of sheep without a shepherd. They could not find a word worth speaking.

The rebbetzin turned to them with a question: "Do you remember what happened here when my son was born?"

One of the older chassidim, R' Yisrael Binyamin Gleiberman — who was later appointed tutor to the *yenuka* — asked, "Is the Rebbetzin referring to what happened before the *bris*? I remember it well."

The rebbetzin nodded her head. "Yes, I'm talking about what occurred before the baby's *bris milah*. Tell the story, and let everyone hear."

R' Yisrael Binyamin told the tale:

"When R' Asher's son was born, he asked his father, R' Aharon, to choose a name for the boy. But his father believed that it was the child's father, and not the grandfather, who should choose the newborn's name. After some discussion, the two agreed that each of them would write down the name he thought the boy should be called. When they checked afterwards, they found that both had written the name, 'Yisrael.'

"R' Asher asked his father, 'Why did you choose the name Yisrael?'

"R' Aharon replied, 'I meant to name him after the Ba'al Shem Tov, and after the boy's two grandfathers — the Maggid of Kozhnitz and R' Yisrael of Rizhin.'

"'I, too, had those three in mind,' said R' Asher.

"R' Aharon sighed, and said, 'All three of them were brought up as orphans.'"

Was this the story the rebbetzin had meant? Apparently not. Her eyes glimmered with tears. The gentle hint now carried a new significance.

She shook her head. "I was not referring to that story. Don't any of you remember what my holy father-in-law said on the *vacht nacht* — the night before the *bris*?"

Then, suddenly, they did remember. How could they ever have forgotten?

An air of jubilation enveloped the holy courtyard of Karlin on the 10th day of Kislev, 5629 (1869), with the birth of a son to the *tzaddik* R' Asher of Stolin. The good news of the newest link in the holy dynasty flew on wings to every place where Karlin-Stolin chassidim lived, and filled them with joy. The nearby train depot of Gorin-Retchitza was thronged with chassidim, and the trains kept spewing out more and more of those who had come to join in the great celebration. More than anything in the world, they wished to be present at the festive *shalom zachar*, the *vacht nacht*, and the *bris milah*.

Still more chassidim arrived in simple wagons or ornate carriages. On the way, they drank many a *"l'chaim"* in honor of the celebration, and blessed each other with happy cries of "Mazal tov!"

In the days preceding the *bris*, tables were set up in the rebbe's courtyard to accommodate the many guests. The chassidim sat with the father and grandfather, whose exalted faces shone with a satisfaction and happiness that brought endless joy to those around them. Every chassid, in turn, pressed forward to greet the elder rebbe, to shake his hand and that of the "younger rebbe," and to wish them both a fervent and heartfelt "Mazal tov!"

On the evening before the *bris*, the celebration reached its peak. It was the *"leil hashimurim"* — the protected night — the *vacht nacht*. The chassidim prepared to recite the *Krias Shema* beside the baby's cradle, to learn the *Zohar*, recite *Tehillim*, and partake of a great feast.

Excitement reached a fever pitch in the newborn's home when the rebbe arrived at the house at the head of a huge number of chassidim. The Beis Aharon had come to offer his blessing and good wishes to his daughter-in-law, mother of the child, and to see the baby. The house was filled with emotional chassidim who had pressed forward to stand as near as possible to the baby's cradle.

As the older rebbe's eyes studied the tiny face in the cradle, he wore an expression that made words superfluous. It was easy to see that the child was destined for holiness. His little face shone with an exalted light. The grandfather gazed at him for a long time, and said slowly, *"Pri chadash*. A new fruit! We can recite the blessing of *Shehecheyanu.*"

Then he sat down on a chair in the center of the room, turned to his daughter-in-law and the chassidim, and said quietly, "I'd like to tell you a story."

Absolute silence descended on the room, vanquishing the happy babble. The chassidim listened intently as the rebbe, with a serious expression, began to speak.

The Chacham Tzvi, R' Tzvi Ashkenazi, was a renowned *gaon*, one of his generation's leading authorities. He had served as rabbi of the holy communities of Amsterdam and Lemberg, had gone through his share of trying times.

He was born in Moravia in about the year 1660, a link in a holy chain. His father was R' Yaakov Ashkenazi and his maternal grandfather was R' Efraim HaKohen, author of the *Shaar Efraim*, a man for whom the Torah and all its commentaries lay spread out like a map. R' Tzvi Hirsch learned Torah from his grandfather and father. By the age of 16 he began writing down his own halachic responsa. After learning Torah from Ashkenazic sources, he decided to study the methods of learning in practice among the scholars of the Eastern countries.

He traveled to Salonika, where he learned Torah from the *gaon* R' Eliyahu Kovo. Not only did he acquire Torah from this great man, but he also embraced Sephardic manners and customs. Afterwards, he traveled to Istanbul, Turkey, to learn from the sages there. It was not long before he had earned the title "*Chacham*," used by Sephardim to honor their learned ones. From there, he went on to the city of Alt-Ofen, where he married the daughter of a wealthy member of that community, who gave birth to his firstborn daughter. Afterward, he and his family traveled on to Bosnia. There, in Sarajevo, he served as the city's chief rabbi and *Av Beis Din*.

His happiness was not destined to last long. It was wartime. One day a shell landed on his house and exploded, killing his wife and daughter.

Alone again, R' Tzvi Hirsch wandered from country to country and from city to city. He spent some time in Venice, Italy, then moved on to the cities of Ansbach and Prague, in Bohemia (today Czechoslovakia). After many years had passed, he reached the city of Berlin, Germany, where his parents lived. But he did not stay there for long .

At that time, serving as chief rabbi of three holy communities (Altona, Hamburg, and Wandsbeck) was the *gaon* R' Meshulam Zalman Neumark-Mirels, renowned for his brilliance and even more for his piety. R' Meshulam Zalman had an outstanding son named R' Zev Wolf Mirels, who resided in Berlin. From the moment of the Chacham Tzvi's arrival in Berlin, R' Wolf had taken notice of his greatness in Torah and his holiness. He wanted the Chacham Tzvi as a brother-in-law, a husband to his sister Sarah.

There was just one problem. Sarah was very young, and the Chacham Tzvi was many years her senior. Moreover, the years of traveling and suffering had left their mark on his face, making him appear even older than his years.

R' Wolf wrote to his father, who lived in Altona (from which city he served the other two communities as well), proposing that he take the Chacham Tzvi as a husband for his daughter, Sarah. He described the prospective son-in-law's virtues at length. True, the Chacham Tzvi was not a young man — indeed, he looked very old — but there was none to compare with him in brilliance and righteousness.

R' Zalman read the letter, then summoned his daughter to the room and laid out the proposal.

"Do you wish to marry this *tzaddik* and *gaon*?" he asked.

Sarah weighed the question carefully. A few days later, she gave her consent. R' Wolf spoke to the Chacham Tzvi. Shortly thereafter, R' Tzvi Hirsch once again picked up his traveling stick, and set out for Altona.

On his arrival in Altona, he was greeted with much fanfare. His reputation preceded him everywhere he went, and Altona's Jews were proud to be his destination of choice for disseminating his Torah. Their joy knew no bounds when, a month or so later, the news came that the great sage had become betrothed to Sarah, daughter of R' Meshulam Zalman Neumark. The wedding was planned for a date in the near future.

Altona turned out in its festive best in honor of the wedding. From every direction came Jews, dressed in their finest and streaming toward the shul. The *chupah* was erected in the open plaza in front of the shul.

Music and song welcomed the guests, courtesy of a group of merry musicians sitting in the courtyard. The illustrious *chasan* sat at the eastern table, surrounded by important rabbinical figures, his face glowing with an exalted holiness. All was ready for the *chupah*. Only one thing was missing — the *kallah* ...

The bride, Sarah, did not come to her *chupah*. They waited and waited, but she did not come!

People were sent to bring her. All too soon they returned, crestfallen. The *kallah* refused to come unless her request was granted.

The *chasan*, the Chacham Tzvi, sent messengers to his bride, asking, "What is your request? It shall be done."

With modesty and humility, Sarah sent back a clear, unambiguous reply: "I will not come to the *chupah* unless the *chasan* assures me that I will merit a son."

When the messengers bore back her answer, the *chasan's* face changed. His expression became unhappy. His bride was worried. He looked like an old man, and she was afraid that she would not have the privilege of living with him more than a short time.

The Chacham Tzvi's brow creased as he closed his eyes in concentration. His lips moved ceaselessly, without making a sound. Then his countenance lifted, and he cried joyfully, "The *kallah* is a woman of wisdom, and she has acted well. With Hashem's help, she will merit a son."

The answer was relayed to the *kallah*, who did not delay any longer in coming to the *chupah*, surrounded by her friends. The signal was given. At once, the *kallah* entered under the wedding canopy amid music and rejoicing.

The young rebbetzin bore three daughters to her older husband, and only afterwards gave birth to a male child. When he was born, the city exulted: the Chacham's promise before the *chupah* had come true! She had, indeed, merited a son! Jews thronged to his house to wish the new father "Mazal tov." All of Altona rejoiced. From nearby cities, as well, came well-wishers in droves, to join in the celebration and participate in the *bris milah*.

At *Shacharis* on the eighth day, the entire city turned out. The big shul was soon filled to capacity. The baby's father had elected to personally serve as the *mohel*. Wrapped in his *tallis* and *tefillin*, he stood ready to fulfill the great mitzvah. The huge crowd waited suspensefully for the child to be brought. But the minutes passed and, to their consternation, mother and child did not appear.

Messengers were sent to bring the rebbetzin and her baby son to shul. They returned empty-handed. Agitated whispers began to sweep the throng. The mother refused to bring her son to the *bris*. Her own mother — the baby's grandmother — had pleaded with her, as had other relatives, but she was adamant. The boy would not be brought to shul.

All this time, the baby's father stood immersed in his exalted thoughts, apparently floating in other worlds as though none of this could touch him. Suddenly, he stirred. "Why aren't they bringing the baby?" he asked.

They whispered, "For some reason, the mother refuses to bring him."

"Go ask her why she refuses," ordered the Chacham Tzvi.

They did as instructed. "The Rebbetzin Sarah says that she won't allow her son to be circumcised until the rav promises that she and her husband, the rav, will merit raising him in Torah and bringing him together to the *chupah!*"

A cloud passed over the rav's face. This time, she had requested a great deal!

Once again, he closed his eyes and began to silently move his lips. The enormous crowd watched tensely. What would he say? Could he guarantee something so distant — that he would live another eighteen years? Was it even possible for him to do so?

At last, the Chacham Tzvi opened his eyes. He looked at his father-in-law and said, "Your daughter is a wise woman. I guarantee that, with Hashem's help, we will merit bringing this son up together, to Torah, *chupah*, and good deeds!"

A resounding "*Amen!*" echoed through the vast shul. A short time later, the boy was entered into the covenant of Avraham Avinu and given the name Yisrael Yaakov. He grew up to be the renowned Torah giant, R' Yaakov Emden, author of *She'elas Yaabetz* (*Yaabetz* being the initials of "*Yaakov ben Tzvi*"), and other works.

The Chacham Tzvi did, indeed, merit the privilege of raising his son together with his righteous wife. When the boy was 17, his parents married him off in the city of Breslov, in the month of Sivan, 5475 (1715). The Chacham Tzvi went on to live three years longer, and was appointed chief rabbi of the city of Lvov-Lemberg. However, just three months into his rabbinate, on the second day of Rosh Chodesh Iyar, 5478 (1718), he departed this world, and was mourned by the entire Jewish nation.

ഏ

A tense silence held the room. Those present did not understand what the Beis Aharon's story was meant to convey to them. No one said a word. The rebbe regarded the listeners for a moment, his expression grave. He seemed to be waiting to hear something.

Then the moment passed. Refreshments were served, and they drank a "l'chaim." The rebbe himself poured a drink for each chassid and accepted each one's "Mazal tov." Afterwards, all the chassidim departed amid enthusiastic dance.

On the following day, the baby boy was entered into the covenant of Avraham Avinu, and was given the name Yisrael. It was the 17th day of Kislev, 5629 (1869). Less than three years later, the great Beis Aharon departed this world. And then, just fourteen months later, his son, the young R' Asher, was snatched away as well.

"Woe is me," wept the widow, Rebbetzin Sarah Devorah. "You all heard the story that my father-in-law told. You thought it spoke of hidden matters. He was trying to hint to you to have the wisdom to ask that I, too, merit raising our son to Torah and to the chupah together with my husband. But you did not understand. You allowed the golden moment to slip through your fingers. We have sustained a grievous loss — a loss that has no compensation.

A short time later, the heir took his father's place as rebbe. There was a huge stir in the chassidic world when a child of just 4 1/2 was appointed rebbe. It was not long, however, before the boy's high level of holiness became apparent to all, and earned the admiration of the generation's great men.

One example of this — among thousands — will be attested to in the following story.

Intuition — or Ruach HaKodesh

WHILE STILL A YOUNG MAN, THE *TZADDIK* R' YISRAEL Yitzchak Meshi-Zahav began to garner the esteem of his generation's Torah leaders. In his home town of Pinsk, he learned Torah and served Hashem devotedly, engaged in no secular matters at all. His home was destitute, but he cared nothing for his poverty. Great Torah figures, studying him with eyes sharpened to keen perception, recognized in this humble and seemingly simple individual a man whose inner life was wholly dedicated to the service of Hashem. They drew him close and showed him honor. When he visited their courtyards, they would shower him with tokens of esteem and respect, seating him beside them at the head of the table. Those standing around understood that beneath the deceptive guise lived a *ben aliyah* — a man on a journey of spiritual ascent. The high level of this young man can be gleaned from the fact that he merited a visit to his home by the Chofetz Chaim himself!

The higher his spiritual stature grew, the more R' Yisrael Yitzchak despised the polluted lands in which he lived. He longed to move to Eretz Yisrael, where the air is pure and holy. From day to day these longings increased in strength, until they gave him no peace. He began to prepare for the journey.

Unforeseen obstacles began to crop up, to block his way. Each time he was nearly ready to set out, something would happen at the last minute to prevent him from doing so. His trip was postponed, again and again.

R' Yisrael Yitzchak's determination increased. He resolved to force himself to leave, in a way that precluded any other option. He set a date for the journey, several months away, and began fresh preparations to meet it. All his affairs were settled, so that when the appointed day arrived there would be no obstacle to his going.

During this period, his wife, Leah, was expecting a baby. To their great joy, just days before their target date a son was born to them.

But their happiness was short-lived indeed. It lasted only eight hours.

The newborn baby was very frail. Unable to meet the demands of life, he died after just eight hours. Joy turned to ashes. The new mother, still weak from childbirth, suffered deeply from the added blow of her baby's death. She wept for many hours. Physical weakness combined with profound grief, to the point where she became ill. It was obvious that she was in no condition to travel. The rigors of the road were difficult even for healthy people. It was no place for the weak or sickly.

R' Yisrael Yitzchak nearly gave up. But he didn't take his wife's strong will into account. Leah was a *tzaddekes*, a truly remarkable woman and a loyal partner to her righteous husband. Understanding that Heaven was testing them to see how deep their commitment ran, she pleaded with her husband to ignore her condition and travel to Eretz Yisrael on his own.

"If you delay, more challenges will crop up," she said. "You go, and when I recover from my illness I will follow."

At first, he would not hear of it. How could he leave his wife behind and travel alone, as though he were a bachelor? He refused to listen to her pleading. However, Leah was able to offer an argument that softened his resistance.

"On the contrary," she urged. "If you move to Eretz Yisrael, the merit of that mitzvah will allow me to recover. I will then be able to travel, and we will soon be together again."

He listened to his wife. Once again, he readied himself for the road.

The great day arrived. R' Yisrael Yitzchak was moving to Eretz Yisrael! He packed his bundles, bid farewell to family and friends, received his devoted wife's parting blessing, and started for the train depot.

For the most direct railway trip he would have to purchase a ticket straight to the port city of Odessa. Instead, he bought a special ticket for a train that would stop in the city of Stolin. He planned to stay there a number of hours, after which he would continue on to Odessa. This ticket cost more than the direct one, but R' Yisrael Yitzchak did not regard the expense.

When he moved to Eretz Yisrael, R' Yisrael Yitzchak was only 33 years old. Years before he had developed a special bond with the holy Karliner Rebbe, R' Yisrael, the "yenuka." At a young age, R' Yisrael Yitzchak succeeded in achieving spiritual levels that most others do not manage to accomplish in many years, The holy rebbe of Karlin, perceiving the young man's rich inner life, drew him close. Given the depths of their friendship and mutual esteem, it would never occur to R' Yisrael Yitzchak to take such an important step without parting from the holy "yenuka" of Karlin, whose home was in Stolin.

A long blast of the whistle announced the train's approach to the Stolin depot. Dozing passengers woke with a start, and wondered where they were. Dressed in his cap and splendid uniform, the conductor passed from car to car, announcing, "We are approaching Stolin. The train will be there for three hours. In three hours, the train will leave. Anyone arriving late will miss the train and forfeit his ticket."

R' Yisrael Yitzchak did not waste a second. He hurried off the train and hastened directly to the rebbe's house. There was only a small window of time at his disposal, and in that short time he must part forever from his dear friend. From the moment he would board the ship that was headed for the port of Yaffo, there was little chance that he would ever return.

The Karliner Rebbe was overjoyed to see his friend, and welcomed him with great warmth. Offering him a seat, he began to talk with his guest with open affection. When he heard that R' Yisrael Yitzchak was moving to Eretz Yisrael and had come for only a very brief visit, his face fell.

"My dear Yisrael Yitzchak," he said sadly, "it is exceedingly hard to part from you. Will you, perhaps, change your mind and stay here for a few days? Then we could sit together and rejoice in one another's company."

R' Yisrael Yitzchak's emotional turmoil was visible on his face. "I wish very much to be able to sit with you more and more. But my time is limited. Soon my train will set out again, and if I do not hurry I will surely miss it."

He was ashamed to admit that financial considerations formed a part of his decision. A new train ticket would cost him 80 rubles. Given his severely restricted travel budget, he simply could not afford this extra expense. His purchase of the ticket that made this stopover in Stolin had already stolen several additional rubles from his empty pocket.

If he thought his answer would satisfy the rebbe, he was mistaken! The rebbe continued to coax him to change his mind and remain for several days. But the guest — who was not one of the rebbe's chassidim, but rather a close personal friend — declined.

They sat and talked together as friends do, while the clock ticked relentlessly on. Suddenly, there was no more time. R' Yisrael Yitzchak jumped out of his seat and began to say his farewells. The rebbe pressed his hand warmly and parted with him amid heartfelt good wishes for a safe journey and peaceful arrival in the Holy Land, where he should live in tranquility and contentment all his days.

R' Yisrael Yitzchak left the house and began to walk rapidly in the direction of the train depot. He had not gone far when he heard a voice loudly calling his name. Turning his head, he saw the rebbe's *gabbai* racing after him. He stopped at once and waited to hear what the man had to say.

A moment later, the *gabbai* reached his side, breathing heavily from his run. "The rebbe sent me to ask you to return to him urgently."

They had just parted, amid blessings and good wishes. What could have happened between then and now to make him have to retrace his steps? Wondering greatly, he turned back with the *gabbai*.

The rebbe was waiting for him at the door to his room, his face betraying his expectation. Seeing R' Yisrael Yitzchak, his expression lightened. "Ah, my dear R' Yisrael Yitzchak!" he exclaimed warmly. "I was afraid you might have gone too far. I have a big favor to ask of you. I would like to use this opportunity to send a letter to the community of Karliner chassidim in Eretz Yisrael. After all, you'll be traveling to their land. Please, do me a favor and give them the letter."

"With pleasure."

But the letter had not yet been written. The rebbe asked him to wait while he wrote it. He entered his room, while R' Yisrael Yitzchak waited outside for him to finish.

If R' Yisrael Yitzchak had hoped the matter would be quickly dispatched, he soon found out how wrong he was. The rebbe closeted himself in his room, the minutes rushing by. R' Yisrael Yitzchak sat as though on hot coals, checking his watch every few seconds. If he hurried with all his might, he could still catch his train. But only silence came from the inner room. It would not be courteous for him to disturb the rebbe as he wrote.

In rising impatience he waited, but the rebbe did not hurry at all. Keenly aware of the passing time, R' Yisrael Yitzchak felt as if he were about to explode. He waited on, standing up and pacing the length of the room.

More precious minutes slipped away. At long last, the door of the inner room opened and the rebbe emerged, a sealed envelope in his hand. He gave this to R' Yisrael Yitzchak and thanked him in advance for his help in delivering it, and the two parted again in great friendship.

R' Yisrael Yitzchak looked at his watch and knew that the battle was lost. It was already 20 minutes past the 3-hour deadline. Unless something extraordinary had occurred to delay his train, it was on its way already, moving from city to city in the direction of Odessa. On that train were all his meager belongings.

He shook his head and tried to think of his next step. The ticket he held was worthless now, but the next train could take him to the port. Shaking his head once again, he set out for the station.

As he neared the train depot, a strange commotion reached his ears. The wide platform bustled with humanity. Clumps and clusters of people were gathered together, all talking excitedly in loud voices. Everything R' Yisrael Yitzchak saw told him that something highly unusual had just occurred. Curious, he approached one of the groups and asked what had happened.

"Didn't you hear the news?" a man asked in surprise. "We've just received word of a terrible accident. Two trains collided with one another! The train that left here for Odessa has crashed into another train. There were a great many casualties. They say that every passenger on both trains, without exception, was hurt to some degree, and that's to say nothing of the large number of people who were killed."

R' Yisrael Yitzchak's hands began to shake. He seemed to see the Karliner Rebbe's face floating before him, delaying his departure on the pretext of having to pen an urgent letter to his chassidim in Eretz Yisrael — as though there were no longer any postal service available. The rebbe had done it to save him! He had lost his meager belongings but escaped with his life!

Thoroughly shaken, he returned to the holy rebbe's courtyard. In the time it took him to reach his destination, he had an opportunity to collect his thoughts. It would not do, he decided, to burst in on the rebbe declaring loudly, "You have *ruach hakodesh*!"

When he reached the rebbe's house, which he had been so visibly anxious to leave just a short time earlier, the rebbe did not seem at all surprised to see him. The entire situation, it seemed, stood revealed to him. Calmly, the rebbe asked, "Why have you come back?"

"Seeing as I've already missed my train," R' Yisrael Yitzchak replied, "I've decided to accept the rebbe's invitation and remain here with him for several days."

A broad smile adorned the rebbe's face. He patted his friend on the shoulder, as if to say, "I know you too well to believe that story!" Then, all at once, his expression sobered. Turning to R' Yisrael Yitzchak, he said, "Tell me why you've really come back. Tell me everything. Leave nothing out."

R' Yisrael Yitzchak was, figuratively, pushed to the wall. There was no evading the question now. He described in detail all that he had heard about the awful collision involving the very train on which he had been meant to travel, and the tragic toll in lives. "I have witnessed for myself that the rebbe has *ruach hakodesh*," he concluded emotionally. "With his visionary eyes, the rebbe was able to look into the future and do all in his power to save me."

"Nonsense!" The rebbe dismissed this conclusion with a wave of his hand. "Don't call it a miracle, and don't link it to *ruach hakodesh*. It has nothing to do with that! I'll tell you this much: I am an expert at reading a person's face — an age-old art based on the Torah's hidden wisdom. I saw on your face that you were about to encounter a trouble that did not belong to you at all. That was why I did my best to save you from the impending danger."

As R' Yisrael Yitzchak listened, thunderstruck, the rebbe continued to astonish him. "In fact, when you arrive in Eretz Yisrael you, too, will acquire this wisdom."

"And now," said the rebbe, without giving his guest a chance to say a word, "don't linger here even one day!" His voice took on a note of urgency. "Take the next train and travel to Odessa. Don't turn right or left. Do everything you can to reach Eretz Yisrael as quickly as possible."

At this point R' Yisrael Yitzchak was completely dumbfounded. Now that he had finally agreed to succumb to the rebbe's pleas and stay with him for a few days, the rebbe was suddenly chasing him away! Why had he changed his mind?

There was no time for further conversation. They parted for the third time, and R' Yisrael Yitzchak boarded the next train bound for Odessa. He reached the ship just before it was due to sail, and was among the last of the passengers to board it.

Very shortly after the ship set sail and moved out into open seas, the world was rocked with the clamor of war. The First World War broke out in all its fury. Chaos descended, roads were filled with soldiers reporting for military duty, trains stopped running, and all land and sea routes were closed. Had he waited even one day, he would have been forced to wait long years before he could move to Eretz Yisrael. Now he understood why the rebbe had urged him not to waste a moment.

On his arrival in Eretz Yisrael, he settled at first in the city of Rechovot, where he found employment in the building trade, as a simple laborer. One day, as he walked to shul for *Shacharis*, he witnessed something that caught his attention.

It was a poor Jew, dressed in rags, whom everyone knew as Menashe. Menashe was surrounded by a group of secular youths, to whom he was lecturing about their wayward behavior. The young people were laughing at him, raucously mocking every word he said. R' Yisrael Yitzchak tried to intervene, but the others were having too much fun to listen. He continued on to the shul.

When he had finished *davening*, he returned home by the same route. Even from a distance he could hear the young people's uproarious laughter. They had not ceased their mockery of the poor man and his admonitions. While Menashe tried to show them the error of their ways through words of Torah and *emunah*, the others were enjoying the experience as a way to pass an entertaining hour or so. What was astonishing was the fact that Menashe seemed completely undisturbed by their laughter. From time to time, when a lull descended, he returned to his words of *mussar*.

Listening from the side, R' Yisrael Yitzchak saw that this was a clear case of, "Just as it is a mitzvah to say things that will be heeded, it is a mitzvah not to say things that will not be heeded." He walked over to Menashe, placed an affectionate hand on his shoulder, and said, "Menashe, enough already! Please, come along to my house and eat breakfast with me."

Menashe went with him willingly, and ate his fill. His host saw that, if not for his invitation, Menashe would have continued his fast. At once, he invited him to return to his house in the days to come as well. Happily, the beggar accepted the invitation. R' Yisrael Yitzchak sensed that his destitute guest was concealing a great secret. This was no simple man.

Several days later, Menashe turned to R' Yisrael Yitzchak and revealed his secret.

He was one of the generation's hidden *tzaddikim*. Sensing the holiness and purity in R' Yisrael Yitzchak's soul, he wished to repay his kindness by teaching him the art of reading people's faces! The Stoliner Rebbe's words had come true.

For more than a year, R' Yisrael Yitzchak studied these amazing arts, using profound works of Kabbalah as his source. And for decades afterwards until his death in the year 5634 (1974), at the age of 93, the *mekubal* R' Yisrael Yitzchak Meshi-Zahav used his wisdom to help hundreds and even thousands of Jews who came to him seeking advice for their various problems. Those who sought him out found themselves facing a *tzaddik* whose entire being was filled with love and devotion for his fellow man. His penetrating answers were outstanding in their clarity and shrewdness, and many supplicants became recipients of mercy and salvation through his efforts. Here, too, he was the beloved of the *gedolei hador,* whose esteem for him was without limit. Residing in the "Mekor Chaim" section of Jerusalem, he was known everywhere as the "*mekubal* from Mekor Chaim." Needless to say, his wife moved to Eretz Yisrael at the War's end, and shared her life with him into their old age.

R' Yisrael Yitzchak often said, with a smile, that once he had acquired the wisdom of reading faces, he knew that the Stoliner Rebbe's claim to have seen impending trouble in his own face had been an obvious evasion. He now knew with certainty that such things are impossible to discern through the art of reading faces.

"I witnessed three wondrous things," he said, smiling. "First: I came to him, and he held me back from the danger that awaited me on the train. Second: I left, and he urged me to hurry to the port of Odessa with all possible speed. And, third: He managed to conceal the fact that he possessed *ruach hakodesh,* using an ingenious argument — simply in order not to arouse people's admiration. And this third wonder was the greatest of them all!"

[This story was passed on to me by R' Yisrael Yitzchak's great-grandson, R' Shmuel Honig, who heard the entire story from the Jerusalem *mekubal*, R' Chaim Dovid Meshi-Zahav *zt"l,* son of the protagonist.]